EATING BITTER

Best Wishes
Regards

Mark

EATING BITTER

A Chinese American Saga

吃苦

MARIA TIPPETT

To order additional copies of this book, contact:
Xlibris Corporation
1-888-795-4274
www.Xlibris.com
Orders@Xlibris.com
81215

CONTENTS

For Ann Cowan and Karen Kovalou

And in Memory of Paul Ho and Bill Liu

The Romanization of Chinese names and places started to employ the Wade-Giles System around the end of the nineteenth century and continued to be used in China and around the world until 1958 when the Chinese government established the new Pinyin System, which was then adopted by the International Organization for Standardization and other organizations in 1982. However, the Wade-Giles System continued to be used in Taiwan. As the people and places in this book include those in both China and in Taiwan, the spelling of names and places often cross the two Romanization systems.

Surnames and personal names in the book have been written according to Chinese custom—surname preceding personal name—tone marks have been omitted.

Acknowledgements

The research for this book began in the living room of Paul and Sonia Ho's North Palm Avenue condominium in an area east of Los Angeles. It culminated in the lovely Garden of Flowing Fragrance at the Huntington Gardens a few miles away where we had gathered there to celebrate Paul Ho's ninetieth birthday.

The seeds for a book on the life of Paul and Sonia Ho were sown on an uncharacteristically rainy evening at the 2006 Asian Excellence in Los Angeles. During that ceremony, which honored David Ho among others, Dennis Avery and Sally Tsui Wong Avery happened to sit at the same table as the Ho family—a week later Dennis wrote to me with a brief outline of their life.

Here was a family whose roots were deep in imperial China. A family headed by a patriarch in his late eighties whose life had been intertwined with the 'interesting times' through which he had lived. A family which now had a formidable record of achievement within American society, recognized in particular by the honors heaped on Dr David Ho for his pioneering work on the treatment of AIDS.

Upon hearing all of this from Dennis Avery I was hooked.

The Ho family made it clear from the outset that they would help me recreate their life story. 'Ask me anything,' Sonia told me, 'no problem.' In between that first meeting in March 2006 and the birthday celebration three years later I accumulated many debts.

The greatest debts I owe are shared between two parties. First, Sally Tsui Wong Avery and Dennis Avery who supported the research and writing of this book and gave me so much encouragement. And, second, the Ho Family who introduced me to Taiwan and China, who answered my many, many questions with humor and wisdom and who, along with their many friends—especially

Lin Li-tai—and relatives—particularly Lu I-wen—were gracious hosts to me and my husband Peter Clarke in Taichung, New York, Los Angeles, Santa Barbara, among other places. All of these people made the writing of this book possible—and enjoyable.

During my research trips to the People's Republic of China the following institutions and people facilitated my work, among them are: National Zhejiang University in Hangzhou; Chinese Overseas Friendship Association, Foreign Affairs and Overseas Chinese Affairs Office in Jiangxi Province; Nanchang Second Middle School and Nanchang University; Xinyu Primary School and Dayi Middle School in Xinyu; Party Secretary Yu in Yongxin; Dr. Zhou Zengquan and Haoyu Qian and their colleagues at the Yunnan AIDS Care Centre; Mrs. Zhang Ying of the Fuyan Aids Orphan Salvation Association in Anhui Province; Youth and Cultural Activity Center, Desa; Longchuan Maternal Child Health Hospital; and Health officials in Longchuan, Guangsong Village, Kunming, and many other people living in the villages and cities of the People's Republic of China.

In Taiwan the following people and institutions deserve many thanks: National Yi-lan Senior High School and the National Native Center for Traditional Art; Guangfu Primary School, Taichung; National Changhua Girls' Senior High School; National Taichung Girls' Senior High School; Lu Family Tempel, Houli; Lu Family Compound, Hsiau-yun.

And in the United States the following institutions should be thanked: Northern Colorado College; Los Angeles Public Library; University of Washington, Seattle; Huntington Museum and Gardens, Pasadena; The Aaron Diamond AIDS Research Centre in New York and, finally, in England, University Library, Cambridge; Churchill College Archives, also Cambridge University.

There were, of course, many individuals who offered their expertise during the writing of this book too. Dr. Diana Lary gave me assistance at an early stage. William Liu, former head of Simon Fraser University's department of translation, graciously offered his knowledge of Chinese history and language throughout the project. Ben Wang provided a brilliant translation and James Osborne produced a screenplay. In both China and Taiwan Ellen Yang proved to be an excellent and sympathetic interpreter. At Simon Fraser University where this project was based, many people including Professor Steven Duguid and Ann Cowan provided administrative assistance and encouragement. The Director of The Institute for Advanced Study in Princeton, Dr. Peter Goddard, gave me a wonderful place to write the final chapters of the book. It was here that I had the good fortune to benefit from the knowledge of Dr. Miaw-fen Lu of the Academia Sinica in Taiwan and one of the Institute for Advanced Study's distinguished professors, Arnold Levine. Alan Packwood, director of the Churchill College Archives drew my attention to the correspondence of Madames Sun Yet-sen and Chiang Kai-shek; Margaret MacMillan, Warden of St. Antony's College, Oxford University along with Anne B. Wood gave their advice as various stages of the project. Lily Lai-Cutugno of the Aaron Diamond AIDS Research Centre in New York helped facilitate travel to and during our trips to China and Taiwan.

Dr. J.P. McDermott of St John's College at Cambridge University read an early draft of the manuscript as did Dr. Fay Bendall, also of Cambridge. My agent Gray Tan found my story a good home. And finally my husband, the British historian Peter Clarke, accompanied me on every step of the way during the making of this book.

He/Ho (何) clan   Kiang (江) clan   Lu (呂) clan

He/Ho (何) clan

- Wang
- Shi 1853 - ?
- Li 1882 - ?
- He Weiqi 1838 - 1878
- Zhou 1848 - ?
- Xueya Wenge 1872 - 1930
- Fu 1899 - 1982
- Hu 1924 - ?
- Buolu
- Xie 1927 - ?
- Zhilan 1924 - ?
- Mingbin Lixiang 1946 -
- Mingwu Jingxiang 1951 -
- Jinlian 1947 -
- Li Wuang
- Hongjian 1938 -
- Xiaozhen
- Qing
- Jun
- Tao
- Bing
- Hai
- Liuliu
- Tangxiang 1939 -
- Zhang Jinxiang 1942 -
- Gu 1919 - 2000
- Chungen/Ken 1968 -
- Xilian 1965 -
- Xiaowu/Sherwood 1974 -
- Xiru 1973 -
- Huang deceased
- Xiangbao 1942 -
- Chen Sicong
- Runzhi (deceased)
- Dongmei
- Yan
- Hong
- He Buji "Paul Ho" 1919

Kiang (江) clan

- Ling-shen (adopted)
- Yuan Han-heng (adopted)
- Kiang Sun-ming
- Lin pen
- Yue
- Bing
- Hsiao
- Tsao
- Lu Din-hsin
- Lou 1903 - 1960
- Dayi/David 1952 -
- Susan 1952 -
- Kiang Shuangrui Sonia Ho 1931 -
- Kathryn 1978 -
- Jonathan 1981 -
- Jaclyn 1987 -
- Hongyi/Phillip 1954
- Michi 1962 -
- Chunyi/Sidney 1967 -
- Lesley 1967 -
- Christopher 1989 -
- Remi 1998 -
- Emily 2001 -
- Charles 2004 -

Lu (呂) clan

- Lu Chiao-hui 1886 - 1955
- Lu Bing-nan

PROLOGUE

We began by looking at a simple tourist map of Chongqing. It charted the outlines of western China's most populous city—at least as big as New York—in the hills of western China, and it showed at once why Chongqing is so strategically sited. We saw from the map that a high-cliff peninsula, rather in the shape of a dog's head, juts out to define the meeting of the waters of two of China's great rivers, the Jialing and the Yangtze. Here was the heart of the historic city, giving it an obvious military significance in struggles waged for its control over many centuries. Chongqing's grisly experience of war in the middle of the twentieth century was, alas, no novelty. But it was the reason for our visit, the start of our quest and a crucial step in the making of this book.

We had not come here to visit the Three Yangtze Gorges, or to explore the Dazu Grottoes, or to enjoy the hot springs—famous sites that now bring not only Western but also many Chinese tourists to the city. We were on a mission of a different sort. The oldest member of our party, Paul Ho, had spent a year and a half in wartime Chongqing as a young man. In March 2007 he was returning for the first time, accompanied by his wife Sonia and two of their sons, Phillip and Sidney. The eldest, David, was to join us later. I was there, along with my husband Peter Clarke and an interpreter, to see whether the fascinating story of the Ho family could be retrieved in its rich and fascinating human detail before it slipped into the anonymity of history.

It was, as I already knew, the story of a notable Chinese-American family who had made good through their own efforts in a new land. They could be seen as immigrants who had fulfilled the American dream of opportunity and enterprise, overcoming the deep-seated racial and ethnic prejudices that Paul in particular had first encountered. Now he was able to enjoy the professional success of all three sons and to delight in the fame of the eldest, Dr David Ho, whose pioneering work in treating AIDS had brought international recognition. But if the family had flourished in the United States, it was in China and in Taiwan that their roots were to be found. This was a story that needed historical context before it could be understood.

The family had been caught up, willy-nilly, in the bitter struggles between the Nationalist dictator Chiang Kai-shek and the Communist leader Mao Zedong. The ensuing rift that spilt his country had seen Paul forced to abandon one family in Communist China and seek refuge in Taiwan. His subsequent marriage to Sonia Kiang, his charming and serene Taiwanese wife with whom he had celebrated a golden wedding anniversary in 2001, had brought them obvious pride in their growing family—but at a price.

Poverty and revolution, war and invasion, were not distant events or empty slogans for Paul Ho. Instead, they had dogged his early footsteps; they had thwarted his scholarly inclinations; they had shaped his life, inflicting misfortunes which he had to suffer, tragedies that he had to endure and dilemmas with which he had to contend. It is a mark of his own fortitude that he snatched opportunity from potential disaster. It is a measure of his own luck—as he would recognize—that he lived to tell the tale.

* * *

Our quest in Chongqing, on that March day in 2007, was to find out where Paul had lived and worked, more than sixty years previously. Relevant documents were lacking on crucial questions. Legwork was the only way to answer them. Most important of all, we needed to tap Paul's own memory, which was asking a lot. As we set out to explore the vast city, we felt that we were looking for a needle in a haystack.

Paul was initially able to give us only a few clues, naturally enough. Now a man whose eighty-eighth birthday loomed, he remained amazingly active and alert, needing no persuasion to throw himself into our task. Indeed he supplied a nice sense of focus, his commitment spiced with an infectious sense of humor. There were moments when his face would wrinkle into a beaming smile and he would guffaw delightedly, 'yes, yes, yes!' He always saw the joke, rarely lost heart, never gave up. His unflagging energy offset his diminutive stature, and we were again made aware of the drive and the resilience with which he had struggled through decades of hardships—many of them the common lot of Chinese people of his generation.

Revisiting Chongqing after a long enforced absence was more than a trip down memory lane for Paul Ho. He was faced with a daunting challenge of recollection, as we all realized. He was certain, however, that the place where he remembered working as an interpreter had been high up—not an unusual location in a city dominated by ridges, cliffs and hills. We had hired a big black Buick, and could have done with an even bigger vehicle. Although it was a tight fit, we all squeezed in. And, after intently studying the map a little longer from his privileged position in the front seat, Paul pointed his finger to a bend in the north bank of the Jialing River: 'It's somewhere above here.'

We had arrived the previous evening in the dark—and in the rain. Our dominant impression of the city had been the decorative lights that lined our route from the airport terminal to the modern thirty-three-storey Golden Resources Hotel that would be our home for the next three days. When we began our tour the following morning, we had a different view of Chongqing. It was not just the dismal weather—a mixture of mist, fog, smog and drizzle—that made the city look so grim. Unlike our hotel, which had been built in the Chinese International Style and was shining with gold and marble, the buildings we now encountered as we drove around the peninsula were not only indistinguishable from one another, many of them had been abandoned in the course of construction and were rusting hulks of iron and steel.

Red lanterns and banners, left over from the New Year's festivities celebrating the Year of the Pig, gave some relief from the vast concrete slab of the new China that had been imposed on the old. So did the general bustle of people. Some were crowded into door-less hole-in-the-wall shops where they sat on small stools eating, or having their shoes shone, or the wax dug out of their ears or playing mahjong. Others shuffled along the sidewalk, carrying their wares on long shoulder poles that bowed under the weight of their load. The presence of many other road-users, driving scooters, buses or private cars, was brought to our attention by the generous use they made of their horns. And there were other sounds, mingling stereotypes of Communist China with those of consumer capitalism, as we drove through downtown Chongqing. Everything from Red Army patriotic songs to Simon and Garfunkel's 'The Sound of Silence' was blasted by invisible loudspeakers across virtually every square and intersection.

Before leaving the commercial area of the city, the Buick took us to the Liberation Monument: the focus of a big square surrounded by high-rise blocks and lit up like New York's Times Square. We paid our respects to a less imposing memorial honoring the thousands of residents who had lost their lives in Japanese air raids during what is generally called the Resistance War of 1937-1945 against the Japanese. The walls of the small, stone, bunker-like building were covered with black and white photographs that could easily have been taken by the Hungarian photographer, Robert Capa, who spent two years in China during the Resistance War. The graphic photographs depicted bodies splayed on the steep stone steps leading to the top of the peninsula. Some people had been crushed under the weight of falling debris; others had been asphyxiated by the smoke or pinned between a wall of fire and the high rocky walls by incendiary bombs. All of the bodies were lined up in neat rows, with chilling precision, ready for their journey to the mass graves on the outskirts of the city. The young Paul Ho had been spared such a fate; his luck had held, as he somberly appreciated on returning to this site of mourning.

Then we drove to a viewpoint at the confluence of the Jialing and Yangtze rivers. The misty view that shifted, evolved and changed every few seconds was in the tradition of the best classical Chinese landscape painters, convincing me once again that nature really does copy art. The inclement weather hid the ugly walls of occupied and abandoned apartment blocks. It made the two rivers look more distant and more mysterious than they actually were. The conditions under which we viewed Chongqing on that dank March day would have been considered 'good' for the city's citizens during the Resistance War. Cloud always made the work of the Japanese bombers more difficult—though not impossible, as the photographs in the war memorial bunker had shown.

It was clearly going to be a problem locating anything that resembled the topography of the 1940s. Moreover, we had not given our white-gloved driver, a slim and wiry young man, readily agreeable to our suggestions, much to go on. But, as we ascended the cliffs, he became caught up in the spirit of our quest. Following Paul's directions, he headed for the district of Jiangbei. This took us above the city's tall buildings, above the mist, and above the cacophony of city sounds. We exchanged asphalt for slime-covered mud tracks and the security of curbs for precipitous drop-off bends in the road.

Suddenly the 'New China' had disappeared. We were in one of the city's poorest neighborhoods. Every building was in need of repair. The small street markets, some located under makeshift blue and white striped awnings, were sparsely stocked. And the shabby dwellings seemingly offered little in the way of public amenities. One ridge seemed to resemble the next. Yet, as we climbed higher, Paul was beginning to find himself. Sensing that he might be in familiar territory, he looked around eagerly, and asked the driver to stop the car.

It had begun to rain again, yet we were happy to stretch our legs. We found ourselves standing next to a three-storey, brown-brick building. Walking around to the entrance, we encountered a small stone plaque. My hopes soared. Was it marking the residence of the Chinese interpreters who had worked for the American Army? No such luck. A quick translation revealed that the plaque commemorated the editor of the *Fangong* (or *Counterattack*) who had published his journal here during the Resistance War. This was clearly the wrong place. Moreover, when Paul looked in the direction of the river, he found that it could not be seen from here. Instead, he pointed to a ridge above our heads. We returned to the car and our obliging driver headed the Buick towards the higher ground. Driving along an increasingly narrow track, we passed windowless, one-storey brick and concrete hovels, abandoned factories and packs of curious dogs. We met vehicles much larger than our own. Where had they come from? Passing them along the precipitous ledges required a lot of skillful maneuvering.

None of us knew where we were going—except Paul, so we hoped. When we reached the top of the cliff the driver stopped. The mist had shifted and we glimpsed an opening down to the Jialing River. The view of the river was the key thing. Likewise, some of the abandoned buildings evidently seemed familiar. Paul, now very excited, was convinced that he was seeing what he remembered from sixty-odd years ago. 'This is where I looked down over tiny plots of land to the river and beyond that to the city.' And the present structures around the site? 'No, the brick building where we worked is no longer here.'

We were standing on an abandoned lot now used as a local garbage dump, looking rather disconsolately for any clues. Paul's son Phillip, who is a dentist, spotted an old tube of Colgate toothpaste. Then he asked his father: 'Did you go down to the city very often?' Paul said that there were seldom any opportunities to do so. But on the few occasions when he and his fellow translators did have some time off, they would walk to an assembly point further down the hill, then catch a lift into town on an American Army vehicle. But there hadn't been much to go down for—portions of the city, as we had just seen in the photographs, had been wiped out by the bombing, there were many refugees, and not enough water and food.

Paul had been open about his fears that our visit to Chongqing would not produce results: 'I don't know anybody there anymore—everyone move back to the coast in 1945; I won't find anything now.' It was true that Paul no longer had any acquaintances in the city, but with the help of our driver and the gaggle of people who answered our questions whenever we stopped the car, Paul had found the site of his old quarters. The trip to Chongqing had not, therefore, been in vain, however unprepossessing the environment. We took Paul's photograph as he stood amidst broken bricks and refuse above the river, framed by the distant row of concrete buildings and one-storey bungalows, and above the limestone cliffs. This was to be the first of many photographs over the next few weeks, charting Paul's formative years in China.

The next day we set off with more confidence that our methods—and Paul's memory—would yield results. Sidney stayed behind with his mother, Sonia, who opted to rest after so much travel. This was wise because we were in for a two-hundred-mile drive due south of Chongqing. Our destination was the remote town of Zunyi in one of China's poorest provinces, Guizhou. The town is widely known for two things: its location near the source of China's popular alcoholic drink, Maotai, and as the place where, during the Red Army's ten-thousand-li Long March in 1934-1935, Mao Zedong had emerged as the leader of the Chinese Communist Party (hereafter CCP). For my purposes, however, Zunyi had another significance. This was where, after Japan's offensive in coastal China, the students and the professors from National Chekiang University in Hangzhou had ended up for most of the Resistance War. Zunyi was thus the place where Paul Ho had begun his student days.

It used to take two days to cover the distance between Chongqing and Zunyi. But a spanking new four-lane highway has replaced this section of the Burma Road, once the route for American supplies and the road that the Chinese had literally built with their hands during the Resistance War. Passing through tunnels and over viaducts as it bites into the Daiou Shan mountain range, the new highway is an impressive engineering feat. It must clearly have cost a huge amount of money to construct yet we found it little used. By the side of the highway we saw remnants of the old Burma Road. There was also a railway that, since the 1950s, has linked Guizhou's provincial capital Guiyang, lying to the south of Zunyi, with Chongqing to the north. But there was little else.

During our three-and-a-half hour journey we passed only a few private cars like our own. Even the old trucks that belched out black smoke from their exhausts (and frequently broke down by the side and sometimes in the middle of the highway) were few and far between. We passed only one gas station. And any thought of finding refreshments was out of the question. What we did see were workers, mainly women, trimming the verges and cleaning the railings dividing the highway's four lanes. On one remote stretch a child, of not more than four years old, walked confidently along the verge. 'Life is more expendable here than back home,' Phillip remarked dryly as we sped past the unaccompanied toddler.

It became obvious that we had moved out of the more cosmopolitan 'New China' of Chongqing into a much more traditional area where people were living close to the land. On all sides, the lower regions of the mountains were terraced. Houses clustered on ledges. We saw the occasional satellite dish, the blank white faces of burial tombs and, elevated onto concrete plinths or poised on rooftops, were larger-than-life-size black and white footballs. As we moved closer to Zunyi, the broad-bottomed valleys were covered in fields of lemon-colored rape seed and in orchards of plum blossoms; we noticed signs of building and more vehicles joined us on the highway.

Zunyi itself proved a pleasant surprise. It was not the depressing place we had been led to expect. People were well dressed and busily occupied with their lives. There were parks along the river—one area had been dammed to make a swimming pool—and there were banks of flowers that enlivened every major intersection. But my heart sank when I realized that, just as in Chongqing, the desire to tear down the past and bring China into the twenty-first century had left few old buildings from the era that most interested us. My husband, Peter, sitting next to Paul at lunch, observed him looking around, rather downcast, and asked if he remembered anything. 'No,' Paul replied flatly, 'everything has changed.' We began to feel that perhaps our luck of yesterday had changed too.

It was not until we arrived in the centre of town that the outlook began to brighten. Paul at once recognized an ancient red stone bridge that spanned a tributary of the Yaxi River and, above it, the remnants of a Buddhist temple. Again, as on the previous day, the scent suddenly became clear. Looking for anyone who might remember what Zunyi had looked like during the Resistance War, Paul approached an elderly man. No good, he was from Nanchang and knew nothing. Another potential informant of the right age also turned out to be a newcomer.

Then, on the corner of the bridge, an old man with a wispy beard turned out to be a local. He was eighty-four and had always lived in Zunyi. Thankfully, he was able to confirm Paul's hunch that we were in the right part of the city. Yes, the buildings fronting the river were new; they had replaced a series of older dwellings that had been seconded to the university during the war. Almost at once, an elderly lady of indeterminate age—she turned out to be a fit eighty-seven—popped up. She was very calm, untroubled by Paul's curious questions, but confident in her answers. She confirmed that this was where National Chekiang University had been—she remembered it all quite clearly in a matter-of-fact way. Paul's mood was now elated. 'A Eureka moment,' was how Phillip described his father's response.

By this time we had attracted a small crowd and the fact that we were strangers became apparent. People stared. Young children approached us with the only word of English they knew—'Hello'. Vendors offered to sell us sesame cakes, a man signaled to an antiquated contraption that could measure both our height and record our weight; and a beggar, who occupied the middle of the sidewalk, cried out for alms.

Paul saw none of this. He was reliving his student days. Clutching Peter's arm, Paul told us just where everything had stood: the men had been housed on the side of the river where we were now standing; the girls had lived on the other side where we had parked our car near the big public buildings. 'Yes,' Paul joked, 'I often crossed the bridge to see the girls.' We helped him climb onto a stone bench beside the bridge. Then we snapped our cameras. Paul looked dapper in his grey tweed sports jacket, and looked more pleased than at any previous point on the trip. We ate the sesame cake, measured our height and weight, gave a few coins to the beggar, and then, eager to tell Sonia and Sidney about our successful expedition, we began the long drive back to Chongqing.

* * *

Paul's excitement was palpable the following day when we boarded an aircraft destined for Nanchang, the capital city of his home province in south-eastern China, Jiangxi. Phillip and Sidney were also upbeat because their wives Michi and Lesley and their children—eight year old Remi and six year old Emily—would be waiting for them at the Gloria Plaza Hotel in Nanchang. Paul and Sonia were aware, however, of the increasingly embarrassing absence of their eldest son, who was to meet us in Nanchang. David Ho, his wife Susan and their son Jonathan were supposed to have arrived by now, but their plane had been delayed in New York by a snowstorm and it was uncertain when they would be able to join us.

Flying to Nanchang we saw nothing of the Wuling and Jiuling mountains, the vast Dongting lake or the majestic Yuan and Wu rivers because, once again, we were flying in the dark. When we arrived in Nanchang, more than two hours late, we were met at the airport by a delegation representing the Chinese Overseas Friendship Association and by members of the Foreign Affairs and Overseas Chinese Affairs Office of Jiangxi's Provincial People's Government. There was no doubt that we were now on Paul Ho's home territory, but the scale of the official reception was evidently reinforced by the celebrity of his absent son David, now so well known throughout the province for his pioneering work on anti-retroviral treatment of HIV patients—the so-called 'AIDS cocktail'.

Our efforts to retrace Paul Ho's formative years in Jiangxi began the morning following our arrival in Nanchang—and necessarily began without the delayed David. The government had provided us with a mini-bus and an interpreter. Our first stop, as we drove among the city's many new buildings, was Nanchang Second Middle School, where Paul had been a student in the 1930s. We found that our visit posed as many questions as it answered—not surprisingly, given the ravages of three-quarters of a century.

Japanese bombs had destroyed a large part of the original school—what remained had been transformed into an electronics factory. The bombs had also incinerated the school's records. The wartime school itself, as we already knew from Paul, had meanwhile been evacuated to the remote village of Shihuiqiao that lay almost two hundred miles south of Nanchang. Moreover, the site that we were now being driven to, lying adjacent to Nanchang's beautiful East Lake on Supu Road, was not even the primary location of present-day Nanchang Second Middle School. Most of the school's three thousand pupils now live and study in a more spacious campus at Honggutan on the outskirts of the city. Today we would not be seeing either the place where Paul had spent those early years of his life, still less finding any records that would give me the precise dates of when he was at the school. What was left to stir his memories?

When our bus drove through the imposing gates of the school's secondary campus we received a fine reception: not only a delegation led by Principal Wu Qin, but also a large red banner welcoming the absent David Ho to the school. Following a great deal of handshaking and card-exchanging, a smartly turned-out Wu Qin led us through a well-treed courtyard to an unheated concrete building. We followed her up a steep flight of stairs to a top-floor classroom that had been transformed into a reception room by nestling the students' desks into a long table. The makeshift table was strewn with bouquets of carnations, roses and white lilies; there were plates of oranges, clusters of bananas and—best of all on a chilly morning—paper cups filled to the brim with steaming tea. It was here that we heard various accounts of the school in the 1930s.

Principal Wu Qin naturally spoke first, and gave us an abbreviated version of the school's motto: 'continuously work hard—that is the whole way', signaling the founder's debt to Confucius. She also told us that, while the school was Nanchang's second high school, it was really the city's first, because its students tried harder—and got results: 'During the last two years more than three hundred students have received first class degrees in the national examination.' She gave a graceful encomium on her guest: 'Paul Ho was not only the best student, he was the first student-exile to return to the school.'

By this time Paul was beaming with pride. It did not matter to him that this was not the building where he had studied. Or that he was surrounded by school officials who were half his age. Or that the primary guest of honor, as the welcoming banner had indicated, was not among us. Paul appeared equally oblivious that the rest of us were shivering from the cold and dampness of the dreary building. When he rose from his chair to address the small group he was, metaphorically at least, back at the school that had shaped the early years of his life. Moreover he now had an opportunity to trade reminiscences with an extraordinary group of four elderly men who had also been at the school.

The wonderful thing was that everyone had a story that they enjoyed telling. The baffling thing was that everyone had a different story. I quickly realized that I would find no easy consensus on all sorts of issues that I hoped to get straight. And this prompted a further reflection: that the telling and retelling of these stories, the refreshment of fond or bitter memories and the revisiting of familiar myths, was important in itself. Paul was not alone in giving me accounts that did not always balance, did not always add up, did not always reconcile. I knew then that this process of inquiry, recollection, discovery and revision would itself be a part of the story I had to tell in this book.

After an intensely packed couple of hours, my mind was full of questions as we climbed back down the steps to the tree-shaded courtyard. How had it been possible for an entire school to move in the midst of war? Why had the school's location changed so often? What, if anything, had the students studied under these conditions? And what about Paul Ho himself? How had he got from Nanchang to Shihuiqiao when the newly built railway and all other forms of transportation had been disrupted by the war? Did his parents know that he had left Nanchang and, if so, where their son had been evacuated? And, in her address that morning, what had prompted Principal Wu Qin to claim that Paul had been a leading student? Was her comment based on hearsay? Politeness? Or had she consulted some document that had survived the Japanese bombs? Above all, I wondered what Paul had been thinking as he sat in that bone-chilling classroom. What about the broken careers of his former classmates? Did their fate show what might have happened to him had he not boarded a boat to Taiwan in July 1947?

The questions that rattled around my head as I walked down the stairs into the thin, cold sunshine were interrupted by the arrival of a large black limousine. David, Susan and their twenty-four year old son Jonathan had finally arrived! Everyone was happy to see them: the school officials who had prepared the banner honoring the distinguished scientist; Paul and Sonia who never saw enough of their eldest son because he and his family lived on the other side of the North American continent; Phillip and Sidney who were looking forward to being with their brother and his family. Following introductions and more handshaking, we moved toward a sunny area of the courtyard where chairs had been set up in a row. The resulting photograph shows Paul and Sonia surrounded by their family and friends, by the school's officials and by men who, like Paul, had never known what it was like to stop learning, during good times and bad.

Our party was at last complete. During the following eight days, David's reputation unlocked every door—an effect discreetly used by him to honor his father and to facilitate my task as biographer. We were overwhelmed by the spontaneous respect shown him by students and teachers alike in schools as well as universities. Even in a remote village, we saw David's name scrawled onto the wall of a derelict building.

It was inevitable that David was expected to sing for our group's supper. And never more so than when we visited the eight-thousand-strong high school, the Dayi Middle School, named after David Ho, in his father's hometown of Xinyu. Speaking in English about the history of SARS, HIV and the 1918 Avian Influenza epidemics, David stretched the linguistic skills of the students. Most of them demonstrated admirably, that they had understood what Dr Ho had said when, at the end of the lecture, they fired off their own questions. 'When did you get married?' That was simple: 1976. 'What do you think has been your greatest contribution to science?' This was perhaps a predictable question, from an enthusiastic young male student, but the answer less so. 'Not developing the AIDS cocktail as you might expect,' David told him, 'but understanding what the virus was doing before anyone else.' Likewise David was asked what was the greatest satisfaction that he had derived from his work. 'Not receiving honors and awards,' he replied, 'but the gratification of having an AIDS infected stranger walk up to me and say: "You have saved my life".' Then a young woman asked: 'What are the qualities that I and the other students here need in order to become successful scientists?' Without a blink David replied: 'Determination and tenacity.' Finally, there came the blunt question that prompted the school principal to bring the session to an end: 'Although you are the honorary president of our school, why do you visit us so seldom?'

Likewise, on the recently built campus of Nanchang University with its 50,000 students, we attended a ceremony proudly admitting David as the honorary dean of its medical school. And when we finally reached Hangzhou in eastern China, there was the inevitable invitation for David to address the medical students at the Zhejiang University, as the former National Chekiang University, his father's alma mater, is now known. Traveling with father and son, the Ho name ensured that we were feted by governors and vice-governors, by party secretaries and mayors, by university presidents and school principals.

Entertaining in China follows a strict pattern, as we soon discovered. Less formal events, like our visit to Nanchang Second Middle School, took place around a table and generally did not exceed an hour or so. More formal occasions, like the banquets that were given in our honor by the governor—a Mao look-a-like—and by the mayor of Nanchang, proved much longer. They invariably began with the guests and their hosts sitting, Mao-Nixon fashion, in overstuffed armchairs covered with lace antimacassars. There followed introductions, during which the accomplishments of the guests and hosts alike were hugely exaggerated—I sat with comely modesty while I was called 'a famous biographer, well known to all of China'. Then we were presented with gifts.

Gift-giving is an art-form in China. David and Paul would be presented with 'national level gifts': perhaps a large ceramic plate or a hand-painted vase. The rest of us received an assortment of wonderful items ranging from strings of pearls and eggshell-thin ceramic vessels to beautifully bound books and silk scrolls. Our hosts, in return, would receive from David a superbly cut-glass apple—that symbol for New York that had been coined by one of the city's jazz singers in the mid-twentieth century. Following the exchange of gifts there would commence a formal dinner during which food was plied with unstinting hospitality. Throughout the meal there ensued a good deal of toasting. These gestures, I learned, are not made across the table. Instead, in China every host approaches his or her guest—at which point you set aside your chopsticks, rise from your chair and, if your host says, 'Ganbei', it's bottoms up! I learned that this considerable to-ing and fro-ing only ends when your host decides that he or she has had enough. So even if you have not finished eating a sumptuous dessert you are invited to abandon your food and leave the dining room.

By the time we left Nanchang, it seemed that every major official in town had honored us. We had been taken to the east bank of the Gan River to see a large reconstructed Buddhist pavilion originally built in 386 for the monk Huiyuan. We had also paid homage to one of the country's greatest painters, Bada Shanren, visiting his water-locked former house on an island in the middle of a tranquil lake, and viewing reproductions of his work.

Paul's hometown, Xinyu, is also in the province of Jiangxi, less than a hundred miles from Nanchang. Yet the differences between the cities are immense. As the capital of the province and the economic centre of the Gan river system,

Nanchang is a self-confident and prosperous city. Our bus soon left the red soil and lush crops that dominate the Gan River Plain and drove into the hills. While it is true that Xinyu is linked to most of the south and southeast of the country by rail and a modern highway, that it is blessed with abundant mineral resources, and that it boasts a population of over one million, it is provincial to the core and the agricultural villages surrounding it are dirt poor.

In Xinyu our bus pulled up in front of a post-modern government guesthouse in the centre of the city. Combining Swiss-chalet and Cape Cod clapboard architectural styles, the building jarred stylistically with the government-run glass palace, the Beihu Hotel, towering above it. When we disembarked from the bus, Liu Zong Ping, the director of the Foreign Affairs Office, and several of his colleagues were there to greet us, as were a larger group of less formally dressed people. These were all members of Paul's family.

The family name is conventionally transcribed into Pinyin as He (though after Paul arrived in America he used Ho, which is the form that I shall use in the later chapters of this book). The family's home village at Songlin, in the foothills ten miles to the south of Xinyu, is alternatively known as Hejiacun, in honor of the clan. Everyone in the village bares the name He. Most of Paul's extended family still reside there and had made the journey into the city to greet him; others, who had moved from Songlin to Xinyu, had walked or ridden their bicycles to the government compound. I surveyed their beaming faces expectantly, looking for any family resemblances, and did not have to wait long.

Out of the crowd emerged Paul's three children from his first marriage, born while he was still a high school student. His eldest daughter, Honglian was sixty-nine; his eldest son, Tangxiang, sixty-eight; and the younger daughter, Xiangbao sixty-five. After embracing their father, they turned to their stepmother, Sonia, and greeted her warmly too.

This was a striking moment in more senses than one. I turned from looking at these three grown-up children to the three sons of Paul's second family: David, a famous scientist, at fifty-five; Phillip, a well-established dentist, at fifty-three; and Sidney, already a successful publicist, at forty years old. I had not been prepared for the enormous contrast. It was not primarily a matter of age, or the contrast between soft and heavily callused hands. Nor was it just a matter of dress, or stance or the condition of the teeth that accentuated the contrasts between the Chinese and American siblings. It was none of these things in themselves, but perhaps all of them cumulatively, revealing a manifest difference in life-chances that set these people apart.

According to the People's Republic of China (hereafter PRC) every member of the immediate Ho family had a 'bad class background.' Thus the family had lost their home and their lands in the early 1950s during the Land Reform. Then from 1966 to 1976 they had been humiliated during the Cultural Revolution. Poverty had been twisted together with politics to deny Paul's first family advantages that his second family had seized with both hands. Phillip had warned me that the effects of the Land Reform, and the Cultural Revolution were written on his step-brother's face. Perversely, it was because Tangxiang and his two sisters, Honglian and Xiangbao, were the grandchildren of a prominent landlord—as well as the children of an American-based father—that they had all been denied a proper education. While Honglian had five years of schooling, Tangxiang and Xiangbao had attended school for only three years.

* * *

Though in sheer numbers the Ho family dominated the reception party that had come to welcome us, it was clear from the outset that the government officials would have centre stage during our visit to Xinyu. They were keen to settle us into the government guesthouse, where the staff attended to our every need, from laundry—and endless cups of tea—to turning our beds and our heating up and down every time we left our room. They were eager to present us with a detailed itinerary. One glance at it assured us that over the course of the next week we would be well fed and entertained. The government officials were also proud to offer us a mini-bus and a driver. Equipped with sirens and flashing lights, we wove through the city traffic, ignoring red lights; and, as the bus sped along the highways, we often exceeded the speed limit, forcing police cars and every other vehicle we passed to the side of the road.

While Xinyu's city officials assured us that they were going to do everything they could to facilitate the writing of the Ho biography, we quickly realized that their help would come at a price. For example, we had little chance to explore the city by ourselves. This was because the tall, slim and handsome Liu Zong Ping and his amiable assistant, Liu Tao, an equally attractive young woman, were never more than a few paces from the front door of the guesthouse whenever we emerged. This energetic pair not only accompanied us to breakfast but to a series of formal luncheons and dinners, the purpose of which was to thank David Ho for the 'strong support' he had given to China after the outbreak of SARS and to ensure him that 'all levels' of government in Jiangxi Province were now doing their best to publicize, prevent and control the spread of AIDS.

Our primary agenda was simple: to visit the family's ancestral home, Hejiacun village in Songlin. On arrival in Xinyu, therefore, after we had unpacked our bags and attended a sumptuous lunch given for us by the local party secretary, Hu Gaoping, we boarded the minibus, along with Tangxiang, Honglian and Xiangbao.

I knew that I should not expect too much when I saw the family's home—their 'bad class background' had seen to that. This meant that I would have to imagine what the family's house and the village itself had looked like when Paul was a child—before the war, before the revolution, before the Land Reform, before the Cultural Revolution and before the village's one hundred households had been depleted by the departure of so many young men and women in search of employment in the fast developing cities of coastal southern China.

When Paul was a child, it took him half a day to walk from Xinyu to Hejiacun village. Now we made journey in less than fifteen minutes. Arriving in the outskirts of the village we encountered several new two-storey concrete dwellings. As our bus approached the centre of Hejiacun, it became apparent that many of the houses were not only in disrepair but had been abandoned. This poor agricultural village had not, however, been entirely depopulated. Instead, when our bus turned a corner and entered a small square, fronted on one side by an artificial pond and on the other by an imposing brick-faced building, we were greeted by a large crowd. As we stepped down from the bus, children of around twelve dressed in plain white cotton uniforms and red hats belted out a simple four-note tune on their pipes, drums and cymbals. Another group—some forty or fifty people—jostled for space around us and sought a view from the stone steps of the ancestral hall which stood on the opposite side of the square.

There was a great sense of occasion, what with the engaging innocence of the band, the red and white banners welcoming David and Paul Ho, the deafening firecrackers and the resulting smoke that stung our eyes. All around, there were the curious onlookers crowding towards Paul Ho, the last surviving son of the village's most prominent landlord; the exile, now the returning champion.

Rather bemused by the wonder of the whole spectacle, Paul looked to his left then to his right at the sea of faces all bearing the He family surname. 'This is my brother's widow, He Xie,' Paul said as he invited an ancient, wizened-faced woman to step forward from the crowd and shake my hand. 'And here is the ancestral hall,' Paul explained as he led us into the dilapidated earthen-floored building that had been stripped of everything except a huge barrel and a few banners left over from the New Year's celebration. 'When I was a child this was the most beautiful building in the village,' Paul assured me.

When we emerged through the rear door of the former ancestral hall, the student-band was there to meet us. And as we made our way down a narrow dirt lane that cut through the centre of the village, we could hear their four-note tune and still smell the smoke from the firecrackers. The ancestral home was duly located and inspected, as was the more modest house in which Paul's mother had spent her last years. But we did not linger, having a more fitting way to honor her memory.

Following a short drive to the edge of the village, our bus stopped at the base of an undulating hill known as Yanshan that rose above us. This is where Paul's mother, Fu, had chosen to be buried. Sonia and the two young children, Remi and Emily, elected to remain on the bus, and the government officials who had accompanied us to Hejiacun returned to Xinyu. The rest of the family group began the climb up the steep slope. The afternoon was now quite hot and we had been able to discard our coats in the bus. It felt good to bare our arms to the sun and to stretch our legs.

During the Cultural Revolution people were prohibited from burying their dead: Mao decreed that everyone had to be cremated. Yet Paul's mother, living until 1982, five years after the end of the Cultural Revolution, had been able to order a fir coffin and to choose a burial site. The path leading to the site Fu had chosen wound through head-high bushes—many of them laden with bright pink azalea blossoms. Someone had attempted to make our climb easier by removing the vegetation that had grown over the narrow path. But it was nevertheless a difficult trek. At one point we caught sight of the adjacent hill, Laojinshan, where Paul's father, Wenge, had been laid to rest so many years earlier. 'Nothing has changed in the countryside,' Paul remarked. After climbing up an even steeper stretch, we saw an outcrop jutting out of the hill. When we got closer to it we could see that there was not just one, but four gravestones on the spur.

Paul had already told me that his mother had not wanted to be buried with her husband or any other members of the village. Moreover, Fu had chosen an unpopular location, one that village gossip predicted would bring either notably good luck or notably bad luck to her descendents. Since her burial in 1983 the success of Paul and Sonia Ho and their children had increased the value of her resting place. Hoping to cash in on the good fortune of the American-based Ho family, villagers who had initially scorned the site had joined Paul's mother on the spur.

Because she was the first person to be buried on Yanshan, Paul's mother had captured the dominant position on the steep bluff that overlooked her home. When we finally reached the spur, we saw a sharp conical pile of earth rising behind her headstone. 'The earth is to keep her warm,' Paul told us. In order to do this and to mark our visit, two members of our party—Paul's farmer nephews, Ming Bin and Ming Wu—added fresh-cut sods to the pile. Finally, in order to ensure that Fu was given nourishment, Tangxiang laid a basket containing three eggs and boiled pork shank at the base of the grave. He also lit several sticks of incense that he placed on the sod and on either side of the gravestone.

Without any word of instruction, first Paul, then his sons—Tangxiang, David, Phillip, Sidney—followed by their sisters, spouses and their children, moved to the front of the grave and bowed three times. It was a simple ceremony, not solemn but certainly serious, and certainly respectful of earlier ways of paying homage. When the ceremony was over we took a few snapshots of the grave with its basket of offerings, incense and sprig of azalea blossoms that Xiangbao had picked on the way up the hill.

Just as we turned to leave, one of Paul's nephews let off firecrackers to frighten the evil spirits from the gravesite. We could hear them crack and sputter as we made our descent. And when I turned around to catch one last glimpse of the grave from a lower viewpoint, large plumes of blue smoke were rising above the spur.

Nobody needed to say that the visit to Fu's grave was a highly significant moment in this family pilgrimage. Paul had had an opportunity to pay homage to his mother in the company of his entire family. Asked what he had been thinking when he stood before the grave, Paul said that he told his mother that there were three generations who had come to pay their respects. He also told Fu that their lives had 'gone smooth'; they had all been diligent students and had worked hard. Finally, Paul told his mother that she was 'a good woman who deserved to be in heaven.' His grandson Jonathan (as he later confided) had been 'overwhelmed' by this first visit to his great-grandmother's grave, and by meeting aunts and uncles of whose existence he had been unaware until just before the trip.

Until now Tangxiang, Honglian and Xiangbao had been on the periphery of our visit. They had not been invited to our welcoming lunch and would be absent from the reception and dinner that was to be given in our honor by the city's mayor, Wang Dehe, at the government banqueting hall that evening. But the act of bowing before the gravestone in order of seniority had its own simple logic and sense of precedence, acknowledging the rightful place of the children from Paul's first marriage within his extended family. 'That was the great equalizer,' Phillip later commented, 'because nobody told Tangxiang that he had to go last and he was very proud to go first.'

This was the climax of a trip that had stimulated so many vivid memories of more than sixty years earlier for Paul Ho. Before going on to explore the early years of Sonia's life in Taiwan, I now needed time to place Paul's life in the historical context of Republican and Communist China. I needed to go back home and resolve the contradictions and competing stories that I had heard over the last three weeks. The family visit had helped me chart Paul's formative years in China, and the three rewarding weeks of traveling, eating, sight-seeing and speaking with his family had brought many flashes of illumination on their story. It had undoubtedly provided me with some answers—but also with a longer list of questions than when I had started out.

Ho family home Hejiacun

Ancestral Hall, Hejiacun

CHAPTER 1

'Strict Father, Kind Mother'

嚴父慈母

'Poor people came into the house to ask father for rice and money.' This was Paul Ho's immediate response, in old age, when I asked him to recall his earliest memory of growing up in the He family village, Hejiacun, in Songlin. As usual, his recollection was sharp but rather understated, leaving unsaid what others might describe in more emotive terms.

No region of Jiangxi province escaped poverty during the early decades of the twentieth century, and it was often extreme. The province's population was rapidly expanding, to about seventeen million, putting pressure on resources. People living in Jiangxi, like so many other people in the countryside, experienced famine made acute by droughts, flooding or invasions of locusts; they also suffered from infectious diseases and high mortality rates. Under such conditions, rents were burdensome, taxes oppressive. In the absence of technological know-how that might have helped cope with some of these problems, it was not unknown for men to sell their children, then their wives, in order to survive. Even starving women sometimes exchanged their babies as food—'You eat mine, I'll eat yours.' One destitute woman was reduced to pounding a brick into a pulp and eating it. 'It made me feel better', she grimly recalled years later.[1]

---

[1] See Ida Pruitt, *A Daughter of Han* (Stanford: Stanford University Press 1945; 1967) and Jack Belden, *China Shakes the World* (New York: Monthly Review Press 1970).

People living in Songlin often had to look starvation in the face. The village lying next to the Kunmu Jiang (river) had few resources and crops were meager. Although southern Jiangxi had plenty of minerals, it was poor compared to the agriculturally rich villages surrounding Poyang Lake—the province's largest fresh-water lake—to the north. The southern county seat of Xinyu could not compare to northern cities like Jingdezhen, which enjoyed a thriving ceramic industry, or even the mountain town of Lu Shan that, from the early twentieth century, provided well-to-do officials from the provincial capital of Nanchang and Western missionaries with an escape from the humid heat of the summer.

Even in the southern part of the province, however, a small privileged class escaped deprivation. And this, of course, is why Paul remembers the poor making their way to his father's house, for his family—unlike ninety-eight percent of the population—had more than enough to eat. Their own problems were to begin much later with the country's spiral into war and revolution.

The style in which the family had once lived could still be easily imagined from what I saw for myself on visiting Hejiacun in the spring of 2007. Paul's ancestral home was, I suppose, much as I had expected it to be. Buildings in this part of China are designed to accommodate high subtropical temperatures and the dwellings, with their generous eaves, are packed closely together. This configuration not only provided shady narrow lanes during the scorching summer heat. In a country where only ten per cent of the land is arable, it allowed for maximum use of farmland.

We saw that the He family home was nestled within a warren of smaller dwellings in the heart of the village. It was built of mud-baked bricks, once covered with white lime plaster, which served to reflect rather than to absorb the heat during the long sun-drenched summer months. The two-storey He family home sported a grey tile roof and, in keeping with the architectural style in this part of China, there were no windows facing the alley. There were earthen floors, four open sky-wells with courtyards below them that broke the roof of the imposing structure, and there had been no fewer than twenty rooms. The absence of windows, Paul assured me, inhibited access to robbers and bandits and kept his family's wealth from 'escaping' through an open aperture.

On the family visit in 2007, we gathered around the main entrance situated in the centre of the wide front of the now shabby building. Above the heavily secured door was a black and white decorative motif and along the sides of the door itself were two red panels bearing faded gatepost couplets. A young man appeared with a long-handled twig broom and energetically scrubbed the surface of the panels so that we could read the faded characters or ideographs. It was no use. The ideographs could not be deciphered. But if we had been able to read them, they would probably have expressed the He family's wish for longevity, health, luck and the other virtues associated with happiness and a long life.

Although Paul's former home, which had once accommodated four families belonging to the He clan, remained the largest domestic building in the village, it had fallen into a sad state of disrepair. The main door that would in the past have led to the common room displaying the ancestral spirit tablets, the family genealogy and offerings of food and incense was not surprisingly locked. Paul directed us to a less imposing door on the right-hand side of the main entrance. The door creaked open. 'This is where I was born,' he told us. We peered inside. The room was surprisingly small, its floor strewn with straw. We had to imagine the brick-heated *kang*—or bed—that had been along one of the walls, and the elaborately carved cupboards and chests that had once furnished a handsome room. Only a cow seemed to live there now. During the Land Reform, Paul's family had been forced to exchange this dwelling for a pigsty. Whatever would his ancestors have thought?

Paul could proudly trace a long line of ancestors, as I was to discover. A couple of days after our visit to Songlin, his eldest son, Tangxiang, greeted us at the government guesthouse carrying a large plastic bag. It contained the He family's genealogy. Within the pages of this tightly bound document were lists of names, birth and death dates, and, in a few cases, essays celebrating the more illustrious male members of the family.

For me, to lay hands on this document was a great coup. During the Cultural Revolution Mao had decreed that all family genealogies should be destroyed. The He genealogy had survived because the relatives had divided it up, then hidden it between the rafters of their homes. Rewritten in 1996 from surviving portions of the original, this formidable document must, of course, be treated with caution.[2] As one scholar has warned, genealogies 'were discovered, invented, fabricated, or otherwise artfully produced for those who came to be accepted

---

[2]   The He family genealogy (家譜) was transcribed in 1996 from the original document by the husband, Cheng Sicong, of Paul's youngest daughter, Xiangbao, who, as Vice Chairman of the Culture and History Committee of the Political Council for Xinyu Municipality in Zongwan County, had a broad knowledge of the region.

socially as Chinese.'[3] The story told in the He's—or later the Ho's—genealogy is what the family wanted to believe and must be read as such.

Western Christians traditionally claimed to be descendants of Adam and Eve; the only problem was to identify the intervening generations. Likewise, many Chinese trace their ancestors to the legendary Chinese sovereign, the Yellow Emperor, or Huang Di, who is said to have reigned from 2697 BC to 2598 BC. The He genealogy duly makes this claim; but we can skip many generations of the Yellow Emperor's progeny to the parts that relate more certainly and directly to the origins of the family that settled in Hejiacun.

In 230 BC, so we are told, the Kingdom of Han was conquered by the Kingdom of Qin and the Han people were scattered along the banks of the Yangtze and Huai Rivers. This is when the family name was changed from Han to He. But many centuries passed before any connection was made with the present Jiangxi area of settlement. It was not until the reign of the first Emperor of the Tang Dynasty (618-907 AD) that a member of the He family, the judge, He Sixing, moved south to Jizhou, which was near Hejiacun in Songlin.

All these painfully reconstructed details are preserved in the precious genealogy, compiled in an era that did not use a fast-forward button. It was at least five hundred years later, during the reign of Huizong in the northern Song Dynasty in the twelfth century, that one of He Sixing's descendants, He Changshi, settled at the base of two hills—Laojinshan and Yanshan—in present-day Songlin, thus establishing its identity as Hejiacun. Paul can thus cite the genealogy in support of a proud claim that his ancestral village dates back at least eight hundred years.

Though everyone in Hejiacun bears the surname He, there are three divisions and six *zhi*—or branches—in the He clan. Paul's branch of the family, it seems, have not always been farmers and landlords. They take pride in the genealogical record that they were also high-ranking government officials and learned scholars. For example, He Guangxu, who taught in Songlin during the latter part of the nineteenth century, is venerated as a great teacher and scholar. Thus the quest for knowledge was, for many male members of the He lineage, a matter of family pride and tradition. A poem survives, written in the late nineteenth century by He Yan Xian, rhapsodizing about the Songlin (or Pine Forest) Academy that he helped to establish:

---

[3]   Patricia Buckley Ebrey, *Women and the Family in Chinese History* (New York: Routledge, 2002) p. 174

Pine trees soaring straight to the sky
Forest deep where hidden fog is rising
Pine trees tower over swirling smoke like dancing ink
Forest permeated with bird songs and reading
Pines and cypresses unite in a common goal
Forest springs provide the desire to study
The classics together.[4]

*   *   *

Paul knew much of this through family legend and it is not difficult to see a connection with his own lifelong pursuit of knowledge. But his own career, of course, took him far from his homeland—he had no genealogy hidden in the rafters of his Los Angeles house. Much of what we know about the recent history of the He family can be credited to the members of the family who remained resident in Songlin after Paul's departure—in particular, his first son, Tangxiang, who proved to be a valuable source in supplementing his father's own memories. Though these living links are vital in reconstructing the family's history, there are natural rivalries, understandable discrepancies and differences, even over names.

Paul gives his father's name as Wenge, though several other names are recorded in the family genealogy.[5] This was the name by which the boy knew him, and which is still venerated as that of a patriarch who casts a gigantic shadow in family legend. There is no dispute that Wenge was a substantial landlord, as his surviving house in Hejiacun, even in its dilapidated state, suggests. Yet his origins

---

[4]
松立干霄翹瞻上達
林深隱霧奮起高騰
松下煙飛同墨舞
林間鳥語雜書聲
松柏有心同勵志
林泉適意共研經

[5] The family genealogy gives Paul father's names as Wenge, Wenge, and Zhencheng in that order. Paul remembers that his father was known as Wenge. Tangxiang adds that his grandfather was also known by the honorific name of Wenge Laoye (meaning, keeper of the literary pavilion) however this name does not appear in the genealogy.

had been humble—that much is generally agreed. The exact circumstances of the formative years of his life, however, are shrouded in some ambiguity. While family members have received one version by word of mouth, the He Family genealogy tells a different story, and both sources deserve our respect.

It is common ground that Wenge was the son of the landowner He Weiqi who met a tragically early death, which threatened to disinherit his only offspring. The family genealogy lists Weiqi (also known as Yahui) as the second oldest son of He Yanyong, who had three sons, although both Paul and Tangxiang put the number higher. Upon his death the ancestral lands passed to Weiqi's brothers rather than to his wife. We know her by her maiden name, Shi.[6] Many Chinese women at this time did not have first names and were simply referred to as eldest, second eldest or youngest daughter, cousin or sister.[7] Throughout their life these women maintained their maiden name; it was only when they married that *Shi* along with their husband's last name was added to their family name to indicate their marital status.

The story told in the He family has it that Wenge was still in his mother's womb when his father died. Weiqi's sudden death thus left his wife, the pregnant Shi, destitute. Forced, according Tangxiang, to leave Hejiacun, she turned her back on Chinese convention, which frowned upon a widow taking another husband, and re-married into the Wang family who lived in Wangjiacun a few miles from the He family village.

The genealogy, however, puts things differently. It states that Wenge was born in 1872, that he was thus five years old when is father, Weiqi, died in 1878, and that it was only subsequently that his mother left the village. The genealogy also suggests that Weiqi had a *Xiao Lao Po*—'little wife' or concubine—named Zhou. Born in 1849, Zhou was—rather curiously for the time—five years older than Shi whom we know to have been born on 8 July 1854.

These two conflicting sources, one oral and the other written, raise several questions. Did Paul Ho's grandmother Shi leave Hejiacun before or after the birth of her son Wenge? Did she do so simply because she had lost control of

---

[6] Shi, which is pronounced in the first tone and is a family name, must not be confused with Shi which has a different Chinese character, a different pronunciation—it is pronounced in the fourth tone—and although it is spelled the same in Pinyin means Mrs. written differently and pronounced with the 4th tone, while Shi the family name is pronounced with the first tone.

[7] Male children were referred to in a similar way.

the household and land? Was this the only reason why Shi left Hejiacun and married into the Wang family? Many of these points can never be resolved. But for the infant Wenge—apparently the helpless victim of his wicked uncles—a more benign plot was to unfold in due course.

What is certain is that Wenge was indeed Weiqi's only son. All sources agree that Weiqi's concubine, Zhou, bore him no children and that by the time Wenge turned fifteen he was not living in Hejiacun—whether or not he had been born there—but in the village of Wangjiacun with his mother Shi.

It was in Wangjiacun that Wenge purchased a wood-wheeled handcart and began transporting coal from the nearby Huagushan Coal Mine to the county town of Xinyu. The twenty-mile round-trip took Wenge through low mountain country that was inhabited by tigers; through a landscape that was heavily forested with pine and cypress and groves of bamboo. The dangerous and arduous journey also took Wenge through Hejiacun, his ancestral village. Possibly through delivering coal to the He household, Wenge thus had an opportunity to cultivate a friendship with his land-owning uncles.

Paul maintained that these 'uncles' were not all blood uncles, which would have meant simply the two brothers of Weiqi, Weikun and Weigan respectively. Thus it is likely that, as a lonely and displaced member of the He clan, Wenge had met men of an older generation who fulfilled a significant role as 'uncles' for him.

This unexpectedly happy twist in the plot is a crucial point in the family's history. For it is almost certainly how, 'over the course of time,' as Tangxiang puts it, that 'good relations' developed between Wenge and his uncles. The relationship became so good, in fact, that Wenge asked them if he could return to his father's village. 'Seeing that he was honest and kind,' Tangxiang reports, 'his uncles accepted his request.'

Once in Hejiacun, Wenge put his wooden handcart aside and began helping his uncles oversee their tenant farmers. He knew how to work hard and how to make the most of what must initially have been a modest income. He learned how to make and to market rice wine, and began studying herbal medicines. Most significant, family legend has it that, since none of the various uncles had sons, Wenge became their heir. This conjunction of events was certainly fortunate for Wenge. As Tangxiang, puts it, 'things got even better' for his grandfather, since he was now set to become head of the He lineage.

According to family tradition, by the latter part of the nineteenth century, Wenge possessed 160 Mu—roughly 26 acres—of land. Cultivated by his tenant farmers, the land yielded soybeans, sweet potatoes as well as rice and other grains.

Since 160 Mu of land could produce roughly 125 bushels of grain a year this meant that, with three bushels a year as minimum consumption per person, the farm could feed about forty people. Wenge's farm was large compared with other farms in the region where the average holding seldom exceeded five acres. Indeed as one mid-twentieth-century visitor to China noted: 'Chinese agriculture was not farming, it was gardening!'[8]

Wenge was thus the biggest landowner in Hejiacun. And, at a time when landlords often acted as civil officials or judges, poets or healers, teachers or scholars, merchants or usurers, he took on other roles too. He continued to produce and to sell rice wine, and to dispense health-giving ginseng root and other blood-strengthening herbal medicines. Yet, according to Tangxiang, 'grandfather never forgot his poor relatives in the country after he became wealthy.' Little wonder that Paul remembered poor people coming to a door that they knew would not be shut in their faces.

As the head of the He lineage, it fell upon Wenge to determine any disputes within the village. Tangxiang assured me that, when a misunderstanding could not be settled, his grandfather used his own money 'to calm down the two sides.' Wenge is likewise remembered for charitable acts. He treated the sick for free. He financed the construction of a pavilion that gave the villagers shade during the sub-tropical summers and shelter from the biting wind and torrential rain during the more inclement months of the year. Wenge also funded the cost of repairing a local bridge. And he paved several *li* of road—one *li* is less than half a mile—lying on the outskirts of the village. Built with large slabs of stone, the newly surfaced road eased the burden of carrying heavy loads on the ends of long bamboo shoulder poles or of pushing big-wheeled handcarts. Its construction also provided much-needed employment. Anyone who was willing to help received one silver *yuan* for every three meters of road they laid.

Little wonder that Wenge's name shines brightly in family legend in terms that contain virtually every cliché the Chinese used to describe the kind-hearted landlord or patron. As Tangxiang puts it: 'Grandfather cultivated his virtue by repeatedly doing good deeds, so he was much honored by the local people.' Nor is it surprising that Wenge's eldest son—Tangxiang's own father Paul—would show filial piety in treading the path of emulation, by manifesting in his turn a strong social conscience that would prompt him to help those less fortunate than himself.

---

[8]   James Cameron, *Mandarin Red* (London: Michael Joseph, 1955) p. 166

*   *   *

Wenge had belatedly come into his own. In his lifetime he witnessed the end of the Qing dynasty in 1911 and the founding, a year later, of the Republic of China. These events in distant Peking did little to disturb his prosperity as a fortunate man who had restored the family fortunes. No longer a virtual orphan exiled with his mother Shi, he had benefited prodigiously from being the only male of his generation in the family. He and his mother—who had also remarkably returned to the He family—had meanwhile established themselves with the 'uncles' in the family home, its twenty rooms still intact in those days, as befitted the leading family in Hejiacun. Wenge now lacked only an heir to perpetuate his own dynasty.

Born in February 1882, Wenge's principal wife, Li, was eleven years younger than her husband. It was a mark of her superior class position that she had bound feet. Begun, it is thought, in the tenth century—some time between the Tang and Song Dynasties—foot-binding aimed to produce a foot that was small, narrow, straight, pointed and ideally, though seldom achieved, no longer than three inches. The golden, or perfumed lilies, as the mangled feet were called, became the most erotic part of a woman's body.

There was no guarantee that the long and painful ordeal—the process took ten to fifteen years to complete—would produce a foot that was round at the heel and pointed at the big toe. Many women's feet became infected and they died of gangrene. Still other women ended up tottering about on their ugly stumps or only walking with the aid of a cane. For those who survived the ordeal to see their feet resemble a lotus bud or the young shoot of a bamboo there were rewards. As a fictional character in Lisa See's *Snow Flower and the Secret Fan* put it, 'my small feet would be offered as proof to my prospective in-laws of my personal discipline and my ability to endure the pain of childbirth, as well as whatever misfortunes might lie ahead.'[9]

Li's mother had been successful in transforming her daughter's feet into a fetish symbol. This had required the five-year-old Li to undergo the painful operation whereby her mother broke the four lateral toes on each foot then bound them to the sole of her foot. Wet when they were applied, the three-meter-long bandages became so tight when they dried that they cut off the circulation in the foot. Li thus acquired a walk that resembled a large lotus flower and duly earned her reputation for endurance and obedience.

---

[9]   Lisa See, *Snow Flower and the Secret Fan* (London: Bloomsbury 2006) p. 43

Maybe she thought all this worthwhile when she won the favor of the wealthy landlord, Wenge. Even so, there was no guarantee that after becoming his principal wife, Li would produce a male heir. She did give birth to one son and to one daughter, but both children died in infancy. Experiencing the death of two children must have been devastating for the young Li. During each pregnancy she had paid strict attention to how she sat and slept, to what she ate—and even to what she thought, lest she have a negative influence on the unborn child. Then, upon giving birth, there was the shame of having produced a female child—and the possibility that the child might be subjected to infanticide. Indeed a box of ashes or a wooden bucket of water was often kept beside a mother's bed in order to facilitate the quick death of a female baby. Bringing up a girl destined to work for another family was as the Chinese saying goes, akin to tilling another man's field.

There was no worse fate for a woman than being unable to produce a male child. It left her husband open to ridicule, since men without sons were considered childless—even bandits did not consider their houses worth robbing. Her failure prevented Li from creating the ideal, if rarely achieved, five-generation family and increased the likelihood that another woman would be brought into the household to produce the much-sought-after heir. Moreover, since sons provided security for the older members of the family, venerated and 'fed' the ancestors, and promised the continuation of future generations, Li's incapacity put every member of the household, including herself, at risk. In particular, Wenge's ailing mother, Shi, had no guarantee that she would be cared for in the event of her son's early death.

It is not surprising, then, that Shi—in all likelihood with the assistance of Li—made it her business to seek a *xiao lao po* or little wife for her son. Tangxiang claims that this was done when his grandfather got 'an introduction from someone else.' The young woman's name was Fu and she lived in a nearby village; Wenge had to marry someone outside Hejiacun because it was taboo to take a wife from his own ancestral lineage. It is likely that it was Shi rather than Wenge himself who was responsible for bringing the thirteen-year-old girl into the He household as Wenge's little wife—or, as her own son Paul put it more directly, 'as my father's concubine.'

Li's junior by at least seventeen years, Fu, whose name meant good fortune or happiness, was born in the village of Fengcheng, up the Gan River northeast of Hejiacun. Fu's birth date, given as the fourth month of the twenty-fourth year of the Emperor Guangxu, is thus stated as 1899 in the family genealogy. She lived with her family in Fengcheng until 1907 when she was given, or more likely sold, to a family living in the village of Shapi in Xiushui County. As a child-wife, or *tong-yang-xi*, Fu was expected to marry the family's son when she reached puberty. Thus at the age of eight Fu had acquired in-laws before she had acquired a husband.

There was nothing unusual about putting a female child up for adoption—although this was generally done at birth and not, as in Fu's case, in late childhood. Many female infants were given, or more frequently sold, to families, for various pragmatic reasons. They might be anxious to cultivate a submissive and obedient daughter-in-law; they might want to avoid paying a go-between or match-maker; they might simply want an easy way of disposing of the child should she prove to be an unsuitable wife for their son.

Unlike Li, Fu did not, therefore, spend the formative years of her life learning to walk on bound feet, learning to be calm and upright, quiet and agreeable and exquisite in movement. Nor could her family have amassed a considerable dowry and bride price. This meant that when Fu entered the household in Shapi, her position was completely different. As a child-wife, she was apprenticed to servitude.

During the course of the next several years Fu's prospective mother-in-law made her feel like a second-class member of the family. This was achieved by crude methods: never giving her enough to eat; making her wear hand-me-downs; forcing her to take on more than her share of the household chores. And, when she was not working, by confining her to a room in the eaves of the family's draughty house where, according her grandson Tangxiang, 'Fu could not escape the wind and the rain and was so cold that she could not stop shivering.'

After enduring five years of this kind of treatment, Fu, who appears to have been insufficiently submissive and obedient, was deemed to be an unsuitable wife for the family's son. In fact, she was about to be sold yet again—this time to a family living in the nearby county of Xiajiang. It was at this point that Shi intervened, evidently having obtained some introduction to the circumstances. Taking pity on the young girl, Shi reunited Fu with her birth-mother, who was in turn persuaded, according to her future grandson Tangxiang, to allow her daughter to enter the He household as Wenge's concubine.

High-born girls like Wenge's principal wife, Li, came with a commensurately high bride-price, of which bound feet was the most obvious symbol. Such girls seldom knew how to work hard and were hopeless at handling money. And, often independently minded with elevated ideas of their own status, they were less likely to be submissive and modest. Fu, by contrast, knew how to work hard and, having survived her sad ordeal as a child-wife, had shown that she was strong. In short, Fu, unlike Li, could be quietly introduced into the He family—and disposed of in an equally quiet way if she proved incapable of producing the requisite male heir.

Being a concubine was a hard fate. As the fictional character, Mingfeng, in Ba Jin's classic novella, *Family*, writes, it brought 'only one reward: tears, blows [and] abuse.'[10] Fu was not only expected to give her body to a man twenty-six years her senior with the sole purpose of producing a son: she was required to work hard for the family. Moreover, as her eldest son remembers, his mother was 'maltreated and beaten' by Li, who doubtless saw Fu's presence in her husband's bed as a constant reproach and affront to herself, as principal wife. At any rate, Li maintained an authoritative control over the illiterate, flat-footed girl—as low-born females with 'natural' unbound feet were called.

It is agreed that, shortly after joining the household as Wenge's concubine, Fu gave birth to the desperately wanted son. It is also said that, although the child survived infancy, he then died at the age of six in 1918. If this is right, he would have been born in 1912; and if Fu had indeed been born in 1899, she would have been, at most, thirteen at the time of her first child's birth. Whatever the exact dating, the dominant and inescapable fact was that Wenge was still left without an heir—and Shi without a grandson—until the Year of the Lamb, and seventh year of the Republic of China, when Fu gave birth to another boy on 24 March 1919.

As an infant he was known as Nieu Gen. As a child growing up in Hejiacun, he was called Rongda (glorious prospects). Later in life he acquired the honorific name, Guangchun, which means supreme. As a mature man, immigrating into the United States, he became known as Paul Ho. For most of his life in China, however, he was known as Buji, which means 'step by step' and 'foundation'—a name apparently chosen by his school teacher, who named his student after the great calligrapher who had lived during the Qing dynasty, He Shaoji. It is Buji that he will now be called in these pages.

*   *   *

After Buji's birth, so his son Tangxiang believes, life got 'a little better' for his grandmother. And things improved even more when, three years later

---

[10]   Ba Jin, *Selected Works of Ba Jin* (Beijing: Foreign Languages Press, 1988 first published in 1931) p. 179

Buji's mother, Fu, produced a third male child, Guangxuan or Buxiu, and after him a daughter, Zhilan. These children, too, happily survived infancy. Yet however much Fu loved all of her children, it was the destined head of the He clan, Buji, who received the greater share of her attention and affection. Even so, in keeping with Chinese tradition, Fu's three children were treated by Li as though they were her own. Indeed, during the formative years of his life, Buji thought that his birth-mother was Li. Not until he was around five or six, as he recalls, did he hear the truth from an unnamed person. Surprisingly, perhaps, it was not Fu herself who made the disclosure. And self-evidently it was not Li—'she took me away from my real mother,' Buji exclaimed in old age.

Buji spent his formative years within the female sphere of the He household. And there was much for the young child to see: the women making—or supervising the servants making—new clothes, especially in anticipation of the New Year's Festival; visits from itinerant fortune-tellers, whose vague and ambiguous pronouncements, given upon hearing a woman's time and date of birth, could be had for a meal. The young Buji watched Fu and the other women preparing rice cakes for the Dragon Feast, moon cakes for the Moon Feast, sugar dumplings and spring cakes, ginger roots, turnips and turnip leaves, 'cheese' made from fermented bean curd for the New Year's Festival.

A first-born son also received a great deal of attention from his father, and Buji was no exception. He would take naps on his father's lap; he learnt how to stand and to sit. But even though his earliest memory was of his father and he recalled that 'sometimes he hug me', their relationship soon changed in keeping with the Chinese proverb, 'Strict Father, Kind Mother'. Indeed, Buji recalled that his father became 'very strict.' Thus the warmth and physical contact with Fu was paralleled not only by the child's growing respect for Wenge, but also by some reserve. The keenly awaited heir was taught how to breathe and to control his hands—lest they touch another person—and where and to whom he should bow or how deep he should kowtow. Most important of all, the young Buji acquired, through his father's instruction, a reverence for the past, a strong sense of continuity and a deep feeling of respect for his ancestors, for his elders and—not surprisingly—for his own father.

Buji would accompany his father to the largest building in the village, the ancestral hall where clan members gathered to honor their ancestors. Here Buji smelled the incense and oil-burning lamps. He also saw the sacred foot-high wooden spirit tablets—resembling miniature gravestones—displayed above a tall narrow alter. Inscribed in black ink with the names of the deceased, the tablets marked the 'seat' of the ancestral spirits. During the many festivals that were governed by the position of the moon and the sun Buji honored the ancestors in confirming the lineage's common roots. At the Qing Ming or Day of Pure Brightness festival, for example, Buji and the other male children in the village accompanied their fathers to the ancestors' burial grounds and helped sweep the graves, burn incense and offer food and drink to the ghosts of the dead. Such practices made a lifelong impression upon Buji, as I saw for myself in the reverence with which he later honored his own parents and those of his wife Sonia.

One of Buji's most vivid childhood memories dates from these early years in the mid-1920s. I could testify to its vividness because in 2007 I was walking with him to his mother's grave in the hills outside Hejiacun. It was rough ground even for fit adults, though the octogenarian Buji still took it in his stride. There were several boggy patches and at one point we had to cross a small stream. As we hiked up past a pond, Buji became animated and gestured towards it, recalling that this was the spot where he remembered hiding from bandits when he was a young boy of five or six; and the story poured out as though it had happened yesterday.

The appearance of a group of bandits one bright night—'the moon just like the daytime'—had sent the terrified villagers scurrying away. It is true that, following the fall of the Qing dynasty in 1911, assaults, kidnappings, murders and muggings had become a constant threat to wealthy families. 'They want to get my father and me because we got money,' Buji explained. After hearing gunshots, Buji and the other inhabitants in the village ran towards the hills. As they made their way through the thick underbrush, Buji became separated from his family. He crawled on his hands and knees for several yards before taking cover in a grassy clearing beside the pond that lies below the present-day location of his mother's grave.

It was here, as Buji assured me on exactly the same spot over eighty years later, that he had a remarkable encounter (which his later conversion to Christianity had rendered all the more significant). The frightened child saw a tall man dressed in an unbleached white garment—the dress of mourning. He remained quite sure that the man 'was not Chinese at all, but a foreigner.' The man did not speak to the boy but merely indicated where he might find cover. Buji followed the man's lead—'from twelve midnight until morning I hide.' By early the next day, everything was quiet. The bandits had left the area. The He family home had not been vandalized. The money that Wenge had hidden in a box, under one of the house's few windows, had not been discovered. No harm had come to anyone in the village. Buji survived, so he told me with implicit confidence, because the mysterious figure 'saved my life.'[11]

While Wenge increasingly played a larger role in his young son's life, it was one of Buji's 'uncles,' He Duanyou, who emerged as the young boy's first teacher. Even though Duanyou had adopted a boy, Xufa, because he had no birth son of his own, he felt free to lavish attention on the eldest male member of the rising generation. Indeed, Duanyou became Buji's proverbial surrogate father since as the saying goes: 'He who becomes the teacher of a child for one day, is the father of that child for life.'

Buji was around six years old when Duanyou put a paintbrush in his hand and told him to fill in the large red outline of a Chinese character with black ink. Tall and thin, gentle and kind, Duanyou eagerly introduced his young pupil to the paraphernalia that was found on every scholar's table. The small vessel that held the water for grinding the ink stick on the ink stone itself; various-sized vessels for washing brushes; wrist-rests crafted out of ivory, porcelain or bamboo; metal rulers and paperweights and cylindrical brush-holders and intricately carved seals.

During the first year under his uncle's tutelage, Buji was introduced to the significance of the physicality of writing, an act that reinforced the memory of the character itself through movement and gesture. And, since knowing how to draw a character initially took precedence over knowing what that character meant, Buji became an artist before he became a scholar. His proficiency as a calligrapher—a skill that owed something to his father who encouraged him to copy characters—was to stand him in good stead throughout his career.

Already, then, Buji's inclinations towards learning were receiving encouragement and the lively boy was being prompted to focus on the importance of education. Learning came easily to him; it was fun; but it was also useful. He was not unlike another future Chinese scholar, Chiang Monlin, who recalled in his memoir: 'Yes, I knew what a scholar was and the advantage of being one. He might climb up, rung by rung, to the top of the ladder and

---

[11] During the Great Taiping Rebellion in the middle of the nineteenth century Hong Xiuquan who lived in Guangxi and became a leader of the Rebellion claimed that he was the younger brother of Jesus Christ. It is perhaps this figure that Paul Ho, in retrospect, saw as the mysterious figure who saved him.

someday become a very high official.'[12] Certainly on Buji's visits to the ancestral hall he had seen the carved panels with their elaborate inscriptions honoring those members of the He family who had passed the first or second level of the civil service examinations. He had seen the old woodblock editions of the Chinese classics—bound in Oxford blue cloth and, just like the scrolls, secured in heavy wooden boxes—which were stacked against the wall in his father's study. From an early age, then, Buji was encouraged to assume that, as the first son of a wealthy landlord, he was destined to become a scholar, just as Buxiu, his younger brother, was destined to oversee the tenant farms and his sister, Zhilan, would marry the school teacher, Luo Keng, and thereby leave the He village.

Duanyou, who had himself passed the very difficult prefecture level of the civil service examination, encouraged the boy. He fully appreciated that learning and scholarship would give his nephew worldly success, bring honor to his ancestors and luck to his future generations. Duanyou also believed that distinguished scholarship would foster morality, thereby producing a contagious goodness with which his nephew would infect others and thereby help create a harmonious world.

The Songlin Academy where Duanyou taught his young nephew had been founded by the He family in the previous century. Its picturesque setting had inspired the Old Master, He Yanxian, to celebrate the Academy's proximity to 'the craggy peaks covered with the deep green of pine and cypress trees,' and the clear streams and soaring cranes that spread 'their snow-white wings' above the clouds. All of this, Yanxian insisted, 'evoked the auspicious signs of the pursuit of the intellect.' The school accommodated all ages but Buji was privileged by sitting at a special desk next to the teacher, his uncle.

Buji's connection with his first school, however, was to prove short-lived. Duanyou was promoted to become head of the county's Board of Education and left the Songlin Academy to settle in the city of Xinyu. Intent that his nephew should continue his education, Duanyou enrolled the eight-year-old boy in the Shuibei Elementary School in the nearby village of Jinfeng. Dressed in the long gown of a scholar, Buji joined fifty other pupils in the village's one-room school.

Here the teacher, Lai Juehan, subjected the students to a stern discipline. Buji and his classmates had to sit with their feet flat on the floor, press their

---

[12]   Chiang Monlin, *Tides from the West* (New Haven: Yale University Press, 1947) p. 39

knees tightly together, keep their back straight and hold their book at a forty-five degree angle to the desk. Subjection to the strict discipline demanded by Chinese teachers must have been unpleasant. Lai Juehan kept a bamboo stick at the front of the classroom. Any student wishing to leave the room had to march to the front of the class and take the stick with him. Buji remembers ruefully that some of his schoolfellows were so reluctant to leave the classroom in the middle of a lesson to relieve themselves that they incurred the worse embarrassment of incontinence at their desks.

This was evidently a strict regime. But Buji did not complain about the discipline imposed on him by his teacher, Lai Juehan. Out of the classroom, he enjoyed playing games with the other boys. One game entailed seeing how long he could keep a coin, that had been covered with feathers, in the air. Another game was played with two lengths of bamboo that were transformed into water guns. Even so, Buji, who boarded at the school was lonely. He missed Hejiacun, the village of his birth, and he missed Fu, whom he now knew to be his birth mother.

At the Shuibei Elementary School, Buji continued learning from the first book that his uncle had introduced him to: the primer known as *The One Thousand Classic Characters*. Consisting of a long poem of some 250 lines, the text introduced the boys in his class to one thousand Chinese characters or ideographs. Led by the teacher, the pupils repeated each phrase or line of the poem one hundred times—fifty while looking at the book and fifty with the book face down. Initially, Buji committed thirty characters a day to memory. As he became more adept, however, the number rose to several hundred. Learning by rote may now seem mind-numbing for children at an age when the urge to play and be outdoors with their friends is strongest. Yet after six years of this process at elementary school, most pupils had committed to memory textual material amounting to several thousand characters.

Buji demonstrated that he had a good memory and was an adept calligrapher. He also showed that he had a good grasp of classical texts, which he recited well into old age. These texts included the writings of the pre-eminent sage, Confucius, and thereby provided a social code that fostered loyalty and obedience and generally guided all forms of behavior. Buji also read histories of China, and poetry by Song and Tang dynasty poets, along with the work of Jiangxi's own poets, of whom Ouyan Xiu, Wang Anshi, Zeng Gong and Tang Xianzu—'the Shakespeare of the East'—are the most prominent.

*   *   *

For all his aptitude, Buji's education posed a problem. He did what he was told, and did it well, under a system that drilled rather than educated young children. Yet by the time Buji entered Shuibei Elementary School in the late 1920s, the old form of learning, based narrowly on study of the Confucian classics in preparation for the imperial examination system, already appeared out of date. In fact, the Confucian academies had been abolished in 1905, six years before the end of the Qing dynasty. Since no other system had replaced it, however, most students continued to study the classic primers. It was only if they happened to live in a large urban center that they found geography, world history and, above all, science incorporated into the school curriculum. Although the Republic of China had been founded by Sun Yat-sen in 1912, it was not until the beginning of Chiang Kai-shek's rule in 1927 that new laws and regulations were introduced to make Chinese education compatible with Western forms of teaching. Even so, the westernized curriculum did not filter down to rural areas of the country where education was controlled by a conservative elite of which Buji's uncle Duanyou, as head of education in Xinyu, was a prominent member.

The result was that many youngsters like Buji continued to receive a classical Chinese education long after the imperial examination system had been abolished. Educators in the backwaters of Jiangxi province were reluctant to bring their school curriculum in line with the new laws and regulations that from 1928 introduced geography, social studies and science into the classroom. Stubborn, independent-minded, and, above all, suspicious of any form of cultural change, they clung to the practice of ancestor-worship and observed rituals and festivals with more tenacity than people living in the urban areas of the province.

The crucial point was that these new subjects were now prescribed as necessary for entrance to high school. Although a traditionalist himself, Duanyou got the message and saw to it that his nephew, now twelve, was taken out of the rural school in Jinfeng and in 1931 enrolled in Xinyu County Primary School, where the curriculum was more progressive. Thirsty for modern knowledge, Buji was all for the move. Yet he soon discovered that even the county's most westernized school did not offer mathematics or social studies. It is a mark of Buji's own commitment that he taught himself these subjects.

One concept that struck a particular chord with Buji during the early years of his education was the phrase, *Bu Gong Ping*, which can be translated as unfairness, inequality or unjust. When he was around the age of eleven—an age he reached in 1930—Buji had the chance to demonstrate the extent to which he had a practical grasp of what that concept meant.

Though professing no doubt that, Wenge, 'did his utmost to do good,' Buji clearly feels that his father could have done more to alleviate the suffering of his lineage's tenant farmers. The total burden of rent and taxes imposed on the tenant farmers was staggering. There were no fewer than 188 general taxes: taxes on tobacco and wine; taxes on windows and stoves; taxes on coal and ammunition. In addition to these annual payments, tenant farmers had to hand over up to fifty per cent of their main crops to their landlord. The percentage was assessed once a year.

It now fell to Buji and not to his ailing father, Wenge, to inspect the crops at the height of the harvest season, with a view to establishing what percentage should be given to their family. This should have been a pleasant experience for a boy of eleven. Tenant farmers took care to prepare a good dinner consisting of home-made wine and a large bowl of soup filled with local ingredients from the land and the stream. With the cost of the dinner often defrayed by the landlord, a good time was usually had by all. But when Buji visited the farms the province was experiencing the effects of a serious famine, which had begun in 1928 and lasted until 1930. The resulting poor harvests brought no compensating gain in higher prices for the farmers since what they received for their crops declined more rapidly than the retail costs of their outgoings.

It is not surprizing, therefore, that Buji found acute poverty on the land—'the people, very poor, had only water and some potatoes to eat.' He also saw that they had little clothing. When he entered their houses, the tenant farmers were huddled around their stoves for warmth. Discovering the farmers to be hungry, ill-clad and cold, Buji refused to calculate what percentage of their crops should be handed over to his father. He had taken with him a large ledger of accounts payable and receivable; but he entered nothing in it.

When he returned home, distraught at what he had witnessed, Buji was far from ashamed to tell his mother what he had done. Fu replied: 'we have enough to eat, enough money.' Buji then went into the kitchen with the ledger and established himself beside a brick stove. Page by page, he condemned the entire book to the flames. 'Year after year—so many years in one book,' he graphically recalled about burning the account books.

It was, not unnaturally, Li who told her husband what his son had done. Though it might be argued that Buji's benevolent act was in line with Confucian virtues, Wenge was, nevertheless, furious. 'He beat me with a big stick,' Buji told me with some glee. But it was certainly no joking matter at the time—'He threw me out.' Buji stayed surreptitiously with relatives in the village for about a month. Then he returned home. By this time his father's temper had cooled and apparently the matter was never spoken of again between them.

Buji's act represented more than the naughty whim of a budding adolescent. He had challenged his father's authority and thereby failed in his obligation as *Xiaozi*—or filial son. While there is no doubt that Buji had violated filial piety, a central tenet in Chinese tradition, and had fallen out of favor with his father, there can be little doubt either that he became a hero to the tenant farmers, as he long remembered with an undiminished sense of doing the right thing. 'The whole area love me—"That kid is real good"—the peasants like me because they did not have to pay no more.'

It should perhaps not be assumed that the absence of the account books prohibited the He clan from collecting any further rents. Nor, certainly, that Buji's act contributed to his father's death. This occurred shortly after the book-burning incident, probably in the winter of 1930. The fact that Wenge, who had long been unwell, had already delegated the vital task of rent collecting to his son speaks for itself. According to Buji, his father 'always smoked his long pipe too much.' Wenge's death thus came as no surprise, least of all to himself.

Every Chinese adult prepares for his or her burial long before the death seems imminent. In fact the cost of a funeral is on a par with a family's two other major lifetime expenditures: marrying a son and building a house. Upon reaching sixty years of age Wenge had commissioned a craftsman to construct his coffin from the trunk of a large pine tree. He had chosen his place of burial on the side of a hill, Laojinshan, not far from the village—which we glimpsed across the valley when we made our own pilgrimage to Fu's grave in 2007. He had also selected his burial clothes and indicated which material goods he wanted to accompany him on his journey to the other world.

Having seen to these tasks, Wenge had fulfilled his responsibilities and could leave the rest to tradition. He did not have to instruct the mourners how to dress—like the mysterious foreigner who had told Buji where to hide from the bandits, most of the mourners would wear coarse un-hemmed, un-bleached hemp clothing. Wenge could rest assured that an auspicious date for his burial would be chosen—in fact, three months after his death—and that his family would know where to build the hut, on the outskirts of the village, which would keep his body until burial. Nor did he need to choreograph, in advance, the procession to the grave. The males always walked in front of the coffin, while the women, whose violent weeping competed with the clash of cymbals and the crackle of firecrackers, walked behind. None of this needed to be arranged in advance because, just like the making, then the burning at the graveside, of paper effigies of houses, garments and food that would shelter, clothe and feed his spirit, everything happened according to custom.

Buji's memory of the event was characteristically dramatic and detailed. He remembered preceding the coffin, carried by eight pallbearers, in the company of other male members of the He family. He remembered walking up the steep hill, its shape resembling a recumbent tiger. He remembered having to traverse a deep water-filled ravine and clinging to one of the ropes that lashed the coffin to the catafalque lest he be swept down the swiftly moving stream. Finally, Buji remembered peering into the opening of the red-earth grave that was shaped like an octagon.

Everyone believed that the spirit, finding it difficult to begin its long journey, would linger around the grave for several days. Buji claimed actually to have seen his father's spirit emerge from the grave, seven days after Wenge was buried. 'The grave gave off a flame which went up to the sky; many people in the village saw it.' This was Buji's last memory of his father: the soul of Wenge rising out of the grave, lifting above the tiger-shaped hill, above the He family farms, above the village, above the county seat of Xinyu, and above the vast province of Jiangxi, as it left its mortal body.

*   *   *

Barely eleven when his father died, Buji was now, at least in name and form, the head of the He household; but he was also an ambitious student with his way to make in the world. Over the next decade these were different roles that it would have been troubling to reconcile under normal conditions. But conditions in China were already moving away from any concept of normality and the distorted shape of Buji's future career was one casualty—among many.

In 1932, two years after his father's death and by now aged thirteen, Buji set his feet firmly upon the academic ladder. He fondly recalled that it was his uncle, He Duanyou, who helped him gain admission to Nanchang Second Middle School. Situated in the heart of the provincial capital, this was a prestigious institution, educating an elite drawn from the whole of Jangxi Province. So that he could sit for his entrance exams at the school, Buji's family hired someone to take him to distant Nanchang in a one-wheel hand-cart, resembling a wooden wheel-barrow.

This was an epic journey, not only in its circumstances but in its consequences. After settling into a hotel, Buji joined 700 other students in a large examination hall. During the day-long exam he wrote a composition about his family. He answered questions relating to mathematics and social studies. Then he waited while the papers were graded. The results of Buji's examination would inexorably determine his future. Failure would almost certainly have ensured that he remain in the village of his birth. A pass would not only secure him entrance to high school but, if he distinguished himself there, open an opportunity to study at one of China's great universities.

'Can the reader blame a village boy like me,' Chiang Monlin asked in his memoir, 'whose steps had never carried him more than a few miles from his own village, for aspiring to become a scholar?'[13] And the stakes for Buji were as high as they had been a few years earlier for Chiang Monlin. Only two per cent of the students who sat for the exam would pass. With 2,500 candidates in all from across the province sitting the examination, it was unlikely that a student from a rural backwater would emerge among the top fifty pupils.

Uncle Duanyou had meanwhile arrived in Nanchang to offer his nephew moral support. While he and Buji waited for the examination results they explored the city. They also went to the cinema, where Buji saw a newsreel featuring China's ongoing conflict with the Japanese in Manchuria, which Japan had occupied in September 1931. He also saw his first American western movie and became a convert to this popular genre. Then, two days later, Buji and his uncle returned to the examination building. The school officials emerged and posted the results on the school's imposing iron gate. Only the names of those students who had passed the exam appeared on the list.

Buji's name was there. Not only had he passed, gaining him entrance to Nanchang Second Middle School, he had received special praise for his calligraphy. He likewise earned the highest mark in Chinese composition. And, if he had not received lower marks in math and social studies—subjects in which he was self-taught—he might have placed even higher. Required to come in the top fifty, he had exceeded all expectations by ranking eighth among the 2,500 candidates. It is not surprising that when the results were announced back in the Hejiacun village, there was much rejoicing. 'I became a celebrity,' Buji recalled gleefully. As with his father's recent funeral, there were firecrackers and cymbals; there was also a day-long banquet attended by everyone with the surname of He, including Buji's proud uncle He Duanyou.

*　　*　　*

---

[13]　Chiang Monlin, *Tides from the West* (New Haven: Yale University Press, 1947) p. 39

When we revisited the Nanchang Second Middle School with Buji in March 2007, the warmth with which their distinguished old pupil was welcomed back contrasted nicely with the chill of the day itself. The occasion also helped demonstrate how far Buji's experience was common to that of a whole generation of high school students in China.

Sitting at one end of the room into which we were ushered, under large windows that revealed the tops of the courtyard trees, were five elderly men. They had been patiently waiting two hours for us to arrive. We sat with them while we heard about the school itself. Founded in 1901 by the Japanese-educated college graduate, Xiong Yuyang (as Principal Wu Qin, explained to us) it prided itself on offering its students a western-style education—with a particularly heavy emphasis on science. As a result, the school became one of the three top private middle schools in China.

'All the famous scientists have studied here,' Wu Qin assured us, as she surveyed the school's history. We heard that the school had continued to prosper until 1937, the year in which the province of Jiangxi became engulfed in the Resistance War against the Japanese. We learned that in the following year, when the Japanese launched a major offensive against the province, the entire population of the school—teachers, administrators and students—had been forced to leave the city; and that over the next seven years, the exigencies of the war compelled the seven hundred students, their teachers and the school's principal at the time, Che Ju, to move more than once.

For the five old men sitting with Buji under the imposing schoolroom windows, nearly seventy years later, none of this came as news. But they all listened intently, nodding at times. Silent during the speeches, waiting courteously until Buji had presented a gift to the school, they now seized on their turn to participate. Their delegated representative, a recently retired engineer named Xong Zhengyi, introduced the men, all of them members of the school's alumni association. One man was an honorary member of the alumni simply because two members of his family had been teachers at the school. Two others—Zou Keqin and Zou Guoqi—were from Buji's hometown, Xinyu, and all had been students at Nanchang Second Middle School either during or a few years after Buji graduated from the school in 1941.

As I listened to their stories, amidst the constant ringing of cell phones, what impressed me most about these men was not just their longevity—most were well over eighty—or their fierce loyalty to the school, but their determination to continue learning despite all hardships. Yu Fenglai, for example, who was dressed in his policeman son's greatcoat and wore his steel-grey hair pompadour style, had worked in the People's Bank of China; then, after teaching himself the rudiments of physical chemistry, had gained admission to Jiangxi Educational College. Although the Cultural Revolution had interrupted Yu's study there, he had eventually graduated and landed a job with the Air Defense Office in Jiangxi.

Xong Zhengyi revealed that his commitment to learning had likewise prompted him to change professions. Following a career in the aeronautics industry, he returned to school and became an earth sciences engineer. His early career was not unlike Buji's in many respects: both suffered hardship and the disruption of their studies—it took Xong nine years to complete his junior and senior high school education—and both, after graduating from university, had changed careers in much the same way.

One of the old men, who wore a stylish cat-skin hat, had remained silent. Who, I wondered, was this dignified-looking man who sat in the place of honor next to Buji? Before I had an opportunity to ask through my interpreter, the old man rose from his chair to speak. Yang Linghe turned out also to be from Xinyu. But he was considerably older than the other men. He had not changed careers, as they had, but had remained a physical education teacher at the school throughout his working life. Indeed, one of his pupils had been the eighty-seven-year-old man sitting next to him, Buji himself.

'When you step into this school,' Yang Linghe told us, 'you immediately feel a wonderful atmosphere of learning.' Nobody who heard him on that chilly morning would have dismissed this as a mere polite cliché. That Nanchang Middle School had lived up to Uncle Duanyou's high expectations was plainly apparent, though he could hardly have imagined the vicissitudes that were to befall this cohort of pupils.

For the young Buji entering Nanchang Middle School was surely the right move, despite everything. The ambitious boy had already shown his devotion to study, not only by soaking up what he had been taught but by demonstrating a determination to educate himself, however and wherever he could. His achievement in the examinations in 1932 meant that he obtained a passport that would take him out of the narrow confines of Songlin and provincial Xinyu, opening up a succession of wider possibilities—as it turned out, even wider than he could have possibly foreseen at the time.

Hijiacun, 2007

Paul's mother, Fu

The Lake above Hejiacun

CHAPTER 2

'I eat everything but the table.'

除了桌子我什麼都吃

Today the road from Nanchang to Xinyu is a well-engineered new highway, much of it dual carriageway, as we saw for ourselves in 2007. Our journey, with a government driver eager to put his foot down, took well under two hours. Seventy-five years previously, when Buji left Songlin, a few miles beyond Xinyu, to begin his studies in Nanchang, things were very different. Riding in the same kind of one-wheel handcart that had transported him a few months earlier to write his high-school entrance examination, it took him three days to cover a hundred miles of rough country roads and tracks, leaving behind the poverty of rural Hejiacun for the sophistication of the provincial capital.

With a population of more than half a million, Nanchang, lying four hundred miles southwest of Shanghai, was not only the largest city in Jiangxi, but also the economic centre of the province. Moreover, as Buji soon discovered, it was a city of great beauty and culture, with uncharacteristically wide streets, thanks to recent urban reform. When Buji arrived for his schooling in 1932, while he found Nanchang itself relatively peaceful, he was aware that war was never far away, with turmoil evident in other parts of China. The military operations that were to escalate into world war had already made East Asia into a battle zone. In faraway Geneva, the headquarters of the League of Nations, attention was focused on the Japanese invasion of the northern region of Manchuria, undertaken in 1931 to widespread international concern and condemnation.

But it sadly revealed the impotence of the League and a corresponding lack of practical support for beleaguered China. Buji had already seen newsreels, as we know, showing how Manchuria was now occupied by Japan's Imperial Army and governed by a puppet government under Puyi, the 'last' Emperor of the Qing dynasty.

Throughout this period, China's internal disunity inevitably exacerbated its external vulnerability. A long-term struggle for political control of the country was under way between the ruling Guomindang (hereafter GMD) under Chiang Kai-shek and the insurgent Communist Party, ultimately triumphant under Mao Zedong. Rather than uniting to fight the Japanese invader, both sides remained intent on fighting each other for the control of China.

Nanchang itself had been occupied in 1926 by Chiang Kai-shek's Nationalist forces during the GMD's Northern Expedition. But his nominal alliance with the Communists was already under acute strain. Little more than a year later, a mutiny among a group of Nationalist soldiers initiated the founding of the Red Army—an event that later earned Nanchang the Communist sobriquet, 'the heroic city'. There ensued a long and bitter struggle throughout the province of Jiangxi between the newly-created Red Army, which fled to Mao's headquarters in the southern part of the province and set up a Chinese Soviet Republic, and the forces that Chiang Kai-shek mobilized in his determination to rid himself of this thorn in his side. Xinyu had been taken and retaken more than once during the course of these struggles. Buji recalls being chased by the Communists while he was a pupil there, probably in 1931, when there were frequent skirmishes between the GMD and the Red Army.

Nanchang's inhabitants were therefore not only acutely aware of the ambitions of the newly formed Red Army but of the strength and determination of Japan's Imperial Army—twin threats to GMD control. Yet education remained not only Buji's own priority but, given the circumstances, it also remained an extraordinarily high priority for the authorities. Like it or not, Buji's immediate interests, in getting a full education himself, were bound up with the survival of the Nationalist regime. Like every student in Nationalist China, Buji recited Sun Yat-sen's 'Three Principles of the People'—espousing nationalism, democracy and the people's livelihood—and sang the solemn Nationalist anthem, *San Min Zhu Yi*, at morning assembly before class.

Nanchang Second Middle School at that time was located in the district of Ximazhuang and bore little resemblance to the buildings that we were to visit in 2007. But its reputation was already renown. As in North America, Nanchang's students spent three years in the Junior Middle School and then, if they passed the qualifying examination, they entered Senior Middle School for another three years.

When Buji enrolled in the Junior Middle School in 1932 he exchanged his long scholar's gown for the school's uniform: black slacks and a dark blue jacket. When he began his first lessons, he found himself studying not only the writings of Confucius and other classical Chinese scholars whose work had formed the bulk of his education to date, but also many of the new subjects that he had been impatient to explore. He took classes in geography and history and was also introduced to contemporary politics. He was at last able to get proper tuition in mathematics, which was to underpin his later interest in engineering. Also significant for his future career, Buji received one hour of lessons in English every day.

There was never any fear that Buji would fail to uphold the school's motto, 'continuously work hard—that is the whole way', or that he would forfeit the admiration of his teachers. 'You are the best student,' they told him before the first year was out. Indeed, Buji's marks were so high that, upon completing Junior Middle School, he was exempted from taking the entrance exam to high school.

Buji's horizons were expanding, intellectually and socially too. His residence in the most exciting city in the province introduced him to a world beyond Hejiacun village. He came as a village boy of thirteen; he was to spend nearly five years of his adolescence at the Nanchang Second Middle School, living as a boarder with boys of his own age but drawn from a much wider background than he had ever experienced before. We have relatively little to go on, year by year, about the shaping of his life: boarding at school during the term, returning to his duties at Hejiacun in the vacation. But there is solid evidence that his time in Nanchang made a lasting impression upon him.

It is not surprising that it was at Nanchang Middle School that Buji made friends with whom he would be in contact—and sometimes in debt—for many years to come. In China, moreover, the code for friendship is exacting. As the writer Han Suyin put it in one of her autobiographical books: 'You must never fail your friend. Even though he be a confirmed cad, you lend him money, encourage him with good advice.' And if the friend happens to be a fellow student you call him 'brother.'[14] Buji relished studying with like-minded pupils and under

---

[14]   Han Suyin *Destination Chungking* (London: Jonathan Cape, 1942; (London: Granada Publishing, 1973) p. 31

enthusiastic teachers like Yang, the physical education instructor in the cat-skin hat whom he met again in our company in 2007. Here was an atmosphere that gave Buji confidence to excel as a young scholar.

But Nanchang was no ivory tower. In fact, Buji was walking through a minefield. Indeed, shortly after he arrived in the city, the GMD commenced building a new airport—it would be one of the largest in the country. The government also introduced an air defense warning system consisting of electric sirens and a system of signals, which Buji long remembered. When one ball was at the highest position on a pole an air raid was possible; two balls indicated that a raid was imminent; three balls signaled immediate danger; and afterwards, a yellow ball gave the all clear. By the time Buji had completed Junior Middle School, Nanchang's Air Defense Command was fully operational.

Events beyond his control increasingly intruded to thwart the very things that Buji had come to cherish. The challenge of the Communists after their break with the GMD in 1927 was sustained despite setbacks. The Nationalist Army's encircling and suppression campaigns in Jiangxi lasted until the autumn of 1934 when the Red Army, accompanied by Mao, began its famous Long March to western China. The obvious beneficiaries were the Japanese, as evidence of their encroachment became increasingly difficult to ignore. Buji's schooldays in Nanchang were thus passed in an atmosphere of constant apprehension and potential disruption from the ever-present threat of military intervention. His biography and the history of modern China were becoming ever more tightly intertwined.

*　　*　　*

Buji turned eighteen in March 1937. Still relatively small in stature, he was now a young man of an age for whom two conventional expectations beckoned—or menaced. One was possible marriage and the other was possible military service.

While Buji was aware that Nanchang was bracing itself against a possible attack from Japan, he was back home in Songlin in July 1937 when an incident—the Lugouqiao Incident on the Marco Polo Bridge on the outskirts of Beijing—set off China's Resistance War against Japan a full two years before the outbreak of the Second World War in Europe. Buji was still absent a month later when a dozen Japanese seaplanes attacked Nanchang's airport and railway station, escaping this first raid on the city because Nanchang Second Middle School was not yet in session. We can be certain that he was back in his native

Hejiacun village, if only because this was the summer that he married a young woman from the nearby village of Gujiacun.

The initiative was not his own. While Buji was completing his fifth year of school in Nanchang, Li, as his father's principal wife, had been negotiating with a matchmaker—or *meipo*—to find a wife for the young man. Now eighteen, Buji was the eldest of his generation and, since the death of his father, Wenge, the head of the He clan in his village. With the end of his high-school education in sight, Li—and no doubt his own mother, Fu—felt that it was time for Buji to appease the ancestors and to provide for their own security by giving them an heir.

This was a highly traditional engagement and marriage. The woman who would be known from now on simply as 'elder brother's wife' had the name Gu, like everyone else in her village. Most information about her necessarily comes from Buji himself—and some of the questions that it seemed natural for me to ask as his biographer illustrate the gap between western and Chinese assumptions in these matters.

When I asked whether Gu had a first name, Buji simply replied, 'no name.' When I asked him Gu's age, he told me, 'three months older than me.' When I asked him if he had met Gu prior to their wedding, he gave a curt 'No!'—as though I should have realized that it was as odd for a woman to have a first name as it was for her to meet her prospective husband before the marriage ceremony. Finally, when I asked Buji whether he found his bride attractive when he had raised her veil for the first time on their wedding day, he shrugged his shoulders, then replied, 'average looking.' Not, perhaps, the stuff of romance as understood in western societies.

We do know that Gu was born on 22 January 1919. We also know that she was illiterate, which may seem to us an odd piece of matchmaking on behalf of a bridegroom who was already distinguished by his literary and intellectual interests. Gu's feet were unbound which is not surprising since fashion had changed and Sun Yat-sen had ordered this custom to stop. So, in this respect, here was a girl more like Buji's mother Fu than like the lady of the house, Li. Gu was an accomplished sewer and embroiderer, again just like Fu. She was tenacious but very honest, sweet and modest. According to her son Tangxiang, Gu was 'the best woman in the world.'

After the He family settled on a suitable bride-price, Gu's family began assembling items for their daughter's dowry: the bridal suite, furniture, as well as silver that was destined to remain with Gu throughout her life. Well before the day of the wedding these items were proudly transported from Gu's village, lying twenty-five miles east of Hejiacun, to her new home. Then, just before the wedding, Gu herself was carried to the He family home on a bridal sedan chair.

During the marriage ceremony, which took place in the ancestral hall, Buji and Gu stood before the imposing altar that marked the 'seat' of the spirits and paid their respects to the ancestors. After bowing three times they turned to the groom's parents and to the rest of Buji's relatives and bowed again. Then they faced one another and mingled two bowls of hot wine and shared a bowl of rice. This simple act signified that their lives were now one. It also marked the end of the ceremony and the beginning of a lavish banquet during which the guests enjoyed eating no fewer than twelve dishes.

After the feasting the couple were led to a room on the right-hand side of the main entrance of the He family house. It was the same room that Buji showed us on our visit to Hejiacun in 2007—'This is where I was born,' he told us while pointing to the semi-derelict room now used as a stall for a cow. But in the summer of 1937 this had been the bridal chamber, furnished with delicately carved chests and a large rectangular brick-heated bed or *kang*.

Nine months after marrying Buji, Gu gave birth in March 1938 to a daughter, Honglian (red water lily). In June of the following year she bore Buji a son, Tangxiang (auspicious fruit), who is also known as Mingqing. Since sons were, as the Chinese saying goes, 'prized as a living purse,' there was much rejoicing. This was not, however, the case three years later when Gu gave birth to a second daughter, who was given the personal name, Xiangbao (fragrant treasure).[15]

This marriage, followed by the birth and survival of three children, secured the future of both Buji's mother Fu and Wenge's widow Li—the two matriarchs whose own natural concerns had largely prompted it. They now shared the family home with Buji's new wife, Gu, and his brother Buxiu. Moreover, the marriage underscored Buji's position, as the head of the He family and indeed of the village itself, just like his father Wenge before him. It was a role that Buji took very seriously. According to Tangxiang, his father was always 'ready

---

[15]   It is interesting that the *He Family Genealogy* only mentions Tangxiang by name and that the entry on Buji, written by his second daughter's husband Chen Sicong, omits to mention Gu's two female children by name—the younger of whom is his own wife. Chen Sicong ensured, however, that his own name appeared in the He family genealogy several times.

to take up the cudgels for a just cause.' In fact, it seemed that every time Buji returned to the village from his studies in Nanchang, or later from western China, 'something unfortunate would happen' that required his assistance and found him ready to oblige.

On one occasion Buji discovered that during his absence several young men in the village had been conscripted into the GMD army—'completely unreasonably and illegally,' according to Tangxiang. Buji thus traveled to the county town of Xinyu and demanded to see the head of the township who had been responsible for conscripting the young men. When the official could not produce a document authorizing his action, Buji is reputed to have slapped him across the face. This brave—perhaps even foolhardy—act produced results: the unlawfully conscripted men were returned immediately to Hejiacun.

Although Tangxiang remembers that his father possessed 'a spirit that dared to struggle against bad people and bad things,' Buji had no desire to remain in the village and simply take on the duties of a landlord. 'I don't like family business, all those rich things, because I burned the books,' he told me; 'I am an intellectual.' True, from the moment of his birth Buji seemed destined to follow the life of a scholar. 'Let not rich people invest in farms and land, for in books is to be found a rich harvest of corn,' as the Emperor Chengzong of the Sung dynasty put it in his *Invitation to Learning*. 'Let those young men of ambition who wish to rise to fame and wealth apply themselves to earnest study of ancient tomes.' This was indeed Buji's general inclination; but it was his particular family circumstances that left him free to follow it.

Buji had this freedom because his three-year-younger brother, Buxiu, would be there to run the family farm and to serve as head of the He clan in his older brother's absence. Thus, following his marriage to Gu in the summer of 1937, Buji was able to return to Nanchang with the aim of completing the last year of his high school education. He could not have foreseen, however, that it would take him another four years to do this.

*   *   *

When Buji returned to Nanchang from his peaceful Hejiacun village in the early autumn of 1937, he found that the Japanese had stepped up their air strikes over the city. Classes were continually disrupted as Buji and his classmates ran for cover in makeshift bomb shelters. Although the Japanese would not occupy Nanchang until March 1939, their relentless air raids over the city continued, as did their advance by land. They successively occupied Beijing, then Shanghai and their drive up the Yangtze valley was made more threatening by the infamous Rape of Nanjing. It is not surprising that Nanchang's government prepared plans for evacuation.

Throughout China, some sixty million people fled westwards in order to escape the Japanese Army's 'Three All Policy': kill all, burn all, destroy all. Some institutions likewise withdrew bodily to western China, as did the GMD government itself, which was repeatedly forced to move its capital: from Nanjing to Wuhan, from Wuhan to Chongqing. By the end of 1938, two-thirds of the population of Nanchang had left the city, including the Nanchang Second Middle School. There is, however, conflicting evidence as to exactly where and when the school's principal, Che Ju, led his seven hundred students, his teachers and his administrative staff out of the city.

I became aware of this problem when I visited the school myself in March 2007. On that lively occasion, it was agreed that the school had moved from Nanchang to the remote village of Shihuiqiao, which lies in the foothills of the Jinggangshan mountains near the county seat of Yongxing in the south of the province. This is the best part of 200 miles from Nanchang, as we found when we made the journey ourselves by bus a few days later—about a hundred miles beyond Xinyu, which lies roughly halfway. How, I wondered, had Buji got to Shihuiqiao when the newly built railway and all other forms of transportation had been disrupted by the war? Did his wife and mother know that he had left Nanchang and, if so, where had Buji been evacuated? And how long did the school remain there? There seemed to be little agreement among the four old alumni who shared their contradictory reminiscences as generously as their hot tea on that cold morning in Nanchang.

Nor could Buji readily resolve the difficulty of establishing how and when he had left Nanchang. In one interview he told me that he made his own way from Songlin to the school's new site: 'how to get there was my business . . . I had a map.' On another occasion, he suggested that he left Nanchang in the company of his fellow classmates. Whichever version is correct, Buji must still have been in Songlin as late as the autumn of 1938 because this was when his second child, Tangxiang, was conceived.

What Buji does remember clearly is the arduous journey from Nanchang at some stage, with a painfully frustrating inability to leave his family with proper information as to his whereabouts. The school would naturally have passed near Xinyu. 'We went on foot walking close to my village,' he recalled, 'but we couldn't go in and tell my mother where we were going.' Where had he stayed during the trek south, I asked? 'We stayed in Kedian, small inns.' How long did it take him to walk to Shihuiqiao? 'More than ten days.' What dangers did the students encounter on the journey? 'Some students tried to cross the river and drowned; others were attacked by bandits.' There is no reason to doubt the seriousness of the hazards the students and staff faced. 'I am lucky,' he concluded with a wry chuckle, 'I go through the mountains.'

In the late 1930s the village of Shihuiqiao boasted handsome stone houses that Buji remembered as 'strong, big and very good.' The district had played a significant role in recent history, not least through its association with the rise of Mao and the legend of the Long March. Though Mao had already left the area by the time Buji and his classmates arrived, the Communists had left their mark. There were few men or boys in the region since some 100,000 'volunteers' had been conscripted, or as Buji baldly put it, 'forced,' to join the Red Army. For example, the family with whom Buji and seven other students boarded in Shihuiqiao consisted only of a woman whose husband had joined the Red Army, willingly or not, and her daughter.

Buji had fond memories of his hostess. Hers was a small household compared to the He family home, though her large stone-built house would have towered over the mud-brick and limestone dwellings in Hejiacun village. And the school itself, where Buji spent most of his time, struck him then as an even more impressive building, as befitted the village's ancestral hall. Though already twenty and the father of two children, he was still at heart a village boy.

Shihuiqiao was clearly an inaccessible spot, but I became strangely fascinated with the fragments I gathered about it during our visit to Jiangxi in 2007. I kept asking questions; most went unanswered. Then, towards the end of our stay in Xinyu, the city officials agreed to help us get to Shihuiqiao to see for ourselves. Whatever would it look like today? Would time have obliterated the rather stately old-world village that Buji remembered? Would a tide of sophisticated economic progress have washed over it? We were provided with a bus driver and a guide, and they in turn enlisted the help of Yongxing's government officials. We learnt a lot one way or another. Buji was sitting next to my husband Peter on the bus, bubbling with memories prompted by his 88th birthday party the night before. Tangxiang and his interpreter brother-in-law, Chen Sicong, who helped me to fill other gaps in the family story, also accompanied us.

It was soon apparent that we were heading off the tourist map. After leaving the largely deserted highway at Ji'an, we bounced along a narrow, ill-paved road that wound through rural towns and villages, through rugged hills covered with pine trees and groves of tall bamboo, and through red-earthed countryside dotted with conical brick kilns, with water buffalo yoked to heavy ploughs, guided by farmers who toiled in their two-crops-a-year fields. It looked as though little would have changed in seventy years. After picking up a government escort in the county town of Yongxing, which struck us as rather drab initially, we made our way a few miles further along a seldom-used road, to arrive at the location of the school itself.

Shihuiqiao turned out to be a desperately poor village, more like Hejiacun than we had expected. Once again we were the focus of attention. Arriving to the clash of large brass cymbals and to the crackle of firecrackers, we were greeted by people who were small in stature, with sun-wrinkled faces. They crowded round when we descended from our bus. Everyone appeared to be dressed in dark blue padded clothing, no doubt to withstand the unheated houses. They were both friendly and curious as they followed us from the main square, where shabby but still imposing stone houses indicated that Shiquiqiao had once been a prosperous agricultural village, then into a high-ceilinged, timber-framed room, again in a dilapidated state.

Yes, we realized, this must be the former ancestral hall, which stood next to a vast derelict shell of a building that had once been the home of the eminent Tang family. So this was where Buji had completed his high-school education. I tried to imagine this enormous space divided into two floors and into several classrooms. As I looked, I could appreciate how this lofty edifice, though now fallen into disrepair and lacking a second floor, had impressed the young Buji.

Once again the government authorities had located one of Buji's teachers who actually remembered teaching the brilliant young student from Songlin. Unfortunately, on the day, the ninety-four-year-old man was too ill to meet us. But they had also found someone who had been a student at the school when Buji was there. The impressive ninety-one-year-old man, with a straggly grey beard yet confident bearing, who stepped foreword was still blithely coming out with formal revolutionary slogans. Three years older than Buji, Yang Chenyuan had been a grade behind him at the school. And he had not been so lucky. After graduating from university he had joined Chiang Kai-shek's Army, for which he had paid dearly by being sent in 1949, after the Communist victory, to a labor camp in a remote corner of northeastern China. Even when Yang was allowed to return to Shiquiqiao he remained under surveillance for many years. He had lived long enough, however, to be rehabilitated and even compensated. With a pension of 1,800 RMB a year, ironically Yang was now one of the better-off men in the village.

Buji, Yang and the rest of our party were led to a small table where we were invited to sit on four wobbly sawhorses. People crowded round, staring at us in a wholly unthreatening way—we were creatures from another world. Someone emerged from the crowd with a bowl of peanuts. A woman emptied a bag of candies on the table with a great flourish. There ensued a moving scene, with the two old men exchanging stories about their schooldays, shrugging about their subsequent experiences.

Yang Chenyuan said that he had recognized Buji immediately. Buji confessed that he did not remember Yang (though students seldom remember those in lower grades to themselves). Buji then turned to Peter and asked him what he should do. Peter suggested that he make a short speech. Buji rose and said how honored he was that everyone had turned out to meet him. Then he declared that he had lived here happily for no fewer than three years, during which time he had completed his high-school education.

It was a graceful rhetorical flourish, catching the mood of the occasion, and much appreciated by all. But I was left uneasily aware that Buji's claim that he had lived in Shihuiqiao for this length of time contradicted what we had been told by the school officials in Nanchang: namely that the school had only been in the village for one year and that the teachers and students did not arrive until 1939, since they had been in Yongtai in Qingjiang County the previous year. Resolving such discrepancies became the focus of our discussion during lunch in Yongxing, a few miles back along the road—and now striking us, by contrast, as relatively sophisticated, with such amenities as indoor toilets.

Party Secretary Yu hosted our modest but agreeable meal in Yongxing. Lithe and young—perhaps in his thirties—Yu bounded into the simple government dining room, with its inevitable color television switched on in the corner. Possessing an eager but authoritative manner, Yu dominated the room in an easy and relaxed way. Obviously a man on the way up, he was set on showing us how to drink. Sticking to juice or, at most, to the tasty local beer, we offered very feeble competition. Yu, however, had a big shot of Maotai, which he gulped down with a grimace, literally holding his nose, before washing it down with a swig of water from a plastic bottle that he kept under the table. After putting away four or five glasses of this fifty-proof drink, he achieved a high level of animation.

Yu launched into a peroration on some significant moments in the recent history of Yongxing. He told us how, as the home of Mao's third wife, He Zizhen Gui-yuan, the city had played an important role in the history of the Communist Party. He went on to remind us that before Mao had embarked on the Long March in 1934, he had made his headquarters in the near-by Jinggangshan mountains. Finally, with no loss of momentum or sense of anticlimax, Yu proceeded to tell us about the evacuation of Nanchang Second Middle School.

According to Yu, the school was only in Shihuiqiao for a year before moving to Taihe located in the most southern part of the province. At this point Yang's equally vocal colleague, Long Wenguang, contradicted this view: 'Nanchang Second Middle School was in Shihuiqiao for two not one year.' But Buji maintained his view that he had been in Shihuiqiao for three years, and I now recalled that Yang Linghe (in his cat-skin hat at Nanchang Second Middle School) had corroborated Buji's story that the school was still in Shihuiqiao in 1941. So I returned to Xinyu later that afternoon in a state of relative enlightenment.

Whether or not Buji arrived in Shihuiqiao as early as 1938, therefore, it seems to be the case that, after two or three school years there, he completed his studies in 1941—and under difficult conditions. While Shihuiqiao, like Songlin, lay well behind the firing line, life was hardly normal. War had disrupted commerce and communications alike, bringing shortages of some basic foodstuffs. 'We ate meat only one day a week,' Buji remembered and 'salt was scarce.' On the other hand, vegetables from the family's farm and fish from their rice paddies were plentiful.

It is not surprising that Buji was always 'very tired' during the years that he spent in Shihuiqiao. Students were kept busy for ten hours a day. Eight hours were devoted to schoolwork. The remaining two hours were occupied with military training. In 1933 the GMD government had introduced a Military Service Law. This made all males between the age of 18 and 45 eligible for military service. Yet full conscription was not enforced until the outbreak of the Resistance War in 1937. As one of the very small proportion of eligible males who were high-school students, however, Buji was exempt from military service. Nevertheless, this did not prevent him from undergoing military training. 'I had a gun but there were no bullets,' he recalled of the time he spent each day under the instruction of the GMD soldiers.

While Buji's former classmates all agree that there was much hardship and disruption during these years, their enthusiasm for learning evidently did not diminish, if anything it grew. Even so, Buji was to feel the pain of being out of touch with his own family. It was not until two months after his arrival that he had been able to establish contact by mail: 'My mother didn't know how to write and my father was dead so I wrote to my uncle.' Any family news thus had to come through his uncle, Duanyou. Many of Buji's classmates' parents meanwhile had moved to the villages surrounding Yongxing in order to be close to their children. Buji was not so lucky. Consequently, he missed his own new family, with two young children fast growing up in his absence. But most of all he missed his mother, Fu.

Buji was not reunited with his family until the early summer of 1941—an absence of over two years on any reckoning. There was much rejoicing. Everyone was happy to have him take his place as head of the family. For Buji at last, after nine years at junior and senior high school, at the age of twenty-two he was a high-school graduate. And like many of his classmates whose education had been interrupted by the war, he was married with a growing family.

As soon as Buji returned to Songlin in the summer of 1941, he attended to two obligations. First, he evidently fulfilled his conjugal duties. This time the child, Xiangbao, was to be a girl; so unlike her brother, Tangxiang, she was considered to be of little value to the family, since once she married she would belong to someone else and any children she would produce would belong to her husband's family. Secondly, in the autumn of 1941, Buji took his first formal employment, unsurprisingly as a schoolteacher.

Students like Buji who had done well in high school were conscripted into the school system as full-time teachers before they embarked on normal school training. This was because the GMD government needed more teachers in order to give every child in China an elementary school education. It was not a bad job. Teachers were paid a fixed salary, given sick leave and even a pension.

Buji spent the greater part of the academic year of 1941-1942 teaching Classical Chinese at Shifeng Primary School. It was a busy year. Besides preparing his lessons and marking exams, Buji visited his old friends from his own school days. Since Shifeng and Hejiacun were a half-a-day's walk apart he was able to spend most weekends with his young wife, Gu, his children and his mother; also with his brother, who had been exempted from military service in order to oversea the family's farms. By this time, the much-feared first wife of his father, Li, was dead.

Though he was happy to be among his family Buji nevertheless devoted time to making plans for further studies. According to the He Family genealogy, his intelligence, his industriousness and his excellent grades allowed him to be 'recommended for admission by the Jiangxi Provincial Government to study in the Department of Education at the state-run National Chekiang University' (now known as Zhejiang University). Buji's acceptance by one of China's great educational institutions was assured because he came third in the provincial university entrance examinations.

* * *

National Chekiang University had been founded in 1897. It was at once one of the oldest universities and one of the most modern-minded educational institutions in the country. As one student remembered, 'the curriculum was very similar to that of the Sino-Occidental school, but the courses were more advanced, more various, and better taught, with less memory work.'[16]

Styled the 'Cambridge of the East' in a series of wartime pamphlets written by the British biochemist and Sinologist, Joseph Needham, who would go on to change the West's misguided perception of China as a technological backwater, the University trained the country's most prominent scientists and had the country's most distinguished scientists on its staff. For example, its president, Zhu Kezhen, was the country's leading meteorologist and headed the prestigious Academia Sinica's Meteorological Institute. No wonder Buji was pleased to have been accepted. Believing that science was synonymous with China's future, Buji was not unlike his contemporaries who wanted to embrace modern technology and to study it for the sake of their country. Nor was Buji dissimilar from his contemporary, Han Suyin, who 'discovered the thrill of new knowledge' and the excitement of fashioning 'a new world free of ancient feuds and prejudices' during her university years.[17]

It is natural to wonder how Buji could have contemplated leaving his home and pursuing his studies in the midst of the war. But in 1942 there were several apparently favorable circumstances that allowed him to do so. That year the He family farm had a bumper crop and, like other sectors of the economy in Jiangxi, would continue to prosper through high wartime prices. Also during the summer of 1942, the Battle of Zhejiang and Jiangxi, which the Japanese had instigated the previous April, resulted in a major set back for them. This meant that, unlike most of Japanese-occupied eastern and central China, the area south of Nanchang lay in the war-free zone of the province (at least until January 1944, when the Japanese launched offensives in southern Jiangxi as part of their Operation ICHIGO). It thus seemed relatively safe and economically possible for Buji to resume his studies.

The bigger problem lay in where he was going. The university to which he had now been admitted was based in Hangzhou on the east coast of the country,

---

[16]   *Op. Cit.*, Chiang Monlin *Tides from the West* p. 49

[17]   *Op. Cit.*, Han Suyin *Destination Chungking* p. 25

a couple of hundred miles south of Shanghai. In the summer of 1937 Japanese troops had made a surprise landing on the northern shore of Hangzhou Bay. This put National Chekiang University, located halfway between the airport and the railway station, in a vulnerable position.

In order to keep one step ahead of the Japanese troops the staff and students, along with their books and scientific equipment, were evacuated from Hangzhou. They escaped on the tops of over-loaded trucks and on bicycles; they squeezed into over-crowded trains and buses; and sometimes they were forced to make their way on foot. Their first and second stops were at two locations in Jiangxi. Then they were again forced to move further west, to Ishan in Guangxi, before finally settling in Zunyi in the province of Guizhou. For some of the sixteen thousand students involved, the evacuation left romantic memories. 'On the trek the students were generally very up-beat,' wrote one student. 'It was almost as if everybody felt that with a wise leader at the top and five million courageous and dedicated soldiers fighting the Resistance War, there was nothing much to be worried about.'[18]

Whether such high spirits were universally sustained over the full 1,250 miles from Hangzhou may be doubted. And Zunyi is almost as far from Xinyu or Songlin—a long and wearying journey, even when we covered most of the ground by road and air (via Chongqing and Nanchang) during the course of our visit some sixty-five years later.

Buji's experience in 1942 was grueling. He left his teaching post in the summer, said good-bye to his family, and began his own long journey to western China. 'It was real hard,' he recalled, 'real terrible.' There was the ever-present threat of the encroaching Japanese army, which forced Buji to travel south through the provinces of Guangdong and Guangxi before heading northwest to Guizhou province itself. There was the difficulty of walking up to fifty or sixty *li* a day (say, twenty miles) wearing only cloth shoes—'Just one step up from straw shoes'—while carrying a heavy canvas knapsack on his back. And there was the fact that every mile he walked took him further away from his family.

Occasionally Buji was lucky and caught a ride on the top of a coal truck or in one of China's antiquated buses. Described by one writer as 'rolling junk heaps,' these charcoal-fired vehicles 'gasped and choked and gave up the effort

---

[18]   Wen Yiduo, 'Reminiscences and Thoughts on Those Eight Years,' *Chinese Education* (Summer 1988) Vol XXI p. 15

when faced with a moderate upgrade journey.' Then there was Buji's lack of funds—'don't have any money no more'—and his shortage of food. He had to survive on a diet of corn. But eating the starchy substance that was pounded into a cake had unpleasant side effects. 'Ha!,' Buji exclaimed ruefully, 'eating that kind of stuff, then I don't drink water much—constipation.' Things did not improve until Buji reached his destination, the city of Zunyi.

Buji was assigned lodgings by the university and did not complain. Anything was better than nothing. Students slept four to a double bunk bed. They ate spicy hot rice noodle soup and were introduced to other regional dishes. They attended class in old dilapidated temples, in ancestral halls and in local schools. And, although the accommodation was modest and the teaching equipment in short supply, the great achievement for the university was to keep going at all.

During his first year at National Chekiang University Buji chose to study a broad range of subjects. Some of these were subjects he had begun in high school: mathematics, Chinese history, Classical Chinese literature and English that was to provide him with a passport to a new life. Other courses such as sociology and psychology were new.

In his ensuing years at university, however, Buji became more focused on educational psychology and pedagogy, educational administration and educational history. Though initially intent on studying engineering, he had to put his preference for science aside because the Chinese government, which still needed teachers, offered to subsidize any student who was willing to enter the Department of Education. 'The government pay everything,' Buji recalled, explaining his need to forego his plan to become an engineer. Even so, the courses that Buji did take 'were more advanced, more various, and,' as a former student recalled, 'better taught, with less memory work,' than at most institutions of higher education in China.[19]

The GMD knew, of course, that they also needed scientists, medics, pharmacists and translators to help them win the war. This was one reason why they facilitated the universities and supported the many students whose funding had been cut off in the occupied areas of the country where they came from. At the same time, however, they insisted that every student continue the rudimentary military training they had begun in high school and take a course dealing with Sun Yat-sen's 'Three People's Principles'.

---

[19]   *Op. Cit.*, Molin, *Tides from the West*, p. 49.

Yet there was more to it than that. Joseph Needham, who was working as the Sino-British Scientific Liaison Officer at the British Embassy in Chongqing and beginning the monumental history of Chinese science and technology, was impressed by the priority that the GMD were giving to education—not because of military demands but despite them.[20] And the British statesman Sir Stafford Cripps, who also had a scientific background, took the same view when he toured several of the re-located universities and colleges. 'It is really nothing short of a miracle that the universities can be kept going at all in such circumstances and it speaks highly for the devotion of the staff and students alike,' Cripps wrote in his diary. For Cripps this was 'another example of the cheerful determination [of the GMD] . . . to continue the cultural and economic life of the country no matter what the Japs do.'[21]

Buji's single-minded devotion to his studies, along with his determination to keep going in the face of hardships, was a lifelong trait, which shaped his whole career. It eventually took him to the United States, in order to realize his opportunities; but his basic values had been formed in his native China. 'To western minds this attitude seems incomprehensible,' a visitor to Free China, Franz Michael, had noted in 1939. 'But the Chinese point of view,' he continued, 'is clear in this vast country . . . [where] the moral front must not be allowed to be destroyed.'[22]

When I visited Zunyi with Buji, sixty-five years after he had enrolled as a first-year university student in the autumn of 1942, he identified the spot where his lodgings stood on the left bank of the tributary of the Yaxi River. We were unable to find the large house itself—subsequently demolished, as we learned—but Buji recalled that it had been formerly owned by a local merchant called Wang. He well remembered where the female students had lived on the other bank of the river, telling me how he had often crossed the old red stone bridge 'to see the girls.' And he told me something about his life as a student radical.

During his second year of university, Buji was elected Secretary-General of the Student Self-Governing Council, a body that was under the direct control of the GMD. His election speaks for itself as testimony to the extent to which Buji was well respected and popular among his fellow-students; and it signals

---

[20]   Joseph Needham, *Chinese Science* (London: Pilot Press 1945)

[21]   Sir Stafford Cripps, 'Diaries,' Bodleian Library, Oxford, 9 January 1940.

[22]   Franz Michael, *China Press* (Shanghai, 23 January 1939)

his own commitment to representing their wider concerns, not simply looking after himself. It also meant that he was obliged to join the GMD party in order to hold this position. It was, nevertheless, in his capacity as Secretary-General that his commitment to social injustice, seen initially when he destroyed his father's accounts ledger and later when he performed the 'good acts' remembered in Hejiacun village, found a wider scope, this time with a political as well as a personal resonance.

By 1944 Chiang Kai-shek's Nationalist government was widely known to be corrupt, ridden with nepotism, and guilty of hoarding public funds. As a character in Pa Chin's classic wartime novel *Cold Nights* lamented: 'We are law-abiding and suffer, while others get rich and become high government officials at our expense.'[23] High-ranking officials in the GMD were not only corrupt, they were increasingly exposed as politically retrogressive, betraying the hopes invested in them by the promise of Madame Chiang Kai-shek's New Life Movement, with its clean and puritanical image.[24]

In 1942, despite the stresses of the war, Chiang Kai-shek spent much of his time on the writing—or on supervising the writing—of a book called *China's Destiny*. Though often criticized as feudal, anti-democratic, anti-western and infused with outdated Confucian ideas, *China's Destiny*, which appeared in 1943, became required reading for every student. At the same time, the government acquired an even tighter grip on education when Chiang appointed Chen Lifu as the minister of education. The latter's stipulation of what university professors should teach was not welcomed. 'The new tricks aroused the general resentment of the professors,' was the verdict of one participant, Professor Wen Yiduo, who maintains that it also made students 'somewhat lukewarm about their academic work and scholastic pursuits.'[25]

There was an even more pressing cause of dissatisfaction. By 1944 the war was still going badly for the Nationalist government. Part of the problem was Chiang Kai-shek's preference for attacking the Communists rather than the Japanese. Indeed the Communists, now based in Kunming to the west of Zunyi, seemed, in the view of some observers, to be doing a more effective job of defending the country than the Nationalists. A related concern among

---

[23] Pa Chin, *Cold Nights* (Seattle, University of Washington Press, 1978) p. 27 first published in 1945

[24] Madame Chiang Kai-shek—May-Ling—was one of the famous Soong sisters.

[25] *Op. Cit.*, Wen Yiduo, *Chinese Education*, p. 17

the student body—subject to conscription at any time—was the government's attitude to its own soldiers. The sick and the wounded were given little attention; leave was unheard of; mail was almost non-existent; food rations were inadequate; and accommodation was poor. Indeed, conditions were so bad that there was only one blanket for every three soldiers.

Buji was aware of the situation: 'the soldiers were not getting medication, food or shoes.' Consequently he and his fellow students decided to act. Stepping in with direct action where the government had obviously failed in its responsibilities, the students themselves collected and then distributed food and clothing to the troops.

During the Resistance War students prided themselves on being the carriers of the country's national conscience. They looked back with pride on earlier student campaigns, such as the May Fourth Movement in 1919, when students had protested against the outcome of the Paris Peace Conference, which sanctioned Japan's occupation of the former German colony of Shandong because of its neutrality during the First World War. Over the next two decades students had continued to protest: against the Japanese occupation of Manchuria and later against the corruption of the GMD.

Buji had never joined any of the student protests but when Chiang Kai-shek, hearing about the students' charitable act towards the needy soldiers, took the credit himself, he was propelled into action. The issue thereby assumed a higher political sensitivity. It fell to Buji, as Secretary General of the Student Self-Governing Council, to write a letter in protest against Chiang Kai-shek's claim that the Generalissimo, rather than the students, had led the campaign to alleviate the suffering of the troops. Buji, fully aware of the dangers to which he was now exposed, did not sign the letter with his own name: 'I use university official seal.' But it was Buji who took the letter to the local newspaper and saw that it was published—a courageous act for someone in his position.

It should be remembered that Buji's bold stand was not part of a general campaign against the GMD, such as the Communists pursued, but was prompted by a particular incident. As he put it later, Chiang Kai-shek 'wrote something that was not true.' This was a moral affront to Buji and it also related to his own commitment against *Bu Gong Ping* (unfairness). But however much Buji and the vast majority of his classmates disapproved of what the GMD was doing, when many of them were called up to join the army a year later they did the honorable thing. As Professor Wen Yiduo noted at the time: 'Since we had been forced by the enemy to go to war, we thought we'd just have to fight it, and talk about it later.'[26]

Buji always knew that he, too, would have to join up. On the face of it, he was now poised to become a soldier. He had undergone rudimentary military training in high school and during his first and second year of university. When, in the spring of 1944, Chiang Kai-shek lifted the immunity for students studying medicine, pharmacy, engineering and foreign languages, Buji's liability for service became more than theoretical. Chiang took this desperate step in order to create an elite force that could rejuvenate his own troops, now under acute pressure from the Japanese during Operation ICHIGO, which had brought the front line alarmingly close.

When the Japanese entered the southern half of Guizhou, not far from Zunyi, Buji found himself in immediate danger—'there was no place to escape to.' Moreover, he and the other students who had not been conscripted did not have enough to eat. Reciting the words of an ancient Chinese saying, Buji recalled: 'I eat everything but the table.'

Buji was therefore forced to leave Zunyi at the beginning of his third year of study in the autumn of 1944, to don a military uniform and to enlist in the Nationalist Chinese Army. Fortunately he did not get beyond the parade ground. 'Ha! I was too small, they are laughing at me because the rifle dragged on the ground when I put it on my shoulder.'

At the time it was no laughing matter. For Buji, it was fortuitous—but crucial—that he escaped conscription because of his height. (As his son, Phillip, was to joke years later, 'he stood about 5 feet 2 inches with platform shoes.') But for this, he would almost certainly have been detailed to march south of Zunyi in order to stop Japan's drive towards Burma. And he might very well have perished, as he well knew. Not only were the Japanese soldiers better equipped but the morale of the Nationalist troops—as the newly-conscripted students well knew—was at an all-time low. This combination spelled disaster for the Chinese—'If I had gone I would have died.' During every discussion of the Resistance War, Buji would tell me: 'I was very lucky, I was very lucky.'

*   *   *

---

[26] *Op. Cit.*, Wen Yiduo, *Chinese Education*, p. 11.

Rejected from the Nationalist Army, Buji resumed his studies. But at this point, his life was changed again when representatives of the American army unexpectedly presented themselves in Zunyi.

The United States had entered the Second World War in December 1941 after the Japanese bombing of the American Fleet at Pearl Harbor in Hawaii. And, in order to protect their interests in East Asia by helping the Chinese troops against further Japanese transgressions, they gave China not only American dollars but also equipment which their pilots flew from Burma to Chongqing over what was known as the Hump. The United States also saw to it that a hundred thousand of their own troops acted as liaison and training officers in an effort to re-train the Chinese Army. Since few Chinese spoke English the Americans—or 'ocean ghosts' as all foreigners were called—needed interpreters in order to help them do this job. And since even fewer Americans spoke Chinese, interpreters would have to be recruited from a relatively small number of English-speaking Chinese students, who suddenly acquired a wholly new importance in the war effort.

Hence the sudden appearance of the contingent of Americans who visited Zunyi in the late summer of 1944. 'They give us a test,' Buji recalled, 'if you pass the test you go to the Americans.' The oral test was easy: the American officer pointed to each facial feature in turn, which Buji had no difficulty identifying in English. The written test, on the other hand, was more difficult: only thirty per cent of the students passed. Once again Buji had 'no problem' with that exam either and a few weeks later he found himself in the capital of Free China, Chongqing. At a bound, now aged twenty-five, Buji had entered a new world of opportunity, albeit in a subaltern position, knowing full well that many of his classmates had meanwhile been conscripted as cannon fodder to Burma.

In 1944 when Buji arrived in Chongqing, it was a city of contradictions. One commentator described it as a dockyard among the mountains; at that time it took great cargo junks fourteen days to sail the 1,200 miles from the mouth of the Yangtze river at Shanghai. At the top end of the social scale there were Nationalist government officials, top military personnel, foreign ambassadors and consuls, journalists and military advisors, missionaries and businessmen, who lived in relative security and even seclusion—particularly those lucky enough to live in Chiang Kai-shek's compound among the forested hills behind the city.

When they were not working, this privileged group attended an unending circuit of cocktail parties, dinner parties and even balls. In October 1944 Madame Sun Yat-sen organized a ball at Victory House in order to raise money for needy writers and artists.[27] Others found the time to put on exhibitions like the Scientific Exhibition of 1944. They watched films—*The Three Musketeers* was a wartime favorite. They ate Jialing goat and Chongqing water buffalo steak prepared by some of China's best chefs who had taken refuge from the east coast. One American journalist based in Chongqing recalled eating 'better food than I have since eaten in any other city in the world.'[28] Another American, Julia Child, who would become famous as the author of *Mastering the Art of French Cooking*, cultivated her culinary interests while living in Chongqing during the Resistance War.

Buji experienced none of this. Instead, he found himself living in an austere and forbidding military compound, the site of which we were to rediscover with him, high above the steep banks of the Jialing River. Indeed he and the two hundred other students had few reasons to make the trek down to the city. On the few occasions when they did go down they saw that for the majority of Chongqing's citizens and the thousands of refugees who had more than doubled the size of the city—unlike the Nationalist elite—the place was wracked by deprivation. Food was scarce. Water, transported in buckets on the ends of long bamboo shoulder poles by porters belonging to the so-called Stick-Stick Army, was in short supply. And electricity was unpredictable—this is why Madame Chiang Kai-shek nostalgically remembered seeing the glow from thousands of calcium carbide lamps from her sanctuary in the hills above the city.[29]

By now deeply scarred, Chongqing's former white buildings were covered in soot and smoke from too many bombs. The cliffs above the Yangtze and Jialing Rivers were pitted with bomb shelters and makeshift dwellings cobbled together from grass mats and rubbish. The only thing that was plentiful were the people. Every narrow passage and street was crowded with sedan-chair bearers carrying more fortunate people up the steep steps that bit into the cliffs; with rickshaw drivers; with peddlers; with processions—weddings and, all too frequently at this time, with funerals. Evening did not make any difference—this was the time that night-soil workers took Chongqing's effluence to the outskirts of the city.

---

[27] Madame Sun Yat-sen also Soong Chin-Ling the sister of Madame Chiang Kai-shek

[28] Theodore White, *In Search of History* (New York: Harper and Row, 1978) p. 71

[29] Churchill College Archives, Sir Horace James Seymour Papers (SEYR 3/2) Madame Chiang Kai-shek to Lady Violet Seymour, 6 September 1949.

Training was intensive—'they needed us yesterday,' Buji recalled—so he and his classmates studied 'day and night.' He learned new English vocabulary: 'names of weapons, medicines, anything in the Army, supplies for the PX and hotels.' He was introduced to American food—butter, salad, French fries and juicy steaks. Initial distaste was soon overcome—'I got used to that kind of food,' he cheerfully admited; 'after six months, everybody likes it.' He was introduced to American military dress, providing sought-after garments for ill-clad students.

Though Buji recalled that the Japanese 'airplanes dropped the bombs where we were training,' he knew how fortunate he was: 'It was a very good job to have at the time.' The Americans were congenial (which tallies with Stafford Cripps's admiring observation, as a liberal-minded Briton, that they dealt with the Chinese in a 'sympathetic and understanding way.'[30]) So they were agreeable enough as bosses when, after completing his course, Buji found himself interpreting ten hours a day 'for five or six Johns and Jims.'

There was one other important respect in which Buji was assimilating to western cultural norms. Because the man who taught him, the Canadian missionary James Endicott, insisted that all the interpreters under his care attend Church parade, Buji was introduced to Christianity. In some ways this proved no less difficult—or no more difficult—than learning the names of weapons. According to Lin Yutang, 'to be a Christian was synonymous with being progressive, western-minded, and in sympathy with the New Learning.'[31] Moreover, it is evident that Buji did not simply renounce his previous beliefs in favor of a new revelation that invalidated them. Instead, he seems to have found it easy to adapt his wide range of beliefs—ranging from Daoism and the ancestor worship of Confucianism, to customary practices associated with spirits and natural phenomena to the doctrines and narratives of Christianity. Consequently, it was now that Buji became certain that the occidental white-clad figure who had saved him from the bandits when he was a child had been no less a figure than Jesus Christ.

Buji's association with the Americans was important in other ways too. His English improved. He was exposed to American ideas and American culture, including Christianity—all of it synonymous with modernization, technological

---

30 *Op Cit.*, Stafford Cripps, 3 January 1940

31 Lin Yutang *From Pagan to Christian* (London: Heinemann, 1959) p. 34

development and scientific expertise. And, above all, his work as an interpreter significantly improved his finances.

Buji had joined the Americans during a period of massive inflation. At the beginning of 1944, for example, the 200-dollar Chinese bill had to be replaced by a 500-dollar bill. By the end of the year people had become accustomed to carrying their money in wheelbarrows and in knapsacks in order to purchase a few groceries. Buji escaped much of this. He was lucky to be housed and fed well by the Americans and, above all, to be paid in American dollars.

It was, however, at his own initiative that he wisely converted his American dollars into the only stable currency in China: gold. 'I couldn't use the US dollars because nobody knew what they were,' Buji recalled, 'so I went to the bank; and the rate just improved and improved and in the end I had several million and everyone else who had Chinese money was destroyed.' After working just over a year for the Americans, Buji had accumulated ten bars or tablets of gold, of slightly different weights, but enough to represent a small fortune. 'I put it in my belt, I was very rich.' The fact that he saved the gold was to be very important.

*   *   *

When the Americans dropped two atomic bombs on Japan in the summer of 1945—the first on Hiroshima and the second on Nagasaki—the Resistance War was brought to an abrupt end. Even so, the Chinese economy was in disarray since trade had stopped, factories had closed, railways had collapsed and the foreign concessions clustered around such coastal cities as Shanghai had disappeared. A staggering total of three-million-plus soldiers along with between fifteen and twenty million civilians had lost their lives. Even those who had been passive observers had not escaped social deprivation, hunger, dislocation and, in the occupied areas of China, political oppression. No wonder Buji remembered thinking, as he heard that the war had ended: 'Don't know if the whole village is alive or dead.'

After Buji was discharged from the American Army, still one year short of completing his university degree, he naturally made his way to Zunyi to complete his studies. Once there, however, he discovered that the students, professors, and the administrative staff were in the laborious process of moving the whole university, library, scientific equipment and all, back to Hangzhou. Until the relocation was completed, the only thing for Buji to do was to go home.

Japanese forces had retreated through Xinyu in 1945 and, according to Buji, had passed very close to Hejiacun, though thankfully they did not enter it. When Buji returned to the village in the late autumn of 1945, he found the He household there to greet him: not only his brother Buxiu, who now had a family, but also Buji's own wife Gu and their three children, and his mother Fu. 'Mother was crying when she saw me,' Buji vividly remembered, 'she could not speak, so she just hugged me.' While the family was now without servants—they had doubtless been conscripted into the Nationalist Army—no member of the immediate He family had starved. Indeed 1945 and 1946 again yielded bumper crops to sustain the family in their ancestral home.

During his absence Buji had been nostalgic for simple local food such as pork and beef, rice noodles and potatoes. He had missed his children, Honglian, Tangxiang and Xiangbao, now aged seven, six and three respectively, and either in school or soon beginning. He had been parted from his wife, Gu, for almost all their married life. He was now reunited with his mother; and he again had the comfort and guidance of his distinguished uncle, Duanyou.

However delighted Buji was to be home, his attention was focused on completing his university degree. One of the activities that could be undertaken in his home province was the year he was required to spend on teaching practice. Accordingly, almost immediately after returning to Songlin, Buji took up a post teaching English at the County Middle School in Xinyu.

Xinyu must have looked lovely to Buji after war-torn Chongqing. The school where he taught and boarded was located on the banks of the majestic Yuan River, which he quickly discovered was a good place for fishing. A Buddhist temple adjacent the school offered him a quiet place to reflect and contemplate. On the other hand, his former school friends were in short supply: 'some old friends, hard to find.' (This was not surprising since between 1937 and 1945 almost ten per cent of the population of Jiangxi had become either refugees, were homeless or had died.) And even though the nearby location of his family meant that he had the possibility of returning home on the weekends, Buji did not visit Hejiacun often. The pressure of teaching might have been one reason. Also relations 'were very strange,' as he put it, with his wife Gu. 'I didn't get together with her again and most of the time I was not in the village, I was teaching.' The years of separation in war-torn China were not easily compensated. There were to be no further children in this marriage and its low emotional intensity was already apparent.

In just over half a year, Buji had completed one half of his teaching practice. He returned to Songlin in the late summer of 1946 and again bade farewell to his family. It was a poignant moment for his eight-year-old boy, Tangxiang, who vividly remembers his father patting him on the head and promising, 'you will come with me on my next trip.' As Buji saw it, he was following the tradition of many Chinese scholars, for whom it was not uncommon to spend a large part of their life away from their families. Just how long he did not, of course, realize as he set out again, this time for Hangzhou, the proper home of the National Chekiang University.

*   *   *

There are many reasons why Hangzhou has been hailed as the most beautiful city in China. A city of manageable size—it had fewer than one million inhabitants in the late 1940s—it was one of the three major centers of China's silk industry. Close to the city is the Grotto of the Purple Clouds with its cave housing a giant statue of the Laughing Buddha. And in Hangzhou itself lies the deep and serene West Lake, ringed with pagodas and pavilions, and overlooked by substantial high-hill villas. No wonder the city had for a millennium attracted poets and men of letters who made it a center of culture. As the popular saying goes in China, 'in heaven there is paradise but on earth there are Suzhou and Hangzhou.'

Even today, modern development has not been allowed to mar the natural beauty of the West Lake—itself partly man-made, of course, with its islands, temples and causeway. In 2007 I spent a couple of relaxing days with the Ho family, exploring the lake and the surrounding hills. Buji recalled that, when he first arrived in Hangzhou, he took advantage of the university's temporary location next to the lake. 'I row on the lake and visit pagodas and temples.' But there had also been much hard work, as the twenty-seven-year-old student had striven to complete his much-disrupted degree course. During our own visit, the Chancellor of the University presented Buji, then a spry eighty-eight, with a copy of his grades, class by class, for the years 1942-47 when he was registered at the university. They also gave him a lunch attended by one of his former professors. (Unfortunately there was no opportunity to interview him because in the middle of lunch the ninety-two-year old man excused himself from the table because he had to teach a class!)

National Chekiang University had opened its doors again in Hangzhou in May 1946—less than a year after closing them in Zunyi. In September 1946, Buji had been welcomed back into the Department of Education where he registered for the seven courses that, in addition to half a year's classroom experience, he needed to complete his degree.

By the following spring he had completed his course work but not his teaching requirement. Buji's overall grade average was 73.9. Interestingly, his marks in English during his first year (65) had been lower than those in Classical Chinese or Confucius (both 74). After this, he took no English courses in his second or third years; and in his fourth year (1945-46), though his linguistic proficiency had obviously increased through his work as interpreter, he was given only 65 in Practical English. Buji's best marks—mostly over 80—were in Education and in Psychology and he also achieved such marks in some of his History courses. Of course, all of these grades, like the sporadic teaching that supported them, were to some extent blighted by the disruptions of the war years.

Buji did not return to Xinyu County Middle School to finish his teaching qualification. Instead, he recalled remaining in Hangzhou in order to 'help the teachers in education.' In China, university teaching assistants were, according to Professor Wang Kang, 'promising young people who were superior in their studies.'[32] They were employed to assist their professors in various ways. Some handled department affairs or acted as teaching assistants. Others helped their professors to undertake research in preparation for publication. It was in this capacity that Buji found himself staying on into the spring of 1947.

He had come to the attention of one of his professors because of the quality of the lecture notes that he took. 'He says something,' as Buji recounted to me, 'I write everything down; at night I re-write it and make a lot of sense.' Since teaching relied primarily on the professors' oral presentations, any student capable of making a virtually verbatim transcript of a lecture was of value. Hence Buji's claim: 'he took my notes for his textbook.'

Buji's facility in note taking, moreover, proved fateful in its unanticipated consequences. A fellow student, Jiang, like many in the class, could simply not understand the professor's heavily accented regional accent. Buji, with his acute ear for languages, could. In fact he passed on his revised notes to Jiang, with the result that he and Buji were the only students who passed the examination at the end of the course. Jiang was overjoyed and sought a tangible means of showing his gratitude. The son of a wealthy ship-owner from Shanghai, he now exerted himself on behalf of his talented fellow student. 'He has friends in Taiwan,' Buji explained, 'his high school teacher was now a high school president and he

---

32   Wang Kang, 'The Lianda Ethos' in *Chinese Education* (Summer 1988) Vol XXI, p. 88

need teachers.' Thus Jiang was not only able to offer Buji a job but to arrange a passage on one of his father's steamboats that sailed between Shanghai and Keelung in Taiwan.

This is how Buji ended up in Taiwan in July 1947. Why, one must ask, did he take up Jiang's offer? The answer to this question surely lies in the political situation that confronted Buji at the end of the Resistance War, and that inexorably foreclosed his own options.

Hopes for China's postwar rebirth proved illusory. The Nationalists had long been fighting on two fronts: against the Communists as well as against the Japanese. Although the Japanese war had ended in the summer of 1945, the Nationalist forces under Chiang Kai-shek and the Red Army led by Mao Zedong remained at loggerheads. Both were attempting to occupy as much territory, evacuated by the Japanese, as they were able to take. Chiang was already dogged by charges of corruption and collaboration with the Japanese; and he now indisputably made many blunders in military strategy during the Civil War, which began in 1946. He overstretched his troops. He was unwilling to negotiate a settlement with the Communist forces while he still had the right cards in his hand. And in prolonging the war to the end of the decade, Chiang alienated his closest ally: the United States of America. A final effort to unite the two factions in a multi-party government was made by President Truman's special envoy, General George C. Marshall, who had been US Chief of Staff during the Second World War. Convinced that neither the Nationalist 'reactionaries' nor the 'irreconcilable' Communists were prepared to make significant concessions, Marshall left China in early 1947, exclaiming in Shakespearian fashion: 'a pox on both your houses.'

The failure of high-level politics, the reality of the civil war, the suppression of student protests, the virtual collapse of the economy, the break-down of social relations and of culture—here were the realities of post-war China. They were dramatized in the popular 1947 film *Nothing But A Dream* through the characterization of young Shanghai architect who sees his post-war hopes for his own country and his country's future dashed. This film made it pretty clear that, amid the chaos that now descended on one of China's largest cities, the educated class to which Buji belonged had no immediate role to play, either under the GMD or the Communist Party.

Buji, in short, found himself trapped. But, ever resourceful, he was ready to travel, ready to try his luck, and open to offers. We know this from the fact that he had recently explored one other avenue, which proved abortive. While in Chongqing, working for the Americans, he had already been introduced to the possibility of continuing his studies in America. 'This is what they promise us,' he told me. 'Of course, everybody thinks that it is good.' It should be remembered that since the latter part of the nineteenth century China had sent many students abroad to study. Even at the height of the Resistance War the GMD promised that one tenth of the 1,224 students who had worked as interpreters would be eligible to study in North America or in Europe at the end of the war.[33]

It was not until early 1947, when he was undertaking the last year of his degree in Hangzhou, that Buji actually sat the exam. He did not, however, make it into the two per cent of successful candidates who were finally selected. Selection, of course, was undoubtedly biased towards GMD loyalists, who could be relied upon to return. China needed foreign technology and ideas as much as it needed regular infusions of American dollars. True, in entertaining the possibility of studying abroad, Buji was not himself planning to immigrate to the United States. 'I thought I would come back to China—because China needs every kind of people,' was how he explained himself; but as so often in his life, the outcome was governed by more than his own intentions.

With his ten bars of gold strapped firmly to his body, Buji boarded a Taiwan bound steamer in Shanghai: 'I hear the houses are made of paper; I thought I take a look'. When he arrived in Taiwan many hours later, no one from Hejiacun knew where he was. As he explained, 'I thought I was going to Taiwan for a trip—I want to go back to my home town.' He also thought that the duration of his visit would be for no more than a term's teaching, during which he would complete the remaining requirement of his teaching qualification, thus gaining his degree, then return to Hangzhou. Had he known otherwise, he said in hindsight, 'I don't go to Taiwan.' But he did go. His own life and that of all his family hinged on that decision.

---

[33] See Y.C. Wang, *Chinese Intellectuals and the West 1872-1919* (Chapel Hill: The University of Northern Carolina Press, 1966)

Paul and Sonia at Second Middle
School, Nanchang, 2007

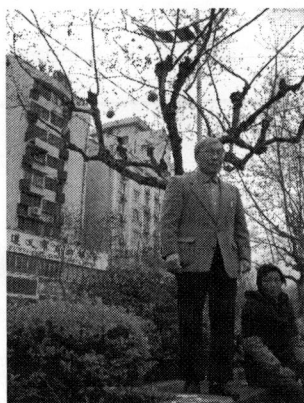
Paul Ho in Zunyi, 2007

Paul greeting Yang Chenyua in Shihuiqiao, 2007

Paul's former Middle School, Shihuiqiao

CHAPTER 3

'Star-crossed lovers'

When he arrived in Taiwan on 16 July 1947, Buji knew nobody. But he had the introduction, duly provided by his friend Jiang, to the principal of Provincial Yi-lan Middle School, Li Zhushou, who needed someone to teach English. Buji had already accepted the offer of 280 yuan a month and now headed from the port of Keelung, serving the capital Taipei, to the north-east coast of the island.

We repeated the journey with Buji on our visit to Taiwan in February 2008. This time we made a day trip to Yi-lan on a chartered bus—a journey of less than an hour and a half through the modern tunnels en route. Buji contrasted this with the four to five hours it used to take in his day over bad mountain roads. And when he had first arrived, he had traveled from Keelung to Yi-lan by train. 'There was no road around the island,' he explained, 'it was very rocky and the sea was very wild.' Yi-lan county is known for its rugged beauty, and Buji had glimpsed the romantic splendor of its thirteen-thousand-foot mountain range through the window of his train; but we were rather disappointed to see little of this from our modern bus.

Then as now, the city of Yi-lan itself has a very different landscape, situated on the north side of the Langyang River and spread across an expansive flood plain rich in alluvial soil. The houses, perched on stilts between neatly squared and banked rice paddies, seem to float on the water. We found the air heavy with dampness. As the family philosopher Phillip Ho elegantly observed, 'you could cut the air, it is so thick and so heavy with the glare from the rice paddies.' Yes, his father nodded feelingly: 'It rained all the time.' With his bed two inches above water Buji felt as though he was 'living on water.' Settled at the beginning of the nineteenth century by fruit-growing Han Chinese farmers, then expanded during the Japanese occupation, Yi-lan had a population of just over four thousand in 1947, though much larger sixty years later, as we soon saw.

We went first to the National Center for Traditional Art: an elaborate complex of modern buildings, art gallery and auditorium, abutting a re-creation of a traditional street. David Ho, even more celebrated in his native Taiwan than in China itself, was obviously the focus of attention: but our visit was organized so as to highlight his father's first teaching post at Provincial Yi-lan Middle School. When we reached the school itself, we entered the main assembly hall, packed with excited pupils. Father and son, David, sat on the stage along with the school principal, who was firm but friendly in steering the occasion: welcome for all, with much applause; presentation of the first of the commemorative plaques showing Buji's tenure as a teacher at the school (similar plaques were to go to each of the schools that we later visited); a short speech from Buji, well received; then questions for his famous scientist son, to which the latter responded with a sensitive touch. There was much enthusiasm throughout and, at the end, it was difficult to see the diminutive Buji amid all the students milling around us. He was understandably moved by the occasion—the last time he had seen Yi-lan was during the year he had worked there.

Remote from the larger centers of Taipei and Taichung, this was where Buji found a job, room and board, and an opportunity to begin his professional career in the summer of 1947. Yi-lan was Buji's first vantage-point in Taiwan or Formosa—beautiful island in Portuguese—as it was then usually known in the West. He found a long-settled population of some six and a half million on an island two hundred and forty miles long and eighty-eight miles wide. Some of the aboriginals or *shan-ti jen* (mountain people) had been on the island since Neolithic times; but the Hakka and Hoklo, who had left provinces like Fujian on the south east coast of Mainland China during the seventeenth century, had long made up the majority of the population. Politically, Taiwan had not become part of China until the latter part of the seventeenth century. Its subsequent status as a prefecture of Fujian Province then only lasted for two hundred years (1684-1885)—a relatively short period in the long span of Chinese history.

Though both the Hakka and Hoklo belonged to the Han Chinese, they were linguistically divided. The Hakka spoke their own distinctive dialect of Chinese while the larger group, the Hoklo, spoke *Min-nan hua* or southern

Min—referred to today as the Taiwanese dialect or language. This was, as Buji discovered in 1947, the language that his Yi-lan students naturally spoke with their family and their friends—though they were forbidden to speak it in the classroom, where Mandarin was now compulsory. It was not only unusual but also in character that Buji decided to learn Taiwanese himself. When I asked the irrepressible Buji what had prompted him to do this, he told me that he liked the sound of the language—which has eight tones, rather than Mandarin's four. He also assured me that he 'had lots of fun.' When I asked him how he eventually learned to make himself understood in this difficult language, he said with a grin: 'Monkey see, Monkey do.'

Obviously Buji was sensitive to the culture in which he now found himself. He did not dismiss it, as most Mainlanders did, but was disposed to accommodate to a new society that he regarded with sympathy. Moreover, the cultural diversity of Taiwan, as he well knew, had other dimensions, mainly as a result of its checkered political history. For in 1895, when Japan defeated China in the Sino-Japanese War, Taiwan had been ceded to the Japanese as part of the indemnity—given up fairly readily by China, as it seemed to many Taiwanese, like a pawn in the game. With Japanese colonial administrators and military officials flooding into Taiwan's major towns, immigration from Mainland China virtually stopped.

Unlike other parts of Asia, which had been briefly and brutally occupied during the war years, in 1945 Taiwan had known nothing but Japanese domination for half a century. During this period, the imperialist Japanese had set out to create a classic colonial economy and achieved considerable success as model colonizers in their own terms. They had built roads and harbors. They had expanded the island's railroads and communication systems; they had increased the production of rice and sugar cane; they had given a boost to the lumber and fishing industries. And they had made education—albeit in Japanese—available to more children than ever before. The result was that Taiwan had enjoyed a higher standard of living than China itself, which helped inculcate a lasting sense of Taiwanese superiority to the Mainland Chinese.

There was an ideological as well as an economic dimension to all of this. Development came at a price, unequally borne; and imperialism was inherently authoritarian. Martial law and the censorship of the press gave no voice to the Taiwanese. The screw had tightened in 1937 when the Japanese implemented the *Kominka* policy. One of its facets was to intensify the use of the Japanese language and the adoption of Japanese names, directly contesting the Han Chinese identity of the majority of the population, and provoking more open dissent. Political activists carried out no fewer than twelve uprisings in an effort to claim a voice in the 'model colony.' The literary community let their feelings be known in other ways. Only a few Taiwanese writers, known as the Komin authors, explicitly advocated collaboration by suggesting how their compatriots might become fully Japanese. By contrast, there were poems of protest, of which Lien Heng's *Flowers of Taiwan* is a good example. Others wrote in secrecy. Wu Cho-liu's novel, *The Orphan of Asia* (1946), suggested the impossibility of creating an identity for the Taiwanese under either Imperial Japan or Nationalist China.

Yet these were the two stark alternatives, as was shown in October 1945, when the island of Taiwan was handed back to the Nationalist Republic of China. This fulfilled the agreement that Chiang Kai-shek had secured from his American allies in the Cairo Declaration of December 1943: a stipulation that all the territories which Japan had 'stolen' from the Chinese be restored to the Republic of China at the end of the war. But by the time that this was done by the victorious Allies in 1945, the effect was paradoxical. Chiang was actually gaining control over Taiwan just when he was losing control over the Mainland.

Buji was simply one of approximately two million Mainlanders, or *Waishengren*, who, in years after 1945, crossed the Straits of Taiwan. Many of those whose financial interests were greater than their loyalty to the beleaguered Nationalist regime moved, stepping-stone fashion, to the British colony of Hong Kong; and some of them, if they were lucky, to the United States. But these well-heeled refugees were in the minority. The majority of *Waishengren* had to settle for exile in Taiwan. Some had claims to high-ranking military or government service. Others traded on their unstinting loyalty to Chiang Kai-shek. Although most of these Taiwan-based exiles were among China's elite, they left Mainland China with few assets but their education. In Buji's case, his educational credentials were usefully supplemented by the gold bars that he had acquired in Chongqing from his earnings as an interpreter for the Americans, and which he now brought with him to Taiwan.

Most of the *Waishengren* thought that they were only 'visiting' Taiwan. Buji had left with only one suitcase, containing a few books and some clothing. These exiles did not imagine that within a few years they would be establishing new lives and new homes: that they would have to re-configure their futures and re-write their pasts.

*　　*　　*

Though the Taiwanese had developed different strategies for coping with imperialist Japan, they were united in their unfavorable view of the *Waishengren*. This hostility is hardly surprising; it was mutual, since the Nationalists now accused the Taiwanese of being 'collaborators' with the Japanese, whereas most Taiwanese felt that they had exchanged one colonial ruler for another. It further reinforced the stereotypes when the Nationalist elite promptly moved into the former homes of the Japanese rulers—the best domestic housing on the island—and took the top administrative posts. They nationalized agriculture, affecting the livelihood of much of the indigenous population. And they insisted that *kuo-yu*, or Mandarin Chinese, become the national language.

The antipathy that existed between the two groups soon came to a head. In response to a provocation by officials working for the Monopoly Bureau, a Taiwanese demonstration was organized on 28 February 1947 demanding a greater voice in the island's government. It enlisted widespread support and publicity alike. The military were called in, with disastrous results. The 'peaceful demonstration' ended in nationwide bloodshed. 'The Taiwanese are now being executed in a holocaust more terrible than anything inflicted upon them by the Japanese,' a Canadian diplomat wrote of the notorious "2-28 Incident".[34] In the view of most Taiwanese, the Japanese 'dogs' had been replaced by the *Waishengren* 'pigs.'

Arriving in Taiwan just five months after the 2-28 Incident, Buji was thrust into a land that was in turmoil and would continue to be governed by martial law for the next forty years. He was in the midst of censorship, of a strictly imposed curfew and of imprisonment and execution for political dissidents. He found himself doubly despised, because ordinary Taiwanese considered *Waishengren* not only as inferior to themselves but also as less sophisticated and less competent than their former Japanese masters. Yet Buji himself was ignorant of the 2-28 Incident when he arrived in Taiwan: 'If I knew that, I would not have come.' It was, however, another matter to retrace his steps and return to Mainland China.

There was an obvious delicacy in his position. As a schoolteacher, Buji was willy-nilly an agent in the post-war re-indoctrination of the Taiwanese population. He taught in a classroom where portraits of Chiang Kai-shek and Sun Yat-sen had only recently replaced those of the Japanese Emperor. He helped the other teachers conduct morning assembly. Here the students

---

34   Chester Ronning *A Memoir of China in Revolution* (New York: Pantheon Books, 1974) p. 110

were taught to raise their hand to the Chinese Republican flag before singing what has been dubbed Sun Yat-sen's battle hymn of the Republic of China: *San Min Chu Yi*. Yet this was not simply the policy of a repressive regime, imposed on a subject people. In its sense of formality and hierarchy, much of it was reminiscent of Buji's own boyhood education. His students stood when he entered or left the classroom. They rose from their desks when they answered questions in class. And they never challenged their teacher's authority. Buji, the teacher who was learning Taiwanese himself, was hardly the model of an alien or authoritarian figure.

The complacency of the Nationalist elite is striking. Confident of their supremacy in Taiwan they were unwilling to admit defeat in Mainland China. They could rely on international support against the Communists, of course. As the wise uncle of Han Suyin declared in her famous novel *A Many-Splendoured Thing*, everyone believed that 'America won't let them take Formosa.'[35] As late as September 1949—two years after Buji had arrived in Taiwan and just after Chiang Kai-shek had likewise become an exile there—Madame Chiang Kai-shek wrote a revealing private letter, professing optimism about the prospect of returning to Mainland China: 'The coming months will be bitter ones but we are facing them unafraid,' she affirmed. 'We know we shall prevail in the end.'[36] Yet the fact is that, by this time, their situation had long become hopeless.

On Mainland China, a million troops belonging to the Communist Army had now crossed the Yangtze River; they had occupied the former Nationalist capital, Nanjing; and they had taken Beijing. Mao Zedong was to declare the founding of the People's Republic of China (hereafter PRC) in a speech on 1 October 1949, given to a crowd of 100,000 people from the top of Tiananmen Gate leading to the Forbidden City: an historic occasion which saw Mao hailed as the leader of 550 million people. Chiang Kai-shek's response to this event was simply to maintain the 'Three No's Policy': no contact, no negotiation and no compromise with Communist China, and (as late as 1958) he continued to proclaim that his intention was *Fan-kung ta-lu*—to re-conquer the Mainland.

---

[35]   Han Suyin *A Many-Splendoured Thing* (London: Jonathan Cape, 1952) p. 2

[36]   Churchill College Archives, Cambridge, SEY R 3/2 Sir Horace James Seymour Papers, Madame Chiang Kai-Shek to Lady (Violet) Seymour, 6 September 1949. Lady Seymour was the wife of Sir Horace Seymour, who had been British Ambassador to China from 1942 to 1946, and the two women had become close friends while living in the wartime capital of Chongqing.

The brute facts of confrontation and non-recognition would determine not only the future of China and of Taiwan as separate and hostile political entities but also the fate of the family that Buji had left behind in the remote province of Jiangxi.

Unlike the typical *Waishengren*, replete with a neo-colonialist attitude and an impatience to return home to civilization, Buji gradually reconciled himself to the fact that he might well be in Taiwan for the foreseeable future. On arrival, he had written to his family but received no reply. He drew somber conclusions and decided to bide his time. This was the path of prudence in view of the steadily deteriorating situation on the Mainland: 'I don't go back there, it was impossible.' But if he was safe, he was also alone: torn by feelings of guilt and responsibility for those he had left behind to an unknown fate that he was helpless to mitigate. He found his predicament 'very sad—don't know what happened to my family. It was impossible for my family to come to Taiwan.'

*   *   *

Buji did what he could, given the limited options available to him in a small town. Day-trips by bus with his teacher-colleagues to the hot springs in the nearby hills and eating 'good noodles' made life in this rain-soaked place tolerable. Nevertheless eight months was long enough for a young man (he turned twenty-nine in March 1948) to vegetate in this remote east-coast town. It had given him a foothold in Taiwanese society, allowed him to complete his student-teaching requirement for his degree. (Buji's National Chekiang University transcript shows that the degree was awarded on 7 August 1948, when he was allowed to graduate in his absence.) But if he were now to make his career in Taiwan, Yi-lan offered too little scope or opportunity, either personally or professionally.

Buji's prospects suddenly changed when he received a letter out of the blue. It came from Huang Pu-gui the sister of a former classmate from Xinyu days. Pu-gui was now the Principal of the Taiwan Provincial Changhua Middle School for Girls, where her brother had taken up a post teaching Chinese literature. Convinced by her brother, Huang Pu-kui, that his old friend He Buji had elegant handwriting and a good knowledge of English due to his employment as an interpreter with the American Army, Huang Pu-gui now offered Buji room and board and a job teaching English. 'Where is Changhua, is it better or worse?' Buji asked his friends in Yi-lan. When they told him 'it's better than Yi-lan,' Buji pulled up stakes in February 1948 and prepared to move to the other side of the island.

Again, it was all new ground for Buji. He discovered that Changhua and its surrounding villages are bounded by two rivers—the Ta-chia to the north and the Hu-wei in the south—by the Strait of Taiwan to the west and, to the east, by the spiky mountain range that forms the backbone of the island. Founded in 1723, the city was longer-settled than Yi-lan as well as much bigger. By the early twentieth century Changhua had become a lively commercial and administrative center for the region. It had less rain than Yi-lan—comfortingly, Changhua's subtropical climate resembled that of Buji's home province of Jiangxi. Moreover with the island's third largest city, Taichung, only a half-hour train journey away, it was far from remote. 'The best is Taichung,' Buji observed years later, 'southern part of the island too hot, Taipei too crowded.'

From the moment he took up his teaching position in March 1948, Buji found himself a busy man, with several outlets for his restless energy. His colleagues remembered that he 'worked very hard and that all of his students paid respect to him.' A devout Christian since working for the Americans, Buji joined the local Baptist Church (where, in due course, he would be baptized by the Texas missionary, Reverend David Hanker in 1953). Eager to explore the area and have some measure of independence, Buji purchased a Phillips bicycle with a dynamo—a luxury item in 1948 Taiwan—with some of the gold bars that he still wore close to his body. Most of his time, however, was spent in the classroom or preparing his lessons.

Changhua had been a major administrative centre for the Japanese government during the occupation, and it showed. Buji found that his Japanese-speaking Taiwanese students added *to*—Japanese-fashion—to the end of every English word which he found 'real funny.' Equally they had difficulty understanding their teacher's heavily accented Mandarin dialect. Buji compensated by giving his students a better written than oral comprehension of the language. He did this by preparing mimeographed hand-outs. These formed the genesis of a textbook, prepared at this time, but not published until 2003.

Growing from the roots that the author first established in his early months in Taiwan, *A Concise English Grammar* embodies half a century of wisdom and experience in teaching English to Chinese students. The book was based on what Buji called 'the five sentence structures of English.'[37] This was a simple taxonomy,

---

[37]   The five sentences are 1. Subject Intransitive verb and modifier; 2. subject, linking verb and complementary; 3 subject, transitive verb and object; 4. subject, dative verb, indirect object and direct object; 5a. subject, fractive, object and complement and

which proved its usefulness in practice to generations of students. 'If you know five sentences,' Buji told me, 'in twenty minutes you are happy—never make a mistake.' This was evidently how Buji taught his students to learn English—and possibly how he had himself been taught to learn the language himself.

So Buji was busy enough: teaching English, exploring the countryside on his bicycle, learning the Taiwanese language, and writing a Chinese-English grammar textbook. Yet in the eyes of his principal, Huang Pu-gui, his life was not complete. It seemed to her that Buji needed something else: a family.

It is not clear how far Huang Pu-gui realized that this thirty-year-old English teacher might already have nurtured such desires in his former life. After all, her brother had known Buji in his Xinyu days. But Mainland China, with the People's Republic formally proclaimed in October 1949, was now a world away from the realities of a settled life in Taiwan. As the school year of 1949-1950 drew towards its end, Pu-gui called Buji into her office. Acting not so much as school principal but as matchmaker, and no doubt spurred on by her brother's student friendship, Pu-gui told Buji that she had someone in mind for him. The candidate for matrimony was, in fact, one of his own pupils.

Now eighteen years old, Kiang Shuang-ru was taller than most of the girls in her twelfth-grade class, and therefore sat in the back row. Among the top students in her year, Shuang-ru was also a favorite student of the school principal—and, so some believed, of her English teacher from whom she received high marks.

Buji must have been perfectly well aware of Shuang-ru's identity, despite subsequent claims to the contrary with which he covered up his initial embarrassment. Even if his memory uncharacteristically failed him on the identity of Shuang-ru, the point is fairly clear. What is likely, however—indeed fully understandable—is that at the time he felt some initial diffidence about the thought of courting a Taiwanese woman—and a student to boot. Moreover, even though Mainland women were scarce, there were obvious reasons why the hated *Waishengren* were seldom accepted into a Taiwanese home or thought to be a good match for eligible Taiwanese girls. Above all there was the obvious but unspoken dilemma: Buji already had a wife and a family somewhere else.

Why was Shuang-ru—ultimately to become Sonia Ho—singled out? Now in her final year at school in 1949-50, she was intelligent, attractive and strong-

---

5.b subject causative, object, and complement. Paul Ho *A Concise English Grammar* (Beijing: Beijing Higher Education Publishing Firm 2003)

---

minded. She came from a good family: her maternal grandfather had been a scholar and a substantial landlord, with many tenant farmers to keep him in style. Her first language was naturally Taiwanese, and it is significant that, schooled in the Japanese educational system until 1945, she was more competent in Japanese than in Mandarin. However, like the rest of her Taiwanese classmates, she formed a less sympathetic view of the Mainlanders than of the Japanese. 'Bad people from China, bad people,' she later assured me. 'They think they are better than us—what a nerve!' Their ignorance was appalling: 'Some of the soldiers see the banana and they see it and eat the skin.' They were barbarians: 'They don't know what a faucet was.'

On the face of it, then, the prospect of a marriage being successfully arranged between Shuang-ru and Buji appears distinctly unpromising. The main obstacle was less the twelve-year gap between their ages or the fact that, unknown to Shuang-ru, Buji already had a family in Mainland China than the apparently wide gulf between them in status, in outlook, in language and in culture. To understand this—and to understand how the gulf could be bridged—more needs to be said about the circumstances of Shuang-Ru's upbringing in Taiwan.

*   *   *

Kiang Shuang-ru was born on 23 June 1931 in the small settlement of Shen-gang near the city of Fengyuan. *Shuang* means 'double' and *Ru* means 'auspicious'; hence double auspiciousness. Kiang, the family name, normally that of the father just as in western practice, means 'river'. [38] The Kiang family compound where Shuang-ru was brought up is impossible to find today: 'Our family house is gone—a highway is now there. You can't find anything.' Yet during Shuang-ru's childhood the compound was impressive: 'We have a big house, very big house. A big gate, courtyard, shrine for the ancestors.' On the right side of the enclosed brick-built U-shaped building, Shuang-ru shared several rooms with her mother, Kiang Lou, and her widowed grandmother, Lin Pen. On the left side of the single-storey dwelling, Shuang-ru's uncle by adoption, Kiang Jin-sen, lived with his wife and their three children. Dividing these two living quarters, at the base of the U, was the ancestral hall with its high altar, sweet-smelling incense, oil-burning lamps and ancestral spirit tablets celebrating the members of the Kiang family.

---

[38] On Mainland China Kiang would be Jiang

The death of Shuang-ru's grandfather, Kiang Su-mei, in his early thirties had long-lasting effects upon the Kiang family—particularly on his wife, Lin Pen. As the Kiang family matriarch, Lin Pen 'had great power over the family' so her grandson Lu I-wen recalls. 'All the girls from the Lin family,' he continued, 'had to kneel down in order to get her approval and blessing.' She was the undisputed matriarch of the Shen-gang family compound. Shuang-ru admits that she was 'afraid' of her grandmother, perhaps not surprisingly, though she is still proud to point out that she came from one of the wealthiest families in the region 'who came from Fujian province [on Mainland China] a long time ago.'

It was in 1754 that the first Lin had settled in the grasslands near present-day Changhua when Shuang-ru's ancestor Lin Shia became a *k'en-shiou* or frontier entrepreneur. During the next century the now expanded Lin family had a business processing and exporting camphor in addition to managing their substantial farmlands. And, during the first half of the twentieth century, Lin Pen's branch of the family used government connections to establish and help run the Changhua Bank.

It is not surprising then, that Lin Pen brought a considerable dowry to the Kiang family at Shen-gang. Nor that she also brought expectations: that her dowry along with her husband's wealth would leave a substantial fortune to future generations; that she would produce sons to carry on the family line; and, as a result, that she would be well cared for in old age. But just like her own (apparently equally formidable) widowed mother before her, Lin Pen was left at an early age to preside over her deceased husband's modest fortune—and their children.

Of which there were many, one way or another. Lin Pen's own first child, Yue, was a female. Disappointed that she was not a much-prized male, Lin Pen was ready to listen to the readings of a village fortuneteller who said that only by giving away the child would the family be blessed with sons and good fortune. So Yue was given to one of the family's tenant farmers and became a *simpu*—or 'little bride', rather like Buji's own mother. Lin Pen's next four children—Lou (later Shuang-ru's mother), Bing, Hsiao, and Tsao—were girls too. These children were not given away. However Lin Pen saw to it that they were all married by the time they reached the age of eighteen. Then, since the loss of her husband also meant the loss of producing a male heir, Lin Pen adopted two boys—Kiang Jin-sen and Kiang Yuan-heng. When the eldest son, Jin-sen, came of age he took over management of the family's considerable properties. His younger brother, Yuan-heng, left the family compound at Shen-gang, moved into Taichung and entered business.

Lin Pen had an uneasy relationship with her adopted son Jin-sen and his children, who lived with her in the Kiang family compound. This stemmed partly from the fact that she did not hide the fact that, the accomplished and beautiful Lou, was her favorite child. And though Lou's daughter, Shuang-ru, found her grandmother fierce compared to her gentle mother, she had no doubt that she in turn was the favorite grandchild. She had, for example, been taught how to bind her grandmother's feet. 'She likes me best that's why she teach me,' Shuang-ru recalled, 'you got to do it right because when she go to heaven she thinks she can walk.' Lin Pen's behavior towards both her daughter and granddaughter was fuelled by a love that they recognized beneath the severity of her manner. Thus the scolding of her precocious and independently minded granddaughter was aimed, Shuang-ru insists, at making her 'like the best girl.' Indeed, Lin Pen showed Shuang-ru and her mother where she kept the family fortune—it was concealed in a large cupboard.

Not surprisingly, Lin Pen's overt favoritism created bad blood—and considerable jealously—within the Kiang compound at Shen-gang. When, for example, Shuang-ru was about to sit for her entrance exam to Taiwan Provincial Changhua Middle School for Girls, Jin-sen's wife, whose own daughter, Hung Ka-miao, had failed to pass the same exam, was discovered before the altar in the ancestral hall praying that her niece would be equally unsuccessful. Lin Pen nursed an obvious anxiety that, when she died, her adopted son, Jing-shen, could not be trusted to look after Lou and Shuang-ru.

The old lady's protective attitude towards her daughter Lou had roots that went back many years. At the age of eighteen, in 1922, the kind and gentle Lou had married—or been married off to—a man called Lu Din-hsin. The marriage, which produced no children, was a disaster. Though Shuang-ru recalls that she was 'not supposed to know about him,' it was common knowledge among the Kiang family that Lu Din-hsin was a drunk and a gambler and that he beat his wife. After seven or eight years, the crisis was finally resolved. 'My mother cry every day,' was the story Shuang-ru had been told. 'Lin Pen got mad and call my mother back to the house because she wanted to take care of her.' At this unhappy juncture, Lin Pen had given her daughter not only shelter but also enough money to establish her own business in Fengyuan. Lou's independence, however, was henceforth limited and she was not allowed to wear any make-up lest she attract attention. Lin Pen's attempts to prevent her daughter from forming another liaison, however, had plainly failed. It was in 1930 that Lou became pregnant with Shuang-ru—and her former husband, Lu Din-hsin, was not the father.

While Shuang-ru knew from an early age about her mother's unsuccessful marriage, she grew up knowing nothing about her own father, as she still laments:

> I wonder, everybody has father, how come I don't have? I go home and ask my mother. My mother never tell me. My mother has four sisters—they all keep secret, they don't tell me anything. I ask my auntie every day, my uncle, nobody tells me.

Unknown to Shuang-ru, she had in fact encountered her father—and on more than one occasion. There were two implicit clues, of which she only later made full sense. First, when she visited her aunt, Kiang Hsiao, who had married into the nearby Lu family, Shuang-ru remembers that a man often watched her playing in the courtyard of the family compound. Furthermore, she also remembers that, when she was seven or eight, she often accompanied her mother to the nearby town of Taichung. A man always met them when they arrived at the bus station: 'I was told to call him uncle'. Curious as to the man's identity, suspicious as to why Lou insisted that the liaison be kept from Lin Pen, and certain that the 'uncle' was more than a friend, Shuang-ru recalls asking her mother: 'Why do you go with this guy?'

The answers to many of the girl's questions turn on the relations of her own family with the Lu family, one of the most illustrious in that part of Taiwan. Originally from Fujian province in Mainland China, the Bei-tuen branch of the Lu family migrated to Taiwan in 1771 and later moved to San Jiao Zi village in Shen-gang. It was here in 1866 that Lu Bing-nan, a highly respected member of the local gentry whose private army had protected the people of the region, ordered the construction of *Hsiau-yun*, or Cloud of Bamboo villa, for his mother. By the time of Shuang-ru's birth in 1931, the Lu compound was being managed by Lu Bing-nan's seven surviving sons. One of them, Lu Mi-shi, married Shuang-ru's aunt, Hsiao—which is why her niece was often to be found playing there.[39]

When we returned to San Jiao Zi with Shuang-ru in the early spring of 2008, we found that *Hsiau-yun* remains impressive despite its dilapidated

---

[39] The Lu children in order of birth: Eldest son, Lu Dun-li; second son, died; third son, Lu Mi-shi; fourth son, Lu Shuang-chio; fifth son, Lu, sixth son, died; seventh son—Shuang-ru's father, Lu Chiao-hu; eighth son, Lu Chi-yuan; ninth son Lu Bu-ling and first daughter, tenth child, Lu Yu.

condition. Much of the structure is now protected by metal awnings and shed-like covers, pending the (very slow) process of restoration. The compound, comprised of several single-storey and two-storey dwellings, is enclosed by high protective walls and entered through an imposing gate. The houses, the ancestral hall and the once-famous library are separated from one another by lush gardens, by rain-washed brick and cobble stone courtyards, by beautifully arched bridges, by artificial stone 'mountains', and by Buddhist pagodas to protect the residents against evil. Surrounded by distant hills and lake-like rice paddy fields, and intersected by a gentle flowing stream, *Hsiau-yun* always had the very best *Feng-shui*.

Constructed over a period of sixty years, the buildings embraced a variety of styles ranging from early Tong-chih (1862-1875) and Kuang-hsu (1875-1908) of the Qing dynasty to Japan's Taisho and Jaohe and to the Art Deco style of the 1920s. Every building in the compound was constructed with the very best materials. The cobblestones came from the nearby Dajia River; the camphor and pine used for the heavy beams from the distant forest. The green-glazed decorative tiles and orange *Yen chih* bricks were brought over from the Mainland. So were the craftsmen who carved the stone, constructed the lattice windows, and painted the exposed wooden surfaces of the lofty rooms.

We saw the extent of the buildings and were even able to gain access to the old library. *Hsiau-yun* in its day boasted a library of some twenty-one thousand volumes and even now the decayed scroll boxes give some idea of the scholarly splendors of a previous century. And it became a cultural center too. Opera and dance troupes performed exclusively for the family. Famous scholars like Wu Tze-kuang, from Canton province, traveled across the Taiwan Straits in order to teach at the Wen-yin school that was founded by the family. 'Those people all loved to study,' Shuang-ru told me, 'and they did a lot of good things for the people.' Their scholarly bent was indeed obvious from the relics around us.

After leaving *Hsiau-yun* on our 2008 visit, we went on to the temple and Lu family mausoleum in the hills above Houli. Built in 1932, the mausoleum contains the remains of many members of the extended Lu family. The four sisters who founded the Buddhist monastery with their mother—the wife of the fifth Lu son—did so rather than submit to marriage and child-bearing. The complex of buildings the women inhabited until their death stands on a hill behind the Kiang and Lu compounds at Shen-gang. Shuang-ru told us that she had sometimes made the journey on foot with her mother—a walk of at least two hours, as we could well believe. The temple is approached via a narrow winding road, snaking up the hill through the flowering shrubs. The structure combining neo-classical and 1930s Japanese styles is much as it has been since its creation but the new silver dome of the near-by mausoleum stands out.

On our visit here in 2008 the Ho family all duly paid their respect to the ancestors, as at Hejiacun a year earlier, bowing three times in front of the high alter. Then we moved to the mausoleum where the urns are stored in racks around the circular wall of the building; row after row, perhaps twenty or thirty feet high, each row identified by number and date of internment. We readily located the urn of Shuang-ru's mother, Lou, on a row at eye level. But then we made a new discovery, one that justified her inclusion in the Lu family's mausoleum. Aided by temple records we saw that only two rows above, and almost immediately in line with the urn of Shuang-ru's mother was her father too.

For over forty years, Shuang-ru had already known his identity—yes, her father had been one of the Lu brothers, actually the seventh of nine (two of whom had died in infancy). It was after Lou's death in 1960 that Shuang-ru learnt this from her fourth aunt, Hsiao. But it was not until this sun-baked February afternoon in 2008 that she now learnt his proper name too. This was a memorable day, bringing together the two sides of her family in death, with a recognition denied to her during the lifetime of her two parents. Lu Chiao-hu as we could now document, had been born on 19 June 1886 and died on 16 October 1955; Kiang Lou had been born on 13 December 1903 and died on 12 June 1960. Their child Shuang-ru was thus born when Chiao-hu was forty-five and Lou nearly twenty-eight.

Lou, it seems, had met Chiao-hu, a noted scholar who had been taught by the great We Tze-kuang, on one of her business trips to Fengyuan. The couple fell in love, Lou became pregnant, and Chiao-hu proposed. It was at this point, according to Shuang-ru, that the matriarch of the Kiang family had asserted herself: 'My grandmother doesn't want my mother to be second wife.' The fact was Chiao-hu's first or principal wife was barren and, even though she did not live within the compound at *Hsiau-yun*, Lin Pen refused to let Lou enter the Lu household. Issues of family honor may well have been at stake—none of her four daughters were second wives or concubines. Even so, the presence of an unmarried pregnant daughter at Shen-gang must have been an embarrassment, which could not entirely be concealed by silence. Buji insists in retrospect that, even though Lou did not move into the Lu household, she was nevertheless 'a concubine.' Indeed, he suggests, this is why they kept it a secret. It may be nearer the truth, however, to say that the anomaly was that Lou had *not* become a concubine due to Lin Pen's wish to keep her at home.

Two years after Shuang-ru's birth, Lu Chiao-hu did marry again—to Lou's best friend. Lou had made the introduction and encouraged the match, for reasons that may conceal mixed motives of her own: not only to promote her friend's prospects but to perpetuate her continuing liaison with Lu Chiao-hu. This second wife produced three boys (one of whom died) and three girls. While Chiao-hu fathered heirs to continue his name, he was determined, according to Shuang-ru, to continue his relationship with Kiang Lou and to take an interest in their daughter. As Shuang-ru insists, 'this man and my mother love each other.'

So why was Lin Pen reluctant to let her daughter marry into the Lu family? Did she simply want to keep the gentle and considerate Lou close to her for company in old age? Or did she see some fragility of character in Lou that would have prevented her from coping as a second wife? Whatever the origins of Lin Pen's decision, it had lasting consequences for the child of this union. The world of *Hsiau-yun*, though familiar to Shuang-ru during her visits to her aunt, was not to become her home and the link with Chiao-hu was not to be acknowledged. Instead Shuang-ru was to grow up, apparently fatherless, in the more modest comfort of a home at Shen-gang where the dominating presence was that of her grandmother, Lin Pen.

*   *   *

'I had a very lucky life when I was young,' says Shuang-ru. Though not as wealthy or as educated as the Lu family, the Kiang family lived well as landlords at Shen-gang, enjoying the rents of a number of tenant farmers. They were able to employ several female servants, who cleaned the house and cooked in the communal kitchen. They had two men to tend the fruit trees on their property—mainly lychee, mango and longyen—and to maintain the vegetable patch and the rice paddies. These men also looked after the pigs—'come to New Year's festival, we eat it'—as well as chickens and ducks and two dogs, one of which belonged to Shuang-ru. Though the family's income declined after the outbreak of the Sino-Japanese war in 1937, when the government bought rice directly from the tenant farmers and thereby eliminated the landlords' profits, Shuang-ru nevertheless insists that her family was 'very rich.'

Shuang-ru's good memories extend to her early school years. She entered the Japanese-style Kogakko (primary school) at the age of seven in April 1938. Her Taiwanese teachers 'were all very nice.' Every day she had a pleasant thirty-minute walk to the Anli Guo Min Primary School. During her first year a female servant carried Shuang-ru to the school on her back. During subsequent years Shuang-ru walked to school with her one-year-older cousin, Kiang Gouchu. Although Shuang-ru had to study 'very hard' from 8AM until 4PM, or until the light in the un-illuminated classroom had faded, she found the schoolwork 'very easy' and consequently enjoyed it. She also enjoyed making new friends, especially with the timid and reserved, Lin Li-tai. Their friendship, which began at the age of six and would last a lifetime, was reinforced by Li-tai's links to the Lin family from which Lin Pen came.

In 1944, at the end of Shuang-ru's six years at the Anli Guo Min Primary School, she and Li-tai won admission to the Taiwan Provincial Changhua Middle School for Girls. It should be noted that Shuang-ru could have gone to the much larger and longer established Taichung Girls Middle School if her grandmother had agreed to change the family name from Kiang to a Japanese one. Changhua Middle School for Girls was a half-hour's train-ride from the family home and Shuang-ru became a boarder sharing a dormitory with nine other girls, including her friend, Li-tai.

The admission of a limited number of Taiwanese girls to the school—only fifty as against 250 Japanese—put Shuang-ru and Li-tai among a small minority. Although happily proficient in the Japanese language, Shuang-ru's predominantly Japanese teachers, in response to the Kominka or national language movement, devoted much time to the teaching of Japanese. They also introduced Shuang-ru to a new subject: ethics. This was designed to make Shuang-ru and her Taiwanese classmates into loyal and subservient subjects in the Japanese social order. 'There were lots of lessons about being obedient to the Emperor, and every morning the students had to salute the Japanese flag and recite something,' Shuang-ru recalls. 'Long Live Emperor Hirohito' and 'Long Live the Glorious Asian Culture' were the usual mantras. 'I hear that,' she now says dismissively, 'but I don't pay any attention to that kind of stuff.'

Shuang-ru entered high school in April 1944 when Japan was in the midst of a world war. Wartime austerity was the order of the day but the fact that only the Japanese received food-ration coupons meant that Shuang-ru ate a lot of 'cold stuff—terrible food' at the school. As well as deprivation, she faced the harsh discipline that her Japanese teachers meted out to their Taiwanese students. 'The Japanese teachers treat us like a dog; they give us a hard time; we have to go and wash the toilet, dirty job; we have to clean the classroom—we got to do everything,' she remembers, with abiding indignation. 'They spank you—hit you with a stick if you are not sitting up straight and you don't have your feet flat on the floor.'

Shuang-ru also remembers the hazards of the air raids that now disrupted her studies. The air bases, from which part of the Japanese attack on Pearl Harbor had set off in December 1941, and which were now in turn being bombed by the Americans, were not the only targets in Taiwan. The school was forced to take precautions. 'In the morning we had to go into the bunker—and there is a lot of water, we have to stay for a couple hours because of the bombs, and then we come out; we were all wet and we had to wash all the clothes. I never forget that.'

On top of this, the colonial Japanese government's creation of work brigades during the latter part of an increasingly desperate war saw adults and students forced to contribute to the war effort. For Shuang-ru this meant that 'we are always doing something else instead of studying.' The work was no token intrusion on their time but involved demanding and physically unpleasant tasks that took their toll on her health. 'We go to the mountain, and we planted potatoes,' she recalls. Climbing the hill, now known as Ba Gua Shan, that rose behind the school was a nightmare of a job for Shuang-ru and the other female students because the designated potato field had been a graveyard. 'We had a hard time, you know we had to use the pick—other people's bones, teeth, skin. I was so scared. I was very sick. I went home for about one month.'

There were compensations during these difficult years. It is interesting to find that, despite her increasingly negative reactions to the regime, Shuang-ru made friends with two Japanese classmates. She also enjoyed wearing the navy-blue sailor-suit blouse uniform and did not mind having her hair fashioned in the severe straight-bang haircut that the Japanese imposed on their children. And of course she had the comfort of her friend Lin Li-tai: 'we study together, we eat together, we sleep together.' When Li-tai got a bicycle Shuang-ru enjoyed riding on the back—even though they once accidentally rode into the river. Finally, during her Saturday visits to the Kiang compound at Shen-gang, home comforts compensated for the sparse rations: 'my mother make a nice lunch for me: rice, meat, vegetable.'

During these visits, Shuang-ru did not elaborate to her mother, Kiang Lou, or to her grandmother, Lin Pen, on the hardships at school. The way she now explains this points to the women's different personalities. 'I don't talk much about the school to my mother very much because she worry,' says Shuang-ru. But she goes on to add: 'I don't talk to my grandmother very much because she is a very tough lady.' Even though the Shen-gang compound was isolated from the Japanese soldiers, her family must have had some idea of what Shuang-ru was experiencing because they always sent her back to school with a little extra food and with a little spending money to help see her through the next week.

The end of the war came as a mixed blessing. The writing was on the wall for the overstretched Japanese empire by 1944, at latest, but there was no prospect of an early surrender or a negotiated peace. Instead, dogged Japanese resistance was met with an increasingly brutal exercise of power from the ascendant Americans. Not until August 1945 did Emperor Hirohito capitulate. And Taiwan, willy-nilly, had been part of his empire. It was handed over, like the spoils of victory, to Chiang Kai-shek and his *Waishengren* followers. For the Taiwanese, the experiences of victory and defeat were curiously intermingled and they had little cause for dancing in the streets—as the Kiang family discovered soon enough.

During the war, their tenant farmers had found themselves better off because they could sell their rice directly to the Japanese government rather than to their landlord. There was no real possibility of a simple postwar reversion to the status quo. The Japanese regime had gone; the successor Chinese regime was mired in a civil war in which the land question was a fundamental source of contention. Echoes of revolution were not confined to the Mainland. The "2-28 Incident", mentioned earlier, thus became the focus of a complex mixture of discontents within Taiwan: not only political and national but also social and economic.

With new-found confidence and a long-held sense of grievance, some of the Kiang family tenant farmers used the disruption caused by the "Incident" to settle old scores. Shuang-ru, who was sent home from school for two months following the Incident, remembers that about six of their tenant farmers in Shen-gang disguised themselves, then broke into the family compound at midnight. 'We had locked the door, my grandmother opened the door, they come in, they take everything.' They were not successful, however, in finding Lin Pen's hidden 'fortune.' The robbery was, nevertheless, a blatant affront, face-to-face, not some minor peculation. 'Daylight robbery at night,' is how Shuang-ru describes it. 'They had official approval; they threatened the family and told them not to report it—they took money and clothes and threatened that they would come back again,' she recalls. 'Everybody was sick-scared for two months.' This local incident, feeding off "2-28", was all the worse because the family knew who the people were: their own tenant farmers. 'The robbers' children were classmates,' Sonia told me, 'I have to pass by their house every morning when I go to school; they cannot look at me.'

*   *   *

The lucky life that Shuang-ru fondly remembers in her childhood was plainly over by the time of her adolescence. She was coming of age within a turbulent society where her family's economic position had declined and their social status was now under challenge. Moreover, her own role within the Kiang household was anomalous, as a lone girl whose paternity was a subject for speculation by herself and—whether openly or covertly—by others too. Neither her mother nor her grandmother had a husband; instead this was a tight-bound matriarchy in which the strong-minded Lin Pen fulfilled her responsibilities as head of the household as best she could, concerned that her favorite granddaughter, Shuang-ru, should not end up in the invidious position of her daughter Lou.

Taiwan Provincial Changhua Middle School for Girls had likewise to struggled to preserve its identity through traumatic changes brought about by the end of the war. No longer was it a haven for the daughters of the Japanese elite, who had departed with rude haste when their colonial regime suddenly collapsed. Shuang-ru, fourteen in the autumn of 1945, was sad to lose touch with the couple of close Japanese friends she had made. On the other hand she was pleased by the introduction of volleyball, and both she and Li-tai played on the intercollegiate team. Moreover, the influx of new pupils, drawn from both Taiwanese and *Waishengren* families meant that Shuang-ru no longer had to bear the brunt of discrimination and discipline from her former Japanese teachers, now departed. They were replaced by Huang Pu-gui, as principal, and by the Chinese staff whom she recruited, many of whom, like herself, were recent arrivals from the Mainland. Among these, of course, was He Buji, installed as the English teacher in March 1948.

The change for Shuang-ru had, therefore, been double-edged. One of her classmates, Wong Gui-fong remembers that 'the Japanese were real teachers while the Mainlanders were not real teachers at all.' Shuang-ru confirms this. Her *Waishengren* teachers struck her as unworthy of her respect—'my teachers were very low class; they don't wear shoes, they scare me, I'm not used to it.' We have her grades for these years, which continued to be good. But her initial inability to speak, read or write Mandarin, the new official language, was used against her, interpreted as a lack of Chinese patriotism among the backward Taiwanese. All of this was particularly difficult for a pupil who had always been among the top students in her class under the Japanese. Even though she had not enjoyed easy conditions under the Japanese—especially during the final years of the Second World War—what she remembers is that 'when the Japanese left it was hard time.'

Indeed the painful transition created a personal crisis in Shuang-ru's education. 'I almost quit school,' she affirms. 'I go home and cry. I say that I don't want to go back to school but my grandmother spank me.' It was Lin Pen's insistence—'You must go back'—that proved crucial in quelling Shuang-ru's short-lived rebellion: 'So I go back.'

It was obvious that the family matriarch felt her own frustrations, now outliving the conventions of the society in which her privileged upbringing had taken place. She saw girls being raised to be independently minded—defying the four quintessential attributes of a gentlewoman: personal virtue, proper speech, proper comportment and diligent work, as had been set out in the advice books that women had been writing since the beginning of the eighteenth century. She had lived to see the lavish hospitality—theatrical and opera troupes, large hunting parties and enormous banquets—presided over by her father Lin Ch-ao Fung replaced by wartime austerity. When, as a child, Lin Pen's feet had been bound, it had been a symbol of her protected status; and she had relied on Shuang-ru's ministrations to help her walk in heaven. But foot-binding was now forbidden. Born in an era when girls did not receive any formal education—she herself was illiterate—she saw girls now demanding to be educated. Lin Pen had also lived to find yet another official language imposed: Mandarin, which she could not understand. She had been humiliated by her own tenants who had openly robbed her house. And finally, Lin Pen was to see her own fortune dwindle when, during the land reform in the early 1950s, landlords like the Kiangs and the Lins lost the bulk of their land as reform programs wiped out landlordism.

Lin Pen was determined not to be disgraced by her own granddaughter. With Shuang-ru about to graduate from high school, she moved to exert her declining authority. 'I wanted to become a teacher since I was little girl,' Shuang-ru recalls. Lin Pen was not opposed to her granddaughter studying. Indeed her third daughter, Bing, had remarkably obtained a degree in Law while living with her husband, Lin Chun-mu, in Japan before the end of the Second World War. Even so, Lin Pen did not want Shuang-ru to attend college in distant Taipei. 'Pretty far,' Shuang-ru admits; 'then my grandmother don't want me to go. So I argue with her.'

If Shuang-ru were to remain near home, the obvious point was that she should marry well—and soon; so Lin Pen hired a matchmaker. 'She has about ten pictures for me to look at,' Shuang-ru recalls, 'but I didn't pay attention to it.' Lin Pen wanted her granddaughter to marry into 'a very rich family.' Her first choice was a doctor, who had a big family—grandparents alive as well as his own parents, a sister and several brothers. 'I didn't like it. I didn't pay attention,' says Shuang-ru. 'I cannot go to a big family, I don't like that, I don't know how to handle that.' The grandmother's choice was clear; but Shuang-ru had other options and a mind of her own.

When we went back to her school, now called National Changhua Girls' Senior High School in 2008, our reception was spiced by more than academic pride in the return of a well-liked pupil and a popular teacher, or even the celebrity status of their eldest son, David Ho. The latter admittedly played up to the situation, and the headline in the local press was not backward in seizing on the opportunity: 'HE DAYI GIVES LECTURE AT CHANGHUA MIDDLE SCHOOL FOR GIRLS AND REVEALS HIS FATHER'S SECRETS.' The 'teacher-student love affair' was reported gleefully, as bearing out rumors that had allegedly been 'circulating at the Changhua Middle School for Girls for many years and had never been proven to be true.'[40] The matter was certainly put to the proof that day.

My arrival in Changhua on the bus, with all the Ho family aboard, had been monitored by Phillip and his wife Michi on cell phones, so that the co-ordination was perfect. As the bus rounded the final corner to the school entrance, we could see the school band and majorettes lined up—girls in their marching uniforms of high peaked caps, red tunics, mini skirts, and high boots. Our route into National Changhua Girls' Senior High School was lined by hundreds of excited pupils who swarmed around us when we disembarked from the bus. Then came a great scene in the school hall. The principal—Kung Chien-kuo the first man to occupy this position—was beaming away as he welcomed Shuang-ru back to the school where she had studied, Buji to the school where he had taught. Documents were produced, as at Yi-lan, showing Buji's engagement as a teacher. But this time the spotlight was on Shuang-ru, who stood on the platform, waving with both arms above her head to receive the renewed cheers. Her school record was presented to her, showing an average of B.[41] Shuang-ru

---

[40] Lian He Bao *United News* reporter Jian Huizhen from Zhanghua, 28 February 2008.

[41] Shaung Ru's transcript from 1949-1950 from Taiwan Provincial Changhua Middle School for Girls confirm an over-all B average.

was not the only member of the Ho family moved by the event. For Phillip Ho 'the feeling was beyond description,' he told me as we left the school hall, 'because this is where my parents met.'

Old members of staff were on hand, as were a number of Shuang-ru's former classmates. I talked to some of them later, once the hubbub had died down. According to one fellow student, Wong Gui-fin, Shuang-ru was 'always smiling and friendly,' had fairer skin and was more 'meticulous about her appearance than the other girls.' Shuang-ru's younger cousin Lu I-wen added that 'she was really smart and had good writing in Chinese characters.' It was Shuang-ru's proficiency in English, more than anything else, however, that made her fellow students pin her name to the back of their English teacher—apparently on more than one occasion.

'It all started with the girls spreading mischievous rumors,' was how Buji explained it when he spoke to the smiling and cheering pupils that day. 'Who could have thought it would come true?' In one of my interviews, he acknowledged that 'all of the students make fun of me and her in the Park; I heard that girl's name and the teacher's name, I don't know who she was.' Of course I already knew that it was not unusual in Taiwan for a girl's friends to take on the role of matchmaker. 'Even before exchanging so much as a half-dozen words,' according to the anthropologist Margery Wolf, 'a young couple may find themselves romanticized by their friends as star-crossed lovers.'[42]

While a member of Buji's class in her last year at school, Shuang-ru claims that she never thought that she would marry him. 'As a teacher he is OK, he is alright. At that time I was so young, I never think about marriage.' But she admits that her friends teased her about her English teacher. Indeed one fellow student, Chang Chiu-yu 'privately revealed,' according to one newspaper report, that Shuang-ru 'often brought litchi nuts to school and only gave them to He Buji.' The newspaper goes on to quote Chang: 'When her classmates found out, they stealthily stuck a piece of paper that said: "Were the litchi nuts delicious?" onto He Buji's back while he was not paying attention.'[43] According to Wong Gui-fin some of Shuang-ru's friends were well meaning but others acted out of jealousy for the teacher's pet. Whatever their motives, however,

---

[42] Margery Wolf, *Women and the Family in Rural Taiwan* (Stanford: Stanford University Press 1972) p. 101

[43] Lian He Bao *United News* reporter Jian Huizhen from Zhanghua, 28 February 2008.

Shuang-ru's fellow students clearly enjoyed participating, if only vicariously, in the 'romance' that was thought to be taking place between their teacher and their classmate.

But what about Buji's own role? 'Of all the teachers,' Wong Gui-fin told me, 'He Buji was the most dedicated and hard-working.' Lin Li-tai, Shuang-ru's companion in class, was impressed when Buji remembered all of their names after calling them out only once. His fellow teachers, like Wei Fui-chen, certainly soon tumbled to what was going on. 'We thought that Shuang-ru might have a thing for Buji. The teachers all knew but nobody confronted him because it was rare for a teacher to form a relationship with a pupil.'

Crucially, Shuang-ru was soon caught up in her friends' enthusiasm because she faced obvious pressure at home, given that training as a teacher in Taipei was ruled out. The issue was no longer whether to marry, but whom. Just before she was about to graduate from school, the principal, Huang Pu-gui asked Shuang-ru if she planned to go to college, with the name of Buji introduced as an alternative: 'If you don't go to college you could marry him.'

Marriage into the large family of the doctor whom Lin Pen had chosen for Shuang-ru offered a different prospect, and one with disturbing possibilities. She might have experienced hostility from the new family, and rejection from an ambivalent mother-in-law who resented Shuang-ru "stealing" her son. Moreover, Shuang-ru had spent her whole life in the tight-knit Kiang household; she had a complex relationship with her grandmother—and, above all, a deep feeling of responsibility for her vulnerable mother, to whom her access would have been restricted. 'I love her so,' Shuang-ru explains, 'I can't leave her alone. If I marry somebody else I cannot take my mother.' There was an alternative, however. Buji did not have a family. 'If I marry him,' Shuang-ru adds, indicating her husband of over fifty years, 'I can stay with my mother.'

After her graduation in the summer of 1950, both Buji and Shuang-ru were ready to respond. As Buji remembers it, 'we came together just like Romeo and Juliet.' (And, one could add, not like the arranged marriage that he had experienced with Gu more than a decade earlier.) As Shuang-ru pithily puts it, 'he chase me.' There is no doubt that Buji was an energetic suitor. He wrote to Shuang-ru every day: 'mailman got so mad,' she recalled. 'Can you tell that guy to write every other day?' the overburdened postman asked the young woman.

When there was now no doubt as to Buji's intentions, and of her own wishes, Shuang-ru did several things. She approached her grandmother—a task that was 'very difficult.' She sought the support of her friend Li-tai because, 'my grandmother trusts her.' Shuang-ru also spoke to her mother. Already cognizant of the teacher's affection for her daughter, Lou had been so angry, according to Wong Gui-fin, that she had visited the school and confronted Buji—'because she knew that he was a Mainlander.' Despite this, Shuang-ru never doubted that she would obtain her mother's support: 'She loves me so much, so whatever I wanted she would like.'

The ground prepared, Shuang-ru took the bold step of inviting He Buji to the Kiang family compound at Shen-gang. During the course of three visits, the ice remained unbroken. 'Grandmother doesn't talk to me, doesn't like me, she wouldn't look at me,' said Buji. True, he had little to recommend him as a possible suitor. As a *Waishengren* he seemed alien. He was much older than Shuang-ru. He was a Christian, while Lin Pen and her daughter were Buddhists. His story that he came from the landed gentry lacked evidence. 'How can I prove that I come from good family?' Buji laments. 'They are far away.' In some respects, of course, this was convenient for his suit, given Lin Pen's inevitable suspicion that, like so many other Mainlanders, Buji might have a family back in China.

The worst mark against Buji, was that he was un-filial. Was he not a Christian, which automatically meant that he was un-filial? Had he not abandoned his own mother and thereby neglected a son's major obligation: seeing to it that his parents were comfortable and happy in old age? And might he treat his future wife and his mother-in-law, and by extension Lin Pen, in the same way? As Lin Pen saw it, the absence of a kinship network also meant that her future grandson-in-law could not be trusted because he could not be dealt with in the normal way. There was no family member to assist him or to exert control over his behavior; no family member whom Lin Pen could seek redress from if things went terribly wrong. Even evidence of Buji's gold bars could not make up for his lack of a family since (as Margery Wolf aptly noted in her study of a Taiwanese family) 'money had no past, no future, no obligations.'[44]

Even so, one of the defining characteristics of elite status had long been learning and the pursuit of knowledge. Buji's position as a schoolteacher certainly counted for something with the Kiang family. 'That guy's a teacher, he's OK,' was Lou's eventual response, according to her daughter. Buji's denial, when Lou asked him if he had a family on Mainland China, counted for something too. His status as a *Waishengren* was not all bad since Mainlanders had access to the best jobs and to the best housing in Taiwan. Moreover, Buji's poverty was less

---

[44]   For an excellent study of the Lin family see Margery Wolf, *The House of Lin* (Englewood Cliffs, New Jersey: Prentice-Hall, 1968)

dire than it seemed since, with several gold bars still in his possession, he had, as Shuang-ru well knew, 'lots of money.' Knowing of Lin Pen's liking for goose liver, Buji carried four live geese on a shoulder pole to Shen-gang—a distance of several miles. Family lore has it that this finally did the trick.

After weighing the pros and cons of her daughter's relationship with Buji, Kiang Lou gave her consent. She herself had had one failed marriage, had clearly not been able to make another. Now there was the prospect that she would become part of the new He household.

This was to be no ordinary marriage. The prospective bride, Shuang-ru, and not the family matriarch, Lin Pen, or even Kiang Lou, had chosen the husband. Because of this Shuang-ru could not expect to have financial support from her family if things went wrong—as her grandmother feared they could. Her fiancé was a *Waishengren*. Had he been married before coming to Taiwan? Had he formed any other relationship with a woman since moving to Taiwan? Buji was likewise faced with some puzzles. For although his fiancée was the granddaughter of a once-prosperous landlord, she had not entered the world through a conventional paternal home. Who was Shuang-ru's real father? There were still many things that each did not know. But each decided to take a chance.

Sonia's
grandmother,
Lin Pen

Sonia as baby

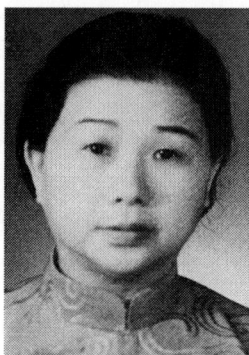

Sonia's parents Kiang Lou and Lu Chiao Hu

Kiang sisters, Lu bottom left

Paul teaching in Taichung

Paul Ho 1950

Provincial Changhua Middle School for Girls

CHAPTER 4

'On Gold Mountain'

舊金山

After becoming engaged sometime during the early autumn of 1950, Shuang-ru and Buji waited the customary year before getting married. During the ensuing year Shuang-ru enrolled in a home economics course. 'I didn't like it,' she says now, perhaps underestimating her own talent, for she did manage to make a suit of clothes for her favorite cousin I-wen, as he fondly remembers. Buji had a more active year. Not only did he change schools and cities, he also acquired an additional job, and one that inescapably carried appreciable political significance in the 1950s, when the GMD regime was consoling itself for the loss of Mainland China by consolidating its hold over Taiwan.

Even though it had only been in operation since 1946, Buji had no doubt that National Taichung Girls' Senior High School, as it is called today, was simply 'a better school' than Changhua Girls' Middle School. Nor is there any reason to doubt Buji's claim that, if he wished to progress, he could 'get ten jobs because lots of principals knew me.' But there was more to Buji's move to the much larger city of Taichung, lying about ten miles north-west of Changhua, than career advancement—or than avoiding the social embarrassment that might very well stem from marrying a former student.

Buji's position at Changhua had been compromised in another way. Towards the end of the school year of 1949-1950, a crisis overtook his colleague Huang Pu-kui, his old school friend who had brought him to Changhua from Yilan. This young teacher was discovered to be a member of the outlawed Communist

Party. Fearing for his life, Huang Pu-kui escaped to Mainland China by boat late one night, thus leaving his sister, who was of course the school Principal, to face interrogation. Huang Pu-gui was not only interrogated but imprisoned. Although released from prision within a few weeks, Pu-gui found herself without a job and Buji correspondingly found himself without a patron. He was now free to move elsewhere.

The fact that he spent the year following his engagement to Shuang-ru in making a career for himself at the larger and more prestigious high school in Taichung served to distance Buji from Huang Pu-gui and her politically suspect brother. Yet his connection with Changhua itself did not end here, again for reasons that have a political dimension.

The Secretary of the GMD in Changhua, Chang Fong Hui, also originated from Buji's own province of Jiangxi. Chang, a party loyalist, had moved to Taiwan with Chiang Kai-shek in 1949. After teaching school for a year, he had entered the local government at the top as Party Secretary. A native of Xinyu, Chang had in his youth formed great respect and admiration for Buji's old teacher and 'uncle', He Duanyou, so much so that his obviously capable young relative was now offered a position in the local government of Changhua. The job entailed writing letters, setting up appointments and translating English, all tasks for which Buji was well suited.

Buji's initial response, however, to the offer of becoming Chang's private secretary was negative—'No, I am happy teaching.' Not easily defeated, Chang proposed that Buji continue teaching at the Taichung High School during the morning while working in Changhua in the afternoon. This was more appealing. Moreover, Chang even offered to have Buji chauffeured from one job to the other in a de-requisitioned American army jeep. On these terms, Buji decided to accept the position, and naturally had to become a party member—about which he simply shrugs his shoulders with a smile when asked about his own degree of political commitment.

Holding down two very different jobs—'hard work', as Buji recalled—must have had a certain glamour, with his attendant jeep and driver whisking him from Taichung to Changhua every afternoon. There was also a solid financial reward. Now in his early thirties, Buji was bringing home two full-time salaries, which was all the more welcome since he was setting up a new household as a married man. He had already rented an apartment on Jenguo Street on moving to Taichung.

This was not, however, where Buji and Shuang-ru used to meet during their engagement. Shuang-ru certainly visited Taichung at the weekends. (This entailed walking for half an hour from the family compound at Shen-gang to the local bus stop then riding into the city.) In Taichung Shuang-ru was welcomed by her mother's younger sister, Kiang Bing, now a housewife, with her Japanese law degree behind her. The young couple spent most of their time together in the comfortable home of Bing and her husband, Lin Chun-mu. Shuang-ru remembers that there were also frequent visits to the cinema and 'sometimes we go out for dinner, just two of us.'

Their marriage finally took place on 26 November 1951. They did not partake in the richly colorful wedding rituals that were the custom among wealthy families in Taiwan—and that Buji had experienced when he had married Gu, some fourteen years earlier, in 1937. But that wedding, of course, had been prominently engineered on his behalf by the He family, whereas now he stood alone. With no parents available to go to his fiancée's home, it was impossible for him to conform to the conventions of a traditional Taiwanese wedding.

For more than one reason, the wedding ceremony was 'not a big deal,' as Shuang-ru admits, adding: 'We didn't marry in the church, because my mother was a Buddhist.' But there was more to it than that. Lin Pen did not give her favorite granddaughter a feast in the family home; indeed the old lady declined to attend, as did Shuang-ru's eldest uncle, the titular head of the Kiang compound, and several other members of the Kiang family, still not reconciled to this unusual marriage to a *Waishengren*.

This 'not too fancy wedding,' as Buji described it, was clearly in the new style. He had chosen the venue himself: a popular restaurant located above a local bookstore. He also chose the menu. 'We had one big dish with ten different things,' Shuang-ru remembers, not twelve dishes as was the custom at such occasions. Nor did the couple exchange bowls of wine or rice, or kneel then bow to the living and the dead ancestors. Moreover, unlike most brides and grooms, Buji and Shuang-ru were well acquainted before their marriage.

A photograph of the wedding party confirms that some at least of the Kiang family were thankfully present. It shows Shuang-ru's second uncle, Kiang Yuan-heng, and his wife prominent among the 'honored guests'. So, above all, is Shuang-ru's mother, Kiang Lou. The bride herself looks characteristically beautiful in a fashionable western-style wedding dress: puffy sleeves a garlanded tiara and a long train carried by two toddlers wearing brightly patterned garments. Dressed in his best dark suit and wearing a large rosette, the groom looks dapper and full of energy. Seemingly oblivious of the social tensions their union posed, Buji appears to be enjoying the occasion. But the camera, they say, never lies. The photographs of his bride reveal a solemn, almost sad, young woman. 'I was very tired that day,' as Shuang-ru puts it, 'I didn't even eat.'

Some sixty people in all occupied half a dozen tables in the restaurant. Though comprising none of the groom's family (through necessity) and few of the bride's relatives (through their choice), the party included five or six of Shuang-ru's old school friends, along with several of Buji's professional colleagues. Indeed this last group dominated the head table: the GMD manager, Shao Huan and his wife who was a former school friend of Sonia's; the Minister of Education Mr. Zhou; and, finally, Buji's boss, Party Secretary, Chang Fong Hui.

The presence of these honored guests was in keeping with Chinese custom. They were there, it could be argued, to reflect the bridegroom's ability to reach high and to demonstrate his deference to his superiors. But there were special reasons why this particular wedding in Taichung in 1951 should have taken on this character. It was Zhou who, in his capacity as master-of-ceremonies and stand-in for Buji's father, wished the bride and groom a long life and a healthy family before pronouncing them man and wife. And then, not missing an opportunity to exploit the occasion, it was the Minister of Education who brought out what might be called the occasion's political agenda.

Most native-born Taiwanese, it should be recalled, remained opposed to *Waishengren* marrying their women, if only for the simple reason that it left fewer women available for their own men. The Kiang family—at least its stay-at-home members that day—were thus representative of wider attitudes. However the ruling GMD saw things differently. For them it was crucial that Taiwanese girls, like Shuang-ru, marry Mainlanders, like Buji—seemingly unattached men seeking new liaisons in a land that would now become their home. So called "mixed marriages" were one way to bridge the gulf between Mainlanders and Native Taiwanese that had been exacerbated by the "2-28 Incident" in February 1947. Little wonder that Zhou made a point of telling the newly wed couple that they were 'a good example of Taiwanese marrying with the *Waishengren*.'

*　　*　　*

Following their wedding, the happy couple went to the two-room apartment on Jenguo Street that lay ready for their occupancy. There was no romantic honeymoon journey, no prolonged feasting, because both of them had to settle down to work, in a pattern that typified much of their subsequent married life.

When we visited Jenguo Street in 2008 with Paul and Sonia Ho, and two of their sons, Phillip and Sidney, we located the apartment with some difficulty— and some mild embarrassment. We knew that the apartment was on the second floor—but of which building? The street had been radically transformed over the years. Was the temple that they remembered still in the same place? And it came out, to some wry amusement, that the street had meanwhile served for a time as part of the city's red-light district.

Jenguo Street, for all of its vicissitudes, had nonetheless survived. This part of Taichung had escaped Japanese attempts to put the whole city on a grid-style street pattern and thereby complete its transformation from a small farming and marketing community to a center of education, commerce, transportation and manufacturing. Paul and Sonia eventually pointed out the second-floor dwelling that they had inhabited for two years—it was No. 19. Then we raised our cameras to make a permanent record of our visit.

It was their recollections of the place that really brought seemingly deserted Jenguo Street to life. A blind couple, who worked as masseurs, had run a clinic next door. A Buddhist temple had stood to the left of No. 19. As we stood there on that March morning, we could suddenly imagine a livelier scene, evoking the street as it was in the early 1950s: calls from street peddlers, knife sharpeners, itinerant healers and cobblers; the clang of Pedi cabs, and the scent of incense from the nearby temple mingling with the smell of fuel oil, cooking fumes and charcoal smoke.

It was not long before we attracted a few curious neighbors. One elderly woman, a long-time resident of Jenguo Street, asked: 'Why are you photographing that building?' When we told her that Paul and Sonia were the parents of the famous scientist David Ho, the woman paused, then said: 'This shows that even a place like this can produce a person of stature.' Her observation bridged the gulf between then and now, for it was in this modest dwelling that the life of Shuang-ru's first child, Dayi—or David as he later became known—began.

The birth of Dayi on 3 November 1952 was from the first a cause for much celebration. The Kiang family had suffered so many previous disappointments when pregnancies resulted in yet more girls. Lin Pen, like her mother before her had been forced to adopt sons in the quest for male heirs. Hence Shuang-ru's comment that 'grandmother was so happy with the boy because for three generations, no boys.' With the arrival of Dayi, then, no member of the Kiang family was more pleased than Lin Pen, as Shuang-ru was relieved to discover when she visited the compound at Shen-gang: 'My grandmother hold the baby all day long, so excited.' Better still, she found that Lin Pen's previous opinion of Dayi's father was accordingly transformed. Whenever Buji accompanied his wife to Shen-gang, Lin Pen was now 'very nice . . . she like him.'

Lin Pen not only acknowledged Buji for the first time: she secured a promise from her adopted son, Jing-shen, that he would take special care of Shuang-ru and her child after she herself had died. The only reservation in the Kiang family was about the name that the newborn heir was given. Since the Chinese believe that an infant's name can determine a child's future, it was crucial what Buji chose to call his first son.

The name Dayi signifies 'boundless hopes and boundless infinities.' In choosing it, Buji hoped that it would enable his son to escape many of the hardships that he had experienced himself. *Dayi* is an elegantly simply ideograph, written with only three strokes. 'I am afraid that you haven't learned to recognize more than a hundred words,' Lin Pen teased her son-in-law. 'How could you just name him with a *da* and a *yi*?' *Da* means 'great' and *yi* means 'the greatest one.' Buji was careful to point out that *da* does not, in this context mean big but great. He remained proud of his persistence in sticking to this name, and admitted with a chuckle that the character's simplicity made 'some people think I am illiterate and others think that I am really deep.'

No doubt Lin Pen's joy would have been threefold if she had lived to see her granddaughter give birth, two years later, to another son, Hongyi (Phillip) and thirteen years after that to a third male child, Chunyi (Sidney). But Lin Pen was dead within six months of Dayi's birth.

Her death was an event of considerable significance not only for the extended Kiang family at Shen-gang but for the little He family in Jenguo Street. It meant that Lin Pen's eldest adopted son, Jing-shen, became head of the Kiang family. And it also meant that her daughter Lou, never comfortable in her adopted brother's presence, could now join her own daughter and Buji in Taichung.

With the arrival of Lou and her maid, A-mi, into the He family, Shuang-ru was free to choose her own way of life. If her previous aspirations to become a teacher had been thwarted, this did not leave her without ambition to fulfill her considerable aptitude outside the home as well as within it. She therefore sought employment—probably with the help of her well-placed uncle, Lin Chu-mu—in the local tax office. Working there with twelve other people, she found herself dealing with income tax and the reports that businessmen had to make of their profits. Though the workday, from 8:30 to 5:00, was long, and entailed a half-hour ride on her bicycle each way, Shuang-ru claims that she 'enjoyed the work and made many friends.' Apart from the few months she took off following the birth of Hongyi in August 1954, she worked at City Hall for seven years in all.

Under the circumstances, it is easy to understand Shuang-ru's insistence that 'money was no problem' during the early years of her marriage. Not only did she and Buji have three incomes between them, but she also had a handsome dowry—money and furniture—from her mother. With more money at their disposal, but cramped living quarters in Jenguo Street, the young couple was able to purchase a more spacious home within less than two years of their marriage.

When we accompanied the family to No 6 house on the Fuhsing Road in March 2008, we could see why Paul had told us on a prior visit to Los Angeles: 'Very good house, like it very much.' Yet looking through the cracks of the imposing wooden fence surrounding the dwelling, the house appeared to be abandoned. Was it awaiting demolition? Or was someone about to restore the building?

Like most of the homes that the Japanese built during their occupation of Taiwan, this handsome dwelling had a low, gently pitched roof, sliding interior doors, many spacious rooms whose size was measured in tatami mats and a generous garden. Phil was pleased to see that two of the trees he remembered as a child—a star-fruit tree and a papaya tree planted by his father—were still bearing fruit. It was a substantial property—a far cry from the two rooms in Jenguo Street. David had earlier told me of running around the house's many rooms; his mother remembers watching him padding along the edge of the nearby canal to visit the children of his grandmother's younger brother's son.

The location next to the Shuan Canal was, Paul assured us, 'good fortune because the canal was flowing directly toward the house.' The house's proximity to Taichung Girls Senior High School was another bonus. The energetic teacher could take a short cut beneath an underpass and, in the early morning, walk to school in a few minutes. Then, in the afternoons, he would get his jeep ride to the GMD offices in Changhua. The amenities of the new house were a tangible compensation for the long hours that the couple put in.

With so much time devoted to work, Buji and Shuang-ru's social life was largely confined to family celebrations. One photograph shows their presence at the Christian wedding of Shuang-ru's cousin Lu Ching-shuang. Nor was this the only event that Shuang-ru attended at her aunt Hsiao's home on the edge of the Lu family compound[45]; indeed she and Buji were evidently drawn into

---

[45]   Kiang Hsiao was married to the fourth Lu brother, Lu Shuang-chio.

the ambit of the extended Lu family on many occasions. What was unknown to Shuang-ru, of course, was the location of her own father's house within the Lu compound, and the attendance on many of these occasions of Lu Chiao-hu himself. Until his death in 1955, Lu thus had some opportunity to watch his daughter, Shuang-ru, blossom into a beautiful woman.

Lu Chiao-hu no doubt took pride in the fact that his own genes were being carried on in his young grandson, Dayi, who was taken to the family celebrations. Thus, by her early twenties, Shuang-ru was in a position to fulfill many of her hopes, as is well captured in a 1953 photograph of her immediate family. In it, she proudly shows off her eldest son, and will soon have a second; she now has the companionship and support of her mother, Lou; she is shown alongside a husband who is resourceful and intelligent, and whose own future, like that projected onto his son, is one of 'boundless hopes and boundless infinities.'

*   *   *

Many of the best family photographs from this period come from the album of Shuang-ru's favorite cousin, Lu I-wen, whose mother Hsiao was Lou's younger sister (fourth out of the five Kiang girls). The two families were to remain close. I-wen, born in the Lu family compound in 1938, recalls that his cousin's formidable husband—Buji was nineteen years older than himself—was 'a very serious man who liked to help other people.' Buji thus introduced the young I-wen to cowboy movies, taught him his 'ABC's in English' and instilled the boy with an appreciation for learning. After studying law and business in Taipei, I-wen was to have a distinguished career as a banker. Buji, not only helped shape the boy's future: he told I-wen of his own plans to study in the United States.

It was hardly a new idea. Before leaving China in 1947, Buji had, we should remember, tried and failed to be admitted to the United States as a student. There were many reasons why he should still have wanted to study in North America. He had pleasant memories of working for the Americans during the Resistance War. America had given him a faith, Christianity, that complemented his idea that technological advancement and scientific control of the environment could lead to social reform and personal happiness. Above all, well before the days of Taiwan's economic miracle, Buji knew that 1950s America enjoyed a far higher standard of living.

Taiwan's future, moreover, seemed precarious in the context of the developing Cold War. The country was certainly regarded as a key ally and base of operations in the American campaign to contain the spread of Communism, as the Korean war of 1950-1953 amply demonstrated. There was a continual threat of invasion from Mainland China that many Taiwanese feared as a real possibility. For Buji, already driven from his first home and first family in Jiangxi, these were understandable reasons to seek opportunity and security for his new family on the other side of the wide Pacific.

Moreover, the United States was a democratic country. In Taiwan, by contrast, the people lived under martial law, with a constant crack-down on freedom of assembly or expression in the press. All forms of advanced learning were isolated from developments elsewhere in the world. Finally, Chiang Kai-shek could not or would not escape the taint of graft and corruption that had characterized his China-based Nationalist regime.

In later conversations about the GMD, Buji often told me, with abiding distaste, that he 'did not like those people.' Even so, as a *Waishengren* himself, he had obviously had the benefit of a succession of teaching positions, a good job in the government and the purchase of a much-sought-after Japanese house. Yet what he regularly witnessed in the Party Secretary's office was a way of doing business that he found increasingly disturbing. 'Giving gifts was common—a box of cookies—but when you opened the box there was lots of money inside.'

He could hardly ignore such evidence of widespread jobbery and bribery, yet found it unnerving to be implicated himself—'I become scared'—in a system that was endemic. 'I wanted to get out of that kind of society,' he explained, 'I don't want to stay there—no future.' Buji profited from his second job to the extent that he drew his own salary without qualm; but clearly he had opportunities for personal enrichment that he spurned for long-held moral reasons, reflecting his whole upbringing and sense of himself. He consistently maintained that 'knowledge, not money' was what motivated him in life—'that is why I go to America.'

By the mid-1950s he was in a position to act on this resolution. With the rejuvenation of scholarly exchange programs, through the Taiwanese-based Educational Foundation and the CIA-funded Asia Foundation, Buji had a second chance to fulfill his wish to study abroad. He applied for a student visa at the beginning of 1956. The process was slow and there was no guarantee that he would be successful. He began by taking a government exam in the area of his choice—educational psychology. Then he took an English exam. So far, so good. His results put him among the ten per cent of candidates who succeeded in progressing to the next stage. Once more, as in his early days as a scholarship boy, his academic abilities shone through.

But the system was not designed simply to reward an elite selected on academic merit: it was geared to choosing politically reliable time-servers. Consequently, the successful candidates were next required to undergo what Buji disparagingly called 'four months of brainwashing.' This was something he naturally wished to avoid and luckily he was in a position to pull strings through his GMD contacts. The intervention of someone Buji refers to as General Liu—and possibly of his boss Chang too—spared him from this exercise. All that remained was an interview at the American Embassy. Asked why he wanted to go to the United States, Buji knew better than to voice any disrespectful remarks about their loyal allies, the GMD regime. Instead he gave the safe reply, true enough for the occasion: 'America is an industrial country; economy real good.'

Any economic gains for his family, however, would be a long time coming, as he well knew. Initially the family's resources needed to be mobilized to finance his initiative. Luckily Buji had the support not only of his loyal wife but of her mother too. Indeed Lou's presence in the household was crucial since it provided Shuang-ru with support, along with a series of maids, in bringing up two young boys. There was not only Dayi but his young brother Hongyi, still only a toddler at the time of his father's departure from Taichung station—and, as he later told me, with a vivid first memory of his father holding him in his arms for a final embrace then being passed over to his mother.

Moreover, Lou was able to offer tangible assistance. Now fond of her son-in-law, she not only fell in with his plans, she made them possible by selling some land, which she had inherited from Lin Pen. This was needed to supplement what Buji could raise by selling the Japanese house and instead purchasing a more modest dwelling for the family whom he would leave behind. Altogether, this gave Buji the enormous sum (at 1950s prices in Taiwan) of $3,500, which the Americans required as a guarantee.

Buji was finally ready to depart for the United States in August 1957. In those days the obvious means of transport was by ship—the cheaper the better. He went to the port of Keelung outside of Taipei, boarding a re-consigned American destroyer that had brought a grain-load of wheat to Taiwan. On the long ocean voyage, the Pacific belied its name and the ship encountered three typhoons. Buji thus found himself at sea for eighteen days, and under extremely taxing conditions. Unable to eat, he lost twenty-three pounds. He arrived at his destination, Portland, Oregon, and duly satisfied the immigration authorities by producing the appropriate papers and evidence of financial support. Thereupon he recalled sending most of the $3,500 guarantee fund back to Taiwan. He was left with seventeen dollars in his pocket and high hopes.

It was a wrenching time for the whole family with two small boys left behind, albeit in the good care of not only their mother, but an attentive grandmother. When Shuang-ru's friends heard that her husband was going to leave for the United States, they told her to stop him because 'he might marry again.' It was not unreasonable advice in the circumstances—and the circumstances were actually more complex than Shuang-ru realized, as Buji was guiltily aware.

Buji had not forgotten that he had a wife and three children in China. He had written to his family in Jiangxi upon arriving in Taiwan in 1947 in order to tell them where he was living and working. In 1956, knowing that he was now about to leave for the United States, he wrote home a second time. Buji addressed the letter to his younger brother, He Buxiu, who had been the head of the family since his departure for university in 1942. Buji did not mention his marriage to Shuang-ru nor the birth of his two sons. He simply wanted to let his Jiangxi family know of his whereabouts. And what he wanted in return, of course, was news—of his brother and his family; of his mother, Fu; of his sister Zhilan; and of his first wife, Gu, and their three children, Hongyian, Tangxiang and Xiangbao. Were they all alive and well? Was the family's farm still yielding high returns? And their palatial home with the many empty rooms that had awed Buji as a boy—what had become of that?

For answers to such questions, Buji had to wait a very long time. In particular, his letter elicited no reply from his brother Buxiu. Nor could it have done so—for reasons that Buji did not learn until more than fifteen years later.

*   *   *

Buji had an evidently close friend from his university days, Qian Zouqin, who was already studying in the southern States. Indeed he was doing so thanks to a loan of $600 from Buji. It was Qian Zouqin who had suggested that Buji apply to Northern Colorado College. It was a good choice for someone in the field of educational psychology. Founded in 1889 as Colorado State College of Education, its main purpose, as its name suggests, had been to train school teachers. Sixty-eight years later the institution had become Northern Colorado College and offered its students courses in virtually every area of undergraduate study. In addition to being a good liberal arts school, Northern Colorado College had a conservatory of music, a natural history museum featuring a large collection of humming birds, and an arboretum with every shrub and tree native to Colorado as well as specimens native to Europe and Asia.

In August 1957 Buji was among the first group of students from Taiwan to travel to America. Yet the influx of Chinese students was nothing new; enrolment from Mainland China before Buji arrived had reached a peak in 1948 with almost four thousand students attending university in America. Indeed the tradition went back more than a century; in 1847 the American missionary, Samuel Robbins Brown, had sponsored three students—Yung Wing, Wong Hsing and Wong Fong. After that, it was not uncommon to find Chinese students and courses on Chinese history and language offered at American universities.

Buji spent his first night in America on a Greyhound bus. 'They change drivers, but I never get off,' as he recalled. 'Thank God, I didn't die.' Already travel sick and emaciated, Buji found the long journey to Greeley, Colorado, both exhausting and exciting. During the journey, he saw his first snow and his first North American wild animals—coyote and bear.

Buji naturally had a preconception of what he could anticipate in America. This was much like that of the character in Lin Yutang's novel, *Chinatown Family* (1948) who felt that 'America was a country made all of machines . . . America should be noisy and full of that rushing motion, speeding motion, going somewhere—click—stopping—click—progress—click, click!'[46] Yet what Buji saw from the window of the Greyhound bus provided nothing to corroborate his belief that America was an industrial country. Instead, he was overwhelmed by the absence of people and by the dramatic landscape that had prompted one nineteenth century visitor to call the state the Switzerland of America.[47] Colorado's Rocky Mountains were indeed comparable to Switzerland's Alps. They were also the setting for many of Zane Grey's best-known tales about trappers and cowboys, which might actually have given Buji, as a fan of western movies, a better clue as to what to expect. When he eventually arrived at his destination, he found simply a town of twenty-five thousand peaceful, temperance-loving souls; he found that Greeley boasted the Spud Rodeo as its annual celebration on the fourth of July.

Students like Buji were traveling in the wake of thousands of men—and, to a lesser extent, women—of Chinese ancestry who had gone to the fabled Gold

---

[46] Lin Yutang, *Chinatown Family* (Taipei: Mei Ya Publications, 1975) p. 5.

[47] Samuel Bowles, *Colorado, Its Parks and Mountains* (Springfield, Massasschutes: Samuel Bowles and Co, 1869) p. 1.

Mountain in order to seek their fortune. It was the discovery of gold north of San Francisco in 1848 that had brought the first contingent of Chinese laborers to America. And it was a reciprocal agreement between China and the United States, the Anson Burlingame Treaty of 1868, that granted Chinese nationals the right of residence in and immigration to the United States.

When the gold ran out in the early 1850s the men who had been engaged in placer mining and manual labor could easily find jobs on the transcontinental railroad. When, in turn, the robber barons had finished building their railroads with the help of 10,000 cheaply employed Chinese workers, the laborers had to find other employment. A small number settled in St Louis and in Massachusetts where they worked in factories or as domestic servants. Others helped build railroads in the Southern states. However, the bulk of the 64,000 Chinese who had come to the United States settled in the West.

Racist attitudes towards the Chinese emerged when it became clear that Chinese laborers were not only more industrious and reliable than their White counterparts, but more willing to work for lower wages. As early as 1852 the Democratic Party passed the first official anti-Chinese resolution. It was not, however, until 1881 that Congress responded to the public's growing anti-Chinese sentiment by suspending immigration from China. A year later it passed the first of many 'exclusion acts' that prevented Chinese citizens from immigrating to, or for those who had already settled in North America, from becoming citizens of the United States. Those who had enough money went back to China. Those who remained as 'alien residents' were subjected, particularly during periods of economic unrest, to accusations that they were not only stealing jobs, but also earning their living through drug-dealing, gambling and running brothels.

The Second World War made some difference, but by no means all the difference. True, by 1943 attitudes towards the Chinese had improved after the United States entered the War and China became an ally. The Magnuson Act granted all Chinese resident in America citizenship. But reform of the exclusion acts stopped here by limiting the annual number of ordinary Chinese immigrants—the only immigrants to be excluded by race and class—to one hundred and five.

There were, however, some special exemptions. Entry was possible for Chinese teachers, tourists, diplomats and a few certified returning laborers. Crucially for Buji, entry to the United States from China on a student visa was permitted on certain conditions. Students were not given the right of abode and most returned to China after they had completed their study. Only after 1950, when many Chinese students did not want to return to Communist China, were they able to apply for a change of status from non-immigrant to permanent resident, which could pave the way to naturalization. But the catch was that if permanent residence were applied for and denied, a student could not regain non-immigrant student status and might thus end up worse off. The view that Chinese students would, unlike other Chinese living in America, make better citizens was reinforced in 1957 when Zhenning (Frank) Yang and Zhengdao (T.D.) Lee, assisted by another Chinese-born scientist, Chien Shiung Wu, won the Nobel Prize in physics. Even so, it is significant that Yang and Lee, who came to the United States to study in 1945 and 1946 respectively, could not obtain permanent status there until 1953 and 1956.

Buji was thus in a different category from most of his earlier countrymen when he arrived in the United States. As the writer Lynn Pan noted, in the minds of most Americans, it was an important distinction—'not to be a student was to be a coolie.'[48] Yet to be a student in the United States, conversely, was not to be a permanent resident, let alone an American citizen. This awkward fact presaged a dilemma that took years to resolve for Buji and his family.

Buji spent most of his time during his year and a half at Northern Colorado College on the east side of the campus in Kepner Hall. Enrolled in the Master of Arts program with a special interest in educational psychology, Buji took a range of courses. He was tutored in student guidance, he discovered what was meant by mental hygiene, he studied personality development and learned how to measure a students' aptitude. Though he was not required to produce a thesis, he did write a thirty-page essay after completing his degree. Written in the autumn of 1958, it was entitled: 'Educational Survey on Taiwan Education system: contemporary structure.' Naturally he played to his strengths in drawing on his first-hand experience here—and, equally naturally, needed to do so as a newcomer in a strange land.

Buji barely scraped through his first semester. This was due partly to his difficulty with the language: 'there were lots of words I didn't know.' Partly, too, it was because he was not used to the North American style of teaching, so alien to his former experience. 'The teachers let their students do whatever they want to do—too much freedom,' he commented. 'In China the teachers tell the students what to do.' It is true that Asian students wrote essays that were largely descriptive and uncritical. They were accustomed to learning by rote.

---

[48] Lynn Pan, *Sons of the Yellow Emperor* (London: Secker & Warburg, 1990) p. 277

They did not take part in tutorial or discussion groups. Above all, they rarely questioned their professors.

Adaptable as ever, Buji soon conformed to the North American pedagogical tradition. He received sympathetic assistance that he gratefully acknowledges— initially from his supervisor, Professor Charles MacLean, with support also from Dean Edward Gates. Here were two men who obviously saw beyond the cultural impediments that inhibited Buji's performance and realized that he could do better. They were proved right when, with very hard work on his own part, Buji's grades improved during his second semester. When he graduated at the end of the academic year in the summer of 1958, he had achieved a 'B' average, which was highly respectable under the circumstances.

Buji had other assistance. His tuition was covered by a scholarship awarded to him by the American Army for having been an interpreter during the Resistance War. This left him to cover his room rent of twelve dollars a month from his own resources, and also his board, though his costs here were minimized because he did his own cooking. To survive, he needed to find work. Living in the heart of Colorado's potato, poultry and sugar beet industry, he knew that there were plenty of part-time jobs to be had.

The first job he found was on a chicken farm, sorting eggs. However there was a problem. 'I had to pick up three eggs in each hand,' Buji recalled, making a joke of his own inability, with his small hands, to pick up three without dropping one. But it was no joke at the time, when, after only a day's work, 'the chicken boss' took Buji off this ill-suited task, dressed him in a plastic hat, pants and long apron, and took him instead into the slaughterhouse. This was grisly work. 'The chickens hang upside down, head towards the ground and after half an hour the chicken cannot move,' Buji explained with distaste. Asked to slaughter twenty chickens at a time, he replied: 'No thank you.' This was the breaking—point for 'the chicken boss', who told Buji's university supervisor that, too incompetent to sort eggs, too squeamish to kill chickens, this under-sized 'Chinaman' would have to go.

It was his professor, Charles MacLean, who now found Buji a more congenial weekend job: sorting books at the college library in Cranford Hall. But though he and Dean Gates were (as Buji insisted) 'real nice' to him, it did not take him long to discover that 'there was a real prejudice.' Rather like the intrusion of the Nazi presence in *The Sound of Music*, Colorado's magnificent scenery could disclose the banality of evil.

The ugly face of Colorado was its combination of typically Southern racist prejudice with the raw Western tradition of easy resort to violence. Antagonism towards anyone who looked or acted differently, or who posed an economic or political threat was still evident in the 1950s. It is true that the Ku Klux Klan were now less active against African Americans; that, in response to the growing Civil Rights Movement, the State had just legalized racial intermarriage; and that the Colorado Supreme Court had outlawed racially restricted covenants on property. Even so, African Americans were subject de facto to segregation, and largely confined to one quarter of the town. They were not welcome at the Lakeside Swimming Pool, at the Crestview Trailer Camp, in thirty-eight of the towns' forty restaurants or, as Buji soon discovered, in any church but the Southern Baptist Church at Five Points, on the non-university side of town.

If the Chinese were treated slightly differently, it was only slightly better. The arrival of the first Chinese person in Colorado in 1870—pejoratively referred to in the press as 'John Chinaman'—had heralded a growth in numbers which reached nearly fifteen hundred within twenty years. Violence against Chinese workers had soon begun, when an angry mob of White miners in Leadville shot three laundrymen and threw their bodies down an abandoned mine shaft, followed shortly by a similar incident against Chinese workers in Rico in San Juan County. In October 1880, thousands of rioters, looking for an economic scapegoat, marched on Hop Alley in the State's capital. As the mob chanted 'Stamp out the yellow plague,' Denver's Chinatown was 'gutted as completely as though a cyclone had come in one door,' a reporter for *The News* noted, 'and passed . . . out the rear.'[49]

Not good memories, and not boding well for subsequent settlement by non-White immigrants. The Chinese population in Colorado, having dwindled to less than three hundred by 1920, was still well under one thousand by the time that Buji arrived. True, the rioting, pillaging and murdering of Chinese workers was no longer seen, but more subtle forms of discrimination still ranked the Chinese with the largely despised African American population.

During his first Sunday in Greeley, Buji donned his best suit and tie and made his way to the First Baptist Church. Like the 7.5 per cent of the Chinese population in America who were Christians, he naturally wished to attend divine service. But he was not welcome into the house of faith that had been founded in 1871. As he recounts with undiminished indignation: 'They kick me out.' He was curtly informed: 'You belong to the Southern Baptist Church

---

49   William Wei, 'History and Memory, The Story of Denver's Chinatown,' *Colorado Heritage* (Autumn 2002) p. 10

with all the Negroes.' When he first told me this story, nearly fifty years later, in the comfortable surroundings of the Ho household in Los Angeles, he wore a puzzled expression, exclaiming rhetorically, 'we are all the children of God—why they do it?' To which his wife Sonia supplied, in her matter-of-fact way, the answer: 'Because you Chinaman!'

Yes, indeed: this revelation of a blatant barrier of prejudice was also something Buji had not expected to encounter in the America of his dreams. Moreover, during his second semester in Colorado he ran into difficulty once again. 'Some of the students give me trouble,' he explained. Concerned that 'Pu-chi', as he was known at the time, was violating his student visa by working in the library, they reported him to the immigration authorities in Denver, sixty miles south of Greeley. It is still a woeful memory, of going to Denver, of hearing the authorities confront him: 'Are you a waiter or a cook?' The implication was woundingly obvious to him: 'The Chinese is always a cook or a waiter or working in the laundry.'

Here, no doubt, was a manifestation of the lingering fear that a foreigner might be getting above himself by taking an American's job. But here too was a kind of xenophobia, newly charged by current events in the world. After all, Buji had arrived in the United States at the height of the Cold War. Anti-Communist feelings, stoked by Senator Joseph McCarthy's Un-American Activities Committee, resulted in thousands of Chinese Americans being questioned about their political views and their loyalty. In 1957, for example, the FBI was investigating the activities of the American-based Taiwanese who, in opposition to the ruling GMD government, supported the Taiwan Independence Movement. Buji duly assured the immigration official that he was not a Communist, not a member of the Taiwanese Association of America, and was not employed in a laundry, or in a restaurant. The matter was dropped at this point. But even though Buji was able to talk his way out of this problem, with the support of the professors who had arranged for his employment in the library, it was an embarrassment he should never have had to face, and one that rankled.

'Some white people were good to me,' he was always quick to add, 'I don't forget about that.' When he had arrived in Greeley, as he remembers, his landlord had met him at the bus station and transported his luggage by horse and cart to his new home. Buji's teachers, moreover, encouraged him to remain at the college for a semester after he had completed his degree. It was during this time that he wrote his essay on educational practices in Taiwan, as well as audited courses in advanced grammar and syntax, in the psychology of adolescence, and in college administration. As usual, he made the best of it, adding to his educational qualifications just as he had planned all along.

* * *

For Buji, it was a narrow life in a big country. He focused his efforts on completing his degree plus sending money back to Taiwan every month, at first one hundred and later two hundred US dollars. Sometimes he sent clothing too. In return, he looked forward eagerly to receiving weekly letters from Shuang-ru. In 1959, when she enclosed a photograph of Dayi and Hongyi dressed in the American-style bomber jackets that Buji had sent them, it was a poignant moment, still fresh in his memory—'I'm crying, so many years I haven't seen them.'

It had, in fact, been only been a year and a half since he had left Taiwan. Even so, the children looked different. They were taller and no longer toddlers but little boys. Dayi was now attending grade school. Hongyi was in kindergarten. Viewing Shuang-ru's image was equally painful for Buji. Even more stunningly beautiful and more fashion-conscious than when Buji left, in these photographs Shuang-ru wears cotton dresses with cinch belts emphasizing her tiny waist, and her thick hair is worn in the currently fashionable bouffant style.

It is not difficult to reconstruct the outline of her life in Taiwan—as narrowly constrained in many ways as that of her absent husband. Until June 1960 she continued working at the Tax Department. During her daughter's absence at City Hall, Lou and a series of helpers: first A-mi, then A-shu then Yu-yen ran the house and looked after the boys. During the weekends Shuang-ru remained at home with Dayi and Hongyi or visited members of her extended family, centered on Lou's four sisters. Closest to home was Shuang-ru's small and frail aunt Tsao whose children played with Dayi and Hongyi and who would tragically die in childbirth at the age of twenty-nine. Lou's elder sister, Yue, whom her grandmother, Lin Pen, had given up for adoption as the 'little bride' of a farmer, lived further away. The farm had meanwhile grown rich producing sugar cane and vegetables. It sticks in the children's memories as a magical place for two city-bound boys who visited with their mother and grandmother. They fondly remember digging up yams and, after building a large fire, baking the succulent vegetables in the earth.

There were equally memorable visits to Shuang-ru's favorite aunt, Hsiao, who lived with her son I-wen on the Lu family compound, *Hsiau-Yun*. Here traditional Chinese culture was still apparent—the formal gardens, the ancestral temple, the opium-smoking, foot-bound grandmother—though the compound now had recently installed electricity and a clay tennis court. I-wen, a young man of twenty by 1958, took a special interest in the two boys during their visits to *Hsiau-Yun* and remembers that 'Dayi was quiet; he liked to be alone and to read.' Hongyi, he recalls, 'was the one who liked to play outside in the big field beyond the compound or to play cards in the house.'

During the summer months the family often visited the temple at Houli that the first Lu son, Dun-li, had built in 1932 for the wife and three daughters of his fourth brother, Shuang-chio (and which we revisited with the whole Ho family in 2008). It used to take Shuang-ru, her mother, the boys and the family servant more than two hours to get there. Walking along the busy road out of the humid, heat-baked city, they passed sugar cane fields and rice paddies. Then they turned right and entered the narrow lane that snaked into the hills through vegetation composed of flowering shrubs and subtropical banyan, acacia and other hardwood trees. As they neared the temple they would see the mausoleum—with a copper dome in those days, not silver, as we saw later—containing the ashes of their ancestors, and then enter the double-storey living quarters that had served as a refuge for the women and their servants in their escape from the strict confines of their previous lives. Here the family partook in vegetarian meals and, for those like the Buddhist Lou, in the practices of the Chinese Dharma.

There were other adventurous outings for Shuang-ru and the boys too. They traveled to Taipei where they visited relatives and, on one occasion, the zoo. They took a bus into the mountains behind Taichung, to the beautiful resort of Sun Moon Lake which boasts the largest natural lake in Taiwan and, towering above it, the majestic Yu—or Jade—mountain.

During my own visit to Sun Moon Lake with the Ho family in March 2008, Sonia and I spent a memorable morning sitting, toe to toe, on a chaise longue in the Lalu Hotel, which now overlooks the serene lake. Located on the former site of a building that Chiang Kai-shek used as his retreat from the bustle of Taipei, Lalu Hotel gave Sonia a relaxing environment, prompting many personal reflections on her life in very different days. Such conversations in Taiwan, at places that served as sites of memory, helped to unlock vivid and evocative recollections—luckily for her biographer, since none of the weekly letters that Sonia had written to her husband during their seven-and-a-half year separation now survive.

For example, during our visit to the house in Li Shing Road, where Sonia and the boys had lived from 1958 to 1965, she helped me understand the many ways in which this neighborhood had changed since her day. Li Shing Road is now paved; the fountain that once stood at a crossing in the middle of the road has been removed. The rickshaw drivers, who once congregated around the fountain waiting for business, are now driving taxis. The rice merchant's shop, where the boys ran errands for their grandmother, is gone. So, too, is the store where the boys surreptitiously used to leaf through comic books. Most of the one-storey brick-built duplex houses with their tiny wooden porches—including their own, again No. 19—have been replaced by concrete two-storey dwellings. There are no longer any open sewers, from which night-soil collectors would remove the human waste in the early morning. And I doubt if any of the children we saw playing in the street make—as the young Hongyi used to—star-shaped toy projectiles out of bottle caps by flattening them on the nearby railway tracks, then cutting them into the required shape. Or that they play street stick-ball either.

In particular, my morning talks with Sonia at Lalu Hotel made me appreciate the extent to which uncertainty dominated her life during these years of separation from her husband. She does not complain herself but those close to her saw her predicament. 'It was difficult for my cousin when her husband left,' I-wen told me, 'because he had no plan of coming back.' Moreover, like everyone else in Taiwan, she was living in a country that seemed under constant threat from Communist invasion; in 1958 tensions between China and the United States over the sovereignty of Taiwan were particularly high. Then there was the enormous responsibility of raising two boys on her own. Determined to refresh the fading memories that each child possessed of his father, she shared her weekly letters from America with them and, when the boys were able to write, had them add a few lines to the weekly missive to their father.

'Letters became a ritual for my brother and myself,' David readily corroborates. Their debt to their mother is something of which they later became even more keenly aware as adults and parents themselves. Sole responsibility for the boys meant that it fell to her to oversee every aspect of their upbringing. She taught them that ways of behaving and commitment to study were more important than amassing material goods. 'I grew up with respect for those who surrounded us and with a deep respect for scholarship,' David affirms. 'No one emphasized the importance of making money.' From both sides of their family, then, these values were consistently imparted, in their father's absence as much as if he had been there to instill the same message.

From the moment that Dayi and Hongyi entered school, they had one goal: to live up to these high aspirations. This initially meant passing the examination, taken in the sixth grade at the end of their study at the elementary school, to enable them to enter the Middle School. 'It seemed like our whole life was geared for that test,' as David wryly comments. Even though the boys' marks were well above average in the examinations they took, 'if you got ninety-nine, you were punished because something was off.'

Determined that Dayi and Hongyi should do well in the examination, Shuang-ru saw to it that they were given extra lessons, even after putting in a long day at school. This entailed a twenty-minute bike ride through the empty countryside where the eerie sounds of frogs and crickets would frequently scare the boys into frenzied peddling home. When Shuang-ru became dissatisfied with the teachers at the local elementary school, she pulled strings through her uncle, Lin Lonh-yun, and moved the boys to another school. Though this meant that Dayi and Hongyi had a longer bicycle ride—arriving home at 7:00 PM—Shuang-ru evidently made the right choice, as I later saw for myself.

When visiting Guangfu School with the Ho family in March 2008, we were greeted by the sounds of a hundred-piece symphony orchestra playing Haydn's Symphony No. 85. When I later had the privilege of meeting some of the students, I quickly realized that Dayi and Hongyi had been enrolled in one of the best schools in Taiwan. The boys throve in this environment. By the third grade Dayi was at the top of his class at Guangfu School. A couple of years later he had become president of the student body.

In 2008, on our visit to Guangfu School, Phillip Ho went back as a respected Californian dentist and businessman of fifty-four; David Ho, at fifty-six, as an internationally renowned scientist. One of the students asked Phillip what it had been like to have such an exceptional brother. The designated philosopher of the Ho family had no difficulty in finding an answer to the question. 'Someone has to come first, just as someone has to come last,' Phillip modestly explained. 'David was always number one, and there can only be one number one.'

But we should not suppose that Dayi was simply a pious prodigy, as his mother well understood. Shuang-ru's responsibility for her children not only entailed taking care of their education and deportment, but coping with all the scrapes that high-spirited boys are liable to get into. It is part of family lore that, during a visit to *Hsiau-Yun*, the Lu family compound, the normally well-behaved Dayi taunted a pet monkey by urinating on him. Not amused, the monkey grabbed Dayi's exposed private parts. I-wen, who witnessed the incident, records with mock-solemnity that Shuang-ru had to take the distressed and embarrassed child 'to one of those traditional temples to help him calm down.'[50]

During Dayi's fifth grade at school there was a more serious incident that required Shuang-ru's full attention. It is ironic, in view of the particular sort of medical research that he later pursued, that Dayi should have contacted what can now be identified as Hepatitis B from a tainted needle while being vaccinated at the local hospital.[51] Needless to say, the effects were serious; he contracted jaundice and came very close to death. 'I remember people talking about my dying,' as he now recalls with a detachment he can afford, since tragedy was averted. But how would Shuang-ru have explained the death of the first-born son to Buji in America? How would she have dealt with that sorrow on her own? And how much did Dr David Ho's later decision to specialize in infectious diseases and their transmission owe to this trauma?

[50] This story has yet another version. According to Phillip, who was an infant at the time, the incident took place in the family garden of the Japanese house and David was simply urinating on the tree when the pet monkey attacked him.

[51] In 1984 David had himself tested for Hepatitis B. Fortunately, he no longer had the B virus, only laboratory evidence of a prior infection.

Paul and Sonia Wedding, 1951

Kiang Lou, Sonia, Paul and David, Taichung

Sonia and Paul's wedding, 1951

Paul in Arizona

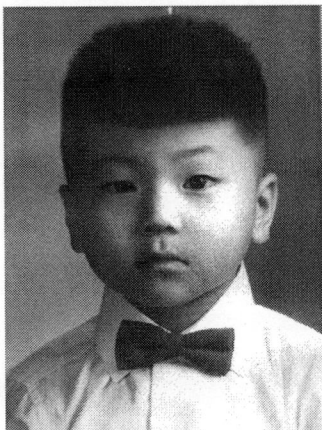

David with bow tie

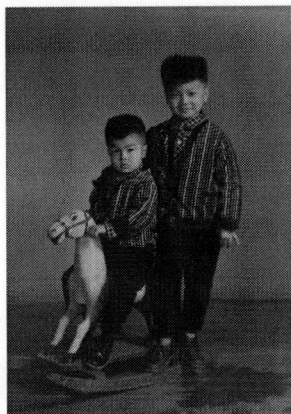

1969年元旦

David & Phillip, Taichung

David and Phillip, Taichung

Sonia, David and Phillip, Taichung

Sonia and Phillip, Taichung

CHAPTER 5

'Eating Bitter'

吃苦

The summer is hot in Taichung. The small house in the Li Shing Road had no air conditioning, of course, and became oppressive in the heat. One day in June 1960 Lou, now overweight and suffering from high blood pressure, retreated to the tiny back garden of the family home. It was there that Shuang-ru's nephew who lived near-by discovered her body. While Shuang-ru and the boys were at the movies, Lou had suddenly died of a brain hemorrhage. Since, as I-wen recalls, 'David's grandmother practically raised him,' Lou's death was a blow from which the seven-year old boy took years to recover. On the other side of the Pacific Ocean, Buji learned of Lou's unexpected death when he was on a routine visit to the US post office, intent on sending money home as usual, and picked up his own mail. 'I did not know that she was dying,' he recalls; 'when I got the letter I was crying in the post office.' The sad event poignantly brought home the fact that he was separated from his family; but it also expedited plans for reuniting them.

With Lou's death, Shuang-ru had lost her closest companion and her best friend. For the time being, she had to quit her job at the tax office in order to look after the boys, though she later returned to work. Now, too, her own family was ready to break a silence that Lou had insisted on maintaining to the end. At last, with the death of her mother, Shuang-ru finally discovered, through her aunt Hsiao, the identity of her father (though his full name, Lu Chiao-hu, was only to be documented for her much later, on our 2008 visit). He was, as she now realized, the man who had watched her play as a child, the man who had met her mother on her clandestine visits to Taichung, and the man in the background at the Lu family celebrations until his death in 1955.

From that moment on, as David remembers, 'we became closer to the Lu family.' They made even more visits to *Hsiau-yun*, the Lu family compound. Moreover, Shuang-ru discovered the further secret, that she had three step-sisters, Lu Hsiao Mei, Lu Hsiao Tzu and Lu Hsiao Wan along with three step-brothers, Lu Wen-shi, Lu Jian-shi and Lu Wei-shi from her father's second wife, and sought them out. For Shuang-ru, then, her family, although diminished by Lou's death, had also in a sense expanded.

But the focus had changed, making Buji's role more problematic. Ever since his departure, nearly three years previously, this was a difficulty that Shuang-ru had had to face, but now she faced it single-handed, at once with more pressure but also with more freedom—including freedom to move, if and when she chose.

Despite the enormous responsibility that fell upon Shuang-ru as a single parent, there were nevertheless advantages to having a husband working on the Gold Mountain. 'They were living well,' as it seemed to I-wen. The monthly cheque for one, then two hundred dollars, as David acknowledges, may now seem 'a small amount, but it went a long way.' The two boys were better dressed than most other children. Their family was the first in Li Shing Road to have an ice box and to make ice cream, albeit in a primitive contraption. Moreover, unlike many of their neighbors, they had hopes that things would get even better.

Like so many of the Chinese students of an earlier generation, who had come to America before the Second World War, Buji initially professed hopes of returning to his native country. 'China need every kind of people,' he told me during one interview, 'I thought I would come back to China.' Yet this earlier way of thinking had already been overtaken by the realities of the 1950s. How could Buji, tainted by his sojourns in Taiwan and America in Communist eyes, possibly have gone back? How could he have contemplated taking his new family to Mao's China? Buji also talked of returning to Taiwan after he had completed his degree. But others, like I-wen, had gained quite the opposite impression from him.

What is now difficult to recover, half a century later, is exactly what plans Buji and Shuang-ru had, and exactly when they made them. This is a matter on which their lost correspondence would obviously have been helpful in pinpointing the decisions they took, the assumptions they held, and the arguments that they doubtless rehearsed. But the broad trajectory of events that ultimately brought them as a reunited family to settle in California is nonetheless clear.

By the time of Lou's death, Buji had been in the United States as a student for nearly three years, but he was far from the average American student in age, experience, culture, outlook or values. There was, to be sure, a general prosperity that nobody had enjoyed for twenty years. But he felt a kind of alienation living in a society that was consumed with rock-n'-roll, with automobiles characterized by soaring tail fins and an abundance of decorative chrome, by television programs featuring ideal families in 'Father Knows Best' and 'Ozzie and Harriet'. It is not surprising that Buji, already thirty-eight when he arrived in Colorado, had little interaction with his much-younger fellow students or little inclination to partake in the college's extra-curricular activities, still less join the men in the informal panty-raids in the girls' dormitory.

If and when Buji returned to Taiwan, his advanced degrees would enable him to secure a better position. Certainly the course that he audited in high-school administration at Northern Colorado College pointed him in this direction. If, on the other hand, he chose to remain in America and put his qualifications to use there, the monthly cheque that he sent to the family could be even larger.

But there was a problem with each of these scenarios. To an extent that he had not fully confided to Shuang-ru—though she certainly sensed it—Buji had never been comfortable living and working in Taiwan. Moreover, there is some evidence to suggest that those who returned from study in America did not always have an easy time of it. Buji insists that he discussed with Shuang-ru the possibility that he might return to Taiwan: 'I said, I'd like to go back—or should I stay on in America?'

Actions often speak louder than words. For it gradually emerged that Buji had made no definite plans for returning to Taiwan. He was by no means the only Chinese student who chose to prolong his studies, and to mark time while the political situation unfolded—as it did on both sides of the Pacific. Like many other Chinese scholars of an earlier generation for whom advanced study required long periods of separation from their families, Buji simply took it for granted that he would not be going home, for the time being at any rate. As long as Lou was alive, this was the default position.

Although Buji could apply for American citizenship, if he were to be refused he would lose his student status. But with a valid student visa in hand, Buji could remain as long as he was enrolled at university. This seems to be the main reason why he decided during the winter of 1958-9 to apply for a PhD in educational psychology at the State University in Tempe, Arizona, close to the state capital at Phoenix. Three more years in America would give him yet another higher degree and more time to send money home. After completing his masters degree in Colorado, he therefore jumped 'from the freezer to the furnace' (his own words) once he was accepted to begin his new studies in Arizona in September 1959.

Meanwhile, however, he obviously needed a well-paying summer job. He had been told in Colorado, 'go to California there are lots of jobs.' When he got to the West Coast in the spring of 1959 he found that this was true. Within a few days of arriving in Los Angeles he had secured two jobs. One, during the graveyard shift, was in a corn flour plant. The other, a daytime job, was for a subcontractor of Lockheed Corporation. By the end of his first month in California, Buji had 'lots of money.' This was necessary because, he explained, 'I want to get my tuition, my own living expense, besides sending money to Taiwan.'

Buji thus chose to go to California, and it proved a momentous choice. Following the Second World War, everyone could see that Los Angeles had become not only the second largest urban area in the United States, and not only the city that Hollywood made world famous, but also a metropolitan centre buoyed up by a vibrant economic base in new industries. As Buji put it, 'California had so many manufacturers and engineers, you can work and you can stay there.' Like thousands of others, he felt the appeal of southern California. The climate seemed never too hot (like Arizona) or too cold (like Colorado) but happily like that of his home province, Jiangxi. The landscape—rugged mountains, fertile valleys and expansive plains—was as varied as the vegetation, with its majestic palms, scent-laden eucalyptus and moss-green oaks. Moreover, the ethnic composition of the state was congenial, as Buji immediately sensed when he arrived: 'So many Orientals!'

Before becoming the first President of the Chinese Republic in 1912 Sun Yat-sen had spent some time in Los Angeles. Thirty-one years later the record audience that crowded into the Hollywood Bowl to listen to Madame Chiang Kai-shek during her fund-raising mission to America was reported to have been spellbound by her eloquence. And in 1959 Governor Edmund G. Brown auspiciously appointed Delbert E. Wong as a judge: the first Chinese American to be appointed to the municipal bench in Los Angeles. It was in California that many Chinese had found a home over the past decades—over half of the country's 240,000 Chinese Americans lived in California. It was here that they grew vegetables, and thereby contributed to the foundation of California's agriculture; here that they planted fruit trees, introducing, among other fruits, the Bing cherry; here that they ran laundries; and, once they became eligible to apply for business licenses, here that they established Chinese restaurants. If the Gold Mountain had a peak and treasures still worth mining, they were surely to be found in California.

Buji had to work hard in California, and under conditions of immediate difficulty. Holding down two jobs in addition to working 'overtime and overtime' took its toll. He was so busy that he could not cash his monthly cheque—a manifestly touching predicament that once led the president of the company to drive Buji to the bank himself. Buji faced exhaustion, worn down with overwork. The bags of corn flour that he heaved onto his shoulder before pouring the corn into the milling machine were heavy, especially for a man of his build. Getting from his rented room near his daytime job in Burbank to his second job on the edge of the city was not easy. 'I don't have a car,' he explained ruefully, 'I have to walk on the freeway.' Normally so stoical, he admitted to shedding tears during his dangerous walk along Highway 5 and to weeping 'every night' as he tried to snatch a few hours' sleep.

Despite all the difficulties and dangers, Buji saw the opportunities that were now open to him—if not in corn flour-milling then in the sort of electronic devices that Lockheed demanded from its sub-contractors. His work in assembling, soldering and testing their equipment introduced Buji to the techniques of electrical engineering, firing his imagination as well as providing a meal ticket.

One knock-on effect was seen when Buji left California at the end of the summer of 1959 and enrolled, as planned, at Arizona's State University in Tempe. In the light of his recent industrial experience, he decided to take more courses in mathematics and physics than in education. When Buji had first entered university in 1942 he had wanted to enroll in the department of engineering. But China—and particularly Buji's home province of Jiangxi—had needed teachers more than it had needed engineers and had been unwilling to subsidize his preferred area of study. His long-time interest in science, it seemed, could now be fulfilled in Arizona, without the exacting English language requirements that had inhibited him in education courses.

But this was to breach the conditions on which his funding had been granted. Although he would take more than three years to complete his doctorate, the university would not renew his scholarship. This meant that from now on Buji would have to find money for his fees in addition to his room and board. It also meant that he would end up with a degree in an area of study, educational psychology, which he no longer wished to pursue professionally.

'When I got my Master's degree I moved to California,' as he recollected, perhaps slightly compressing the chain of events. He remembered thinking, 'Oh, I got the wrong place—Colorado is an agricultural state. Only California is an industrial state, they have everything: defense and factories.' Might California offer a new career for himself, a new home for his family, and educational opportunities that his boys could seize?

By early 1960, in fact, Buji's exposure to the American educational system had convinced him that he would never teach in the United States. 'There was no respect for teachers,' he recalled dismissively, 'in the US the teachers got beat up by the students.' He was now seeking a vocation that lay outside the classroom. When he returned to California in the late spring of 1960, it was to a better job, in a science-based industry, and with no intention of returning to complete his PhD in Arizona. Little wonder that he recalled thinking: 'Oh, this is the right place.' It was in California that he shortly learned of Lou's death. It was in California that the aspirations of his reunited family were ultimately to be realized.

*   *   *

In 1960, at the age of forty-one, Buji committed himself to a career in electrical engineering. He aimed to put himself among twenty per cent of Chinese residents in America who were now in professional employment—it had been only 2.5 per cent in 1940. And he was encouraged to discover a number of role models. Almost a decade earlier the electronic engineer An Wang had founded the successful computer firm, Wang Laboratories, and companies like IBM and Westinghouse were beginning to place Chinese scientists in both professional and supervisory positions. It was a significant step for Buji when, in late 1960 or early 1961, he joined the staff of the Toledo-based Haughton Elevator Company in Glendale, Los Angeles. During the course of designing the relay circuits that controlled the descent and ascent of the elevator, Buji got a taste for the various ways that he could apply his ongoing university studies to his work as a professional engineer.

Apart from his own insatiable thirst for knowledge, it was incumbent upon Buji to retain his student status for immigration purposes. The University of Southern California (USC) made it easy for him to enroll as a full-time student—in addition to his full-time job, of course. 'That school is real good,' Buji recalled affectionately, 'they have same course day and evening.' Moreover, he was now registered for a Bachelor of Science degree, which would open professional doors otherwise closed to him. It needs to be remembered that Chinese Americans were welcome neither into the teaching, medical and dentistry professions, nor into the civil service—even if they could get into university in the first place, since many institutions had quotas on the number of Asian students it was willing to accept. Hence Buji's abiding gratitude to USC for throwing him a lifeline.

Until 1965, when the Naturalization and Immigration Act repealed all discriminatory entry quotas, it was impossible for Chinese 'sojourner' students (or *liuxuesheng*) to remain permanently in the United States, let alone to bring their families to join them. What Buji could do, however, was to acquire residency status by obtaining a green card and from that proceed to American citizenship. He approached the president of Haughton Elevator Company for help. The results were favorable. Buji's own potential as an electrical engineer obviously underpinned the application, as did his personable nature—'they like me,' he recollected with a big smile. The company thus helped him secure his green card in 1961. With his residency status in hand, Buji was at last entitled to apply (under the War Bride Act of December 1945) to bring his wife and children into the United States as non-quota immigrants.

The green card was a document of enormous significance for the family. Coming in the year after Lou's death, it meant that the question of their immigration to the United States was no longer hypothetical but real and urgent. Buji recalled that it was Shuang-ru who made the final decision for him, when she said: 'we have to think about the education of the children, this is the most important thing.'

Buji now had a definite goal to work towards. And work he did. When I once asked him if he ever took any time off, he shook his head, laughed, then exclaimed: 'I don't have any spare time.' There was neither the time nor the money—'all friends poor'—to take an excursion to fashionable Mulholland Drive to view the lights in the San Fernando Valley, or to attend the Dodgers' home games, or to ride the Pacific Electric train to Venice. Indeed, all Buji's energies were focused on paving the way for his family's eventual arrival. 'I have to have enough money, a very good job, a house,' he told me. These were not easy objectives and he had to put up with many hardships along the way.

It would be naïve to suppose that prejudice against Chinese-Americans, which had made California the hotbed of agitation against 'John Chinaman' in the 1870s and 1880s, no longer existed. The newest arrivals, as usual, bore the brunt, looked down upon even by their own kith and kin. Most of his friends, Buji recalled, 'were the sons of Mainlanders and some were sons of Taiwanese'—people whom naturalized Chinese Americans would pejoratively refer to as FOB's: 'Fresh off the Boat.'

The majority of male immigrants, like Buji, still lived a bachelor existence. Sometimes, around 11:30 PM, Buji and Wong Yao and Chen Guan with whom he shared a house near the university would gather for a late evening meal. Even eating in one of the city's many Chinese restaurants was 'out of the question.' Buji still takes pride in the fact that he did most of the cooking for Chen and Wang. 'They know I am a very good cook so on Saturday and Sunday I go to the [Alexander] market to prepare one week of food.' The only trouble with this arrangement, Buji confided, was that 'when I go to evening class they eat everything.' Although his flat-mates used to 'steal my food,' thus making him 'very mad,' this infraction was offset by the companionship offered by other men like himself who were all trying to establish new lives for themselves in America.

Though Buji also wanted to get further along with his degree in engineering, holding down a stable job took priority over everything else. This too presented repeated difficulties for an immigrant who was still not fully qualified. Even the Haughton Elevator Company, which had helped Buji get his green card, did not keep him on the pay roll permanently. He did not have an easy time before finding a job with the Harden Camera Company, designing digital flash circuits. The sobering thought must have dawned on Buji, that Asians like himself were usually the last to be hired and the first to be fired. But the possibility of being dismissed simply made him work harder than ever.

Buji's ambition, not only for himself but for his family, was fierce and indomitable. He was determined to set them apart from the first wave of Chinese immigrants who remained linked to the ethnic sub-economy and its institutions located in predominantly Chinese neighborhoods. He was also determined to challenge the low place that Americans had ascribed to the Chinese in the ethnic pecking order. By 1965 he had saved enough money for a down-payment on a modest art deco house at 940 Venango Avenue in Los Angeles. 'I find out which school's best,' he explained, 'then I bought a house.'

This is why he chose the future family home in a predominantly White area that was far from the Chinese department stores, restaurants and businesses at South Broadway and West 7th Street. He knew that the location of one's house and the proximity to it of a good school for the children mattered as much as how one spoke the dominant language. This is why he told Shuang-ru not to let Dayi and Hongyi learn to speak English until they arrived in America, lest they meanwhile acquire the kind of accent that sometimes made his own English difficult for Americans to understand.

In early 1965, then, Buji was half way through his degree in electrical engineering. He had purchased a second-hand Pontiac that he had not yet ventured to drive on the highway. The house he had chosen would soon be available for occupation. And his job at the Harden Camera Company seemed secure. At last his reunion with his family was no longer a dream but a definite, practicable, imminent proposition.

Now twelve and ten, Dayi and Hongyi were happy to hear that they would soon be joining the father whose absence in America had stretched to seven and a half years. Dayi was (so he remembers) 'relieved in some ways' from the pressure of the Middle School examination entrance, for which he had been groomed since entering elementary school and which he was poised to take shortly before he left Taiwan. As the boys packed their books and their favorite puppets, their mother left her job in order to make all the necessary arrangements. Shuang-ru gave away the wedding dress that she had worn some thirteen years earlier. She sold the house in Li Shing Road, and all of its contents too, in accordance with her husband's instructions—'You can buy everything here.' The money just covered the cost of three one-way airline tickets from Taipei to Los Angeles.

With their remaining possessions packed in only a few suitcases, Shuang-ru and her two sons were now ready to leave Taiwan at the beginning of March 1965. A small group of relatives, all too aware that they might never see them again, since the Taiwanese government did not (until 1979) grant tourist passports, saw them off at Taichung railway station—'all crying,' as Shuang-ru recalls. Her favorite cousin, I-wen, accompanied the trio to Taipei, and waved good-bye to them at the airport. It was an uneventful trip to Los Angeles. During their stopover in Tokyo, Shuang-ru practiced her old skills in Japanese, while Dayi and Hongyi 'went crazy' watching television—the first they had ever seen. All three were not only excited but also apprehensive at what lay ahead.

*   *   *

Every time David Ho walks through the colored, ceramic-tiled passage-way leading to the arrivals gate at Los Angeles International Airport he 'sees' his father at the end of the tiled corridor. It was the welcome to a new life—and to a new identity. The boys had to get used to the new forenames—David and Phillip—that their father had selected from the Bible and their surname that was pronounced Ho and not He.[52] Ever since Americans in Colorado had had difficulties in pronouncing, let alone spelling, Buji—he had increasingly been known as Paul. It was an apt name for a Christian convert. He had also chosen a name for Shuang-ru that was based on the Japanese variant that she had been given as a child: Sonia. These are the names by which they now became known in their American life.

Paul Ho had come to the airport that day with a friend, Wei Wei, who had driven his car for him, since the journey entailed driving on the highway. The two men stood at the end of the long tiled passage. When they met the arrivals, Paul first embraced Sonia, then, immediately recognizing the boys from photographs, bent over and hugged them too.

Paul jokes when he refers to the family's separation as 'the seven-year itch.' At the same time he admits that it was difficult to start again with the boys. For the two fictional characters in Lin Yutang's novel *Chinatown Family*, it seemed strange to meet the father they had never known on arriving in New York, because 'the "father" in their minds was a dream, a legend, a reality so remote it was unreal.'[53] It was little different for David and Phillip. 'We had trouble calling my father, father,' Phillip, who was two-and-a-half years old when his father had left Taiwan, recalls. It seemed equally odd to be speaking to him in Mandarin while they naturally spoke to their mother in Taiwanese.

Paul and Sonia Ho and their two sons had to find temporary accommodation until their own house was ready for occupation in the summer of 1965. They settled for what they could get in the short term: a second floor apartment in a broad bottomed Edwardian house on tree-lined 29th Street in the predominantly African American area, adjacent to the University of Southern California campus, known as Watts.

There were many challenges for Sonia to face. True, in many obvious ways she was in a historically privileged position. Many previous Gold Mountain wives had been abandoned by husbands who had been unable to keep up the monthly remittance payments or who had established new households and new families in America. Virtually every female Chinese immigrant of an earlier era had to enter the country as indentured laborers, as prostitutes or as mail-order brides. Sonia, by contrast, was spared the lengthy interrogation and the long wait that often followed at the detention centre in San Francisco's

---

52 Saint Philip the Evanglist and Saint Philip the Apostle and, of course, King David.

53 Lin Yutang, *Chinatown Chinese* (New York: Mei Ya Publications 1948) p. 6

Angel Island, through which all newcomers from Asia had once passed before entering the United States. Even so, she was confronted with a new situation in a new continent.

Loneliness was one fear. She was without the support of her family and friends. Expectations were so different in this brash, new Californian culture. The ideal American woman projected in magazines, on billboards and on the television seemed to be blond, blue-eyed and big breasted. The celebrity whom most Chinese women idolized was the sexy and talented half-Chinese actress, Nancy Kwan, with her well-known portrayal of the prostitute in the film *The World of Suzie Wong* (1960). This may indeed have represented a step forward from the China-doll and dragon-lady roles that, in a previous generation, Anna May Wong had been forced to take during her long film career; but it was an ambivalent kind of fame from the point of view of respectable Chinese Americans. In this respect Kwan's next big hit in *The Flower Drum Song* (1961) offered a more sympathetic role model for new immigrants, though still stereotyping them in crude Technicolor.

More immediately, financial insecurity was an abiding worry. As a Gold Mountain Wife, Shuang-ru had lived better than many of her friends, but how would she live now? She already knew that her husband's employment was less secure than they had anticipated. It was 'unbelievable,' so Paul recounted, when the Harden Camera Company showed him the door shortly before the family's arrival in March 1965. How would he fare in his new job, with the Xerox Company? How would their standard of living compare to the average middle-class family in America? And how would they pay the mortgage when they moved to suburban Hollywood?

During her first month in America, Sonia recalls, 'I just stay home, I have nothing to do, I can't stand it.' How was she going to get a good job, though, with her own English as yet only rudimentary? As her son Sidney, who was born two years after her arrival in America puts it, she was 'never a stay-at-home Mom.' Sonia took a bus to an employment agency in 'Little Tokyo' in the eastern part of Los Angeles. Here at least, the language barrier could be surmounted. Fluent in Japanese, she landed a job on the assembly line in the Jewish-owned Segal Company, producing costume jewelry for Macy's, Bullock's and other leading department stores. Her Japanese was put to good use since the company's supervisor, Betsy Yamada, was from Japan. 'Start next week at 8:00,' the employment agency told Sonia. This seemed incredible to Paul. Astounded that Sonia had landed a job so quickly he exclaimed: 'You don't even speak English!' That weekend Paul showed Sonia the bus route. On Monday morning she got up at 5:00 AM and made the boys' lunches, thus beginning a routine that would last thirty years.

In some ways, Sonia and the boys had arrived in America at a more favorable and tolerant moment than those before them. The Naturalization and Immigration Act was about to be enacted in the autumn of 1965, and during the following ten years it allowed 205,000 Chinese from Taiwan and Hong Kong into the United States. At this time, too, there were many ethnic groups within the population who were becoming preoccupied with their own origins, taking a new pride in what had previously been regarded as shameful or at least embarrassing. And the civil rights movement was afoot, with mixed success. Even though many Americans were willing to take a more pluralistic view of their society, others were not ready to acknowledge or to remedy the low standard of living, the poor schools, the high rate of unemployment and the police brutality to which African Americans were subjected on a daily basis.

With an address in Watts, however, the Ho family was in the eye of the storm as things came to the boil in the late spring and summer of 1965. It was not until August that the looting, fighting, vandalism and worst of all, arson, reached a horrifying climax, reported across the world, and resulting in thirty-four deaths, a thousand injuries and nearly four thousand arrests. But already tensions between the African American and White communities were high. For example, two months after the Ho's moved into the area, a white police officer pulled over, then shot, an African American man (Leonard Deadwyler) who was doing nothing more than rushing his pregnant wife to the hospital.

David and Phillip thus had a sobering introduction to America when they entered the predominantly African American 32nd Avenue School in Watts. Paul obviously realized that the boys' first months in America were 'very hard,' but kept his feelings to himself, as he watched them struggling to master English under these adverse circumstances. 'Just use the five-sentence structure' he told them, in reference to the system that he had developed for learning the language so many years earlier. The boys recall a traumatic beginning, with racial and language difficulties intertwined—'The blacks, they think those two brothers are dumb because they can't speak.' For someone who had been at the top of his class, 'being laughed at by classmates who thought I was dumb' was an experience that temporarily undermined David's confidence: 'I became a very quiet and introverted child.' When Sonia asked David and Phillip 'Do you like school?' the frustrated boys answered: 'No, we don't know anything.'

Needless to say, as soon as the mortgage on the Ho family's new home in Hollywood came through, they were happy to move. Their new home was a two-bedroom bungalow, attractively built in the art deco style, at 940 Venango Avenue in the suburb of Silver Lake. Sonia continued to work in downtown Los Angeles, a pattern only broken temporarily in 1967 by the birth of her third son, Sidney. He was to have the obvious advantage of learning English from the start, the obvious disadvantage of lacking equal fluency in Chinese or Taiwanese, which his parents spoke at home. And even more significant, unlike David and Phillip, 'I had him as a father from Day 1.'[54]

It took his elder brothers a couple of years before they felt comfortable speaking English. Television was a help. Phil recalls picking up 'a few phrases here and there and some mannerisms' by watching *The Three Stooges*. And the first sentence in English that David understood—'This is my office'—came from the cartoon *Mr. Magoo*. He insists that 'it was much better' when they moved into Hollywood, partly due to the fact that the Thomas Starr King Junior High School had a program for English as a Second Language (ESL). This was doubtless one reason why Paul had made it such a priority to seek a house near to the school.

Likewise with the John Marshall High School, to which the boys duly progressed. Indeed David skipped a grade in Junior High. Here there were sympathetic teachers, fondly remembered—Mr Cross in mathematics, Mr. Hickman in English, Mr. Walker in physics—who quickly realized that the boys were anything but 'dumb.' The rigorous and highly competitive school system in Taiwan, with its elaborate examination system, its emphasis on memorization and industriousness and the fact that it was tailored to the American system helped David and Phillip to overcome their difficulties with the language and to excel in virtually every subject they took. By the time David graduated he was the top student in math and took the top prize in science. It was to be a familiar story, as recognized in Phillip's later comment: 'someone had to be first and it was always David.'

Initially the boys had few friends, no doubt because, as David recalls, 'I was not very confident in the new environment.' Not surprisingly the first boys they got to know—Wilson Wu and Caden Wang—were, like themselves, 'Fresh off the Boat'. In due course, however, their social contacts grew alongside their academic confidence. David and Phillip met other boys with whom they would climb the high school's chain-link fence to the enclosed basketball court. They invited friends to their house to play ping-pong in the cemented back garden of

---

[54]   Sidney Ho, Memorial Speech, 15 November 2009

their home—a game that was all the rage after Zhuang Zhedong won the world championship for China. And, as Phillip recalls, he, David and Sidney shared many happy evenings with their parents. 'Father's idea of splurging was taking us out to the Friday night $2.99 steak dinner at Norm's for a steak dinner.' 'It took a while for the message to sink in but we learned,' Phillip continued, 'that the pleasure is found not in the flavor or ambience but in sharing communion with the family.'

When the family had arrived in America, Paul had just begun working for the Xerox Company—the third major position he had held since returning to California in 1960 but again, not a long-term appointment. Even after he completed his Bachelor of Science degree in electrical engineering at USC in 1968, he continued to move from one job to another, vulnerable to the fluctuating economic fortunes of the different firms for whom he worked as an engineer. After settling in with Scientific Data System in El Segundo City, it came as a notable setback when he found himself among the employees who were laid off. Phillip remembers his father being unemployed for the first time in 1968—'He had a hard time going to the unemployment line.' (Paul would not have collected his unemployment insurance if Sonia had not urged him to do so.) Yet he bounced back, resilient as ever. When the only job he could get entailed a lengthy commute—it took Paul four hours to drive back and forth to the Bendix Corporation—he put up with it until he was in a position to give his notice. Not until 1971 did his luck change, when he landed a position (with Bell and Howell Laboratory) which he was to hold for the next dozen years and which was to lead to recognition of his pioneering work in a new field—computers.

Meanwhile it is evident that Sonia's career was also crucial in securing the family's finances. It was fortunate that the Segal Company prospered during the late 1960s and early 1970s. Sonia worked well on the assembly line—though, as her third son Sidney protests on her behalf, 'for a low wage.' When her Japanese supervisor left to establish his own business, she took her place. Then, within a year, she became assistant manager reporting directly to the CEO. When the Segal Company needed to add more workers to their predominantly Asian and Mexican staff, they looked to Sonia Ho for help. She found them by advertising in Los Angeles' *Chinese Daily News*. 'I pick all the Chinese ladies to work,' she explains, 'they didn't have a job.' She also arranged to bring over some thirty women from Taiwan. Initially, she was supervising about seventy or eighty Asians. She also learnt a little Spanish so that she could communicate with the Mexican supervisor who oversaw a group of Mexican women. By the time

Mr. Segal handed over the company to his son-in-law, Jack Gordon, and it became Contemporary Creations, Sonia was responsible for over one hundred employees—including her three sons who worked in the shipping department during their summer vacations.

Within a very few years Sonia had reached an impressive position in the firm. She had been able to capitalize on her high status within Taiwanese society, with a born air of leadership, and transplant it onto American soil, exercising authority over fellow-immigrants who lacked her upbringing, education and initiative. Her language skills were thus put to good use within a predominantly Asian environment. Paul, by contrast, had to make his way within the White workplace where Asian professionals like himself—'Up-Town Chinese'—were still earning less than Whites with equivalent levels of education, and were still regularly bypassed for promotions and managerial positions.

What with the birth of Sidney in 1967, and the increasing contribution of Sonia's salary, a larger house became both necessary and affordable. It needed to be located in the same area of the city, near to the Thomas Starr King Junior High School and the John Marshall High School. The ideal solution was eventually found: a modest ivy-covered clapboard house at 2042 Sanborn Avenue, which nevertheless to this day gives a spacious feeling, partly because it is built on a slope, with a lovely view of the distant Hollywood hills. It was here that David and Phillip recalled picking up their young brother from Happy Land Nursery. It was also from here that Sidney later walked to and from Franklin Elementary on his own. 'The first thing I had to do when I returned from school,' he recalls, 'was to call her [Sonia] to say that I was home.' Even so, there was no doubt in Sidney's mind 'who the head of the household was, whom I had to answer to, and who laid down the law': it was his father.

By the time the family moved into this attractive house in the Franklin Hills in 1971, they had developed a social circle at the Evangelical Formosan Church, where Sonia and both boys were baptized. 'Without going to church,' Sonia comments, 'you would not have a community.' These were happy years for the family, as they warmly recall: Paul and Sonia look back on Sanborn as their favorite house, the boys look back on happy as well as successful schooldays. For within a few years of arriving in California, David and Phillip had already joined the 'model minority'—a term that would describe the next generation of Asians who took most of the year-end prizes at high school and university. Paul's great gamble in transplanting his family from Taiwan to California—so long contemplated against all odds—at last seemed set to pay off.

*   *   *

Though Paul had lived outside of Mainland China since 1947, and in America since 1957, he was still emotionally attached to the country of his birth. He relished meeting former classmates from school and university who, like himself, had settled in California. He also kept up with his former Taiwanese flat-mates. He attended lectures given by returning Chinese. He read Los Angeles' *Chinese Daily News*. He listened to China's Central Radio and Beijing People's Radio stations. He watched the news in Chinese on American-Chinese television, seizing hopefully on indications of America's growing closeness to China. True, as early as 1967, the former hard-liner Richard Nixon, with his eyes now set upon the White House, had written in *Foreign Affairs* that 'we simply cannot afford to leave China forever outside the family of nations.'[55]

Paul had never given up hope of resuming contact with his family in China. The fact that he had sent a letter from Taiwan to his brother Buxiu in 1956 shows as much, as does Paul's decision, after a further seven years of silence, to write again in 1963. This time he wrote from California, of course, revealing that he was now living in the United States—and disclosing for the first time that he had remarried and had two sons. Again there was no reply, no news of the Hejiacun family in the sixteen years since he had left them.

Paul Ho did not give up. He was crucially encouraged by the turn of international politics: by the détente in the Cold War once the Americans were talking about withdrawing from Vietnam and by the new policy towards China that President Nixon and his Secretary of State Henry Kissinger were tentatively developing. At the beginning of 1972, Paul was fully alert to the signals—'China-American relations have taken a turn for the better'—and on 2 February, just two weeks before Nixon made his historic visit to China, Paul wrote to his brother once again.

There was much to report. In 1963 David had been a ten-year-old at school in Taiwan; now he was a young man approaching eighteen, having secured entry to Massachusetts Institute of Technology in Boston. Phillip was following in his footsteps at High School. And there was now a third son, five year-old Sidney, about to enter primary school. Paul told of how his wife was 'busy all day, every day.' It was a chronicle of hard work reaping its just rewards in a

---

[55]   see: Mei-ling T. Wang, *The Dust that Never Settles* (New York: University Press of America, 2001) p. 151

land of opportunity; it was the American dream, Chinese-style, with plenty to look forward to—for Paul and Sonia Ho, settled in their Hollywood home, for David, Phillip and Sidney, with their feet on the ladder of academic and professional advancement.

The letter, however, had another aspect. Written to his brother Buxiu, Paul was seeking to remedy more than twenty years' ignorance of what had happened to his family. 'Are Tangxiang, Honglian and Xiangbao all married already?' Paul expressed his remorse: 'I have not used all my efforts to fulfill my responsibilities for their education and upbringing, and I feel very bad about this.' He sought to absolve his first wife, Gu, of any blame: 'If the person from the Gu family has remarried it was the right thing to do.' He naturally asked: 'Is mother still living?' And his final question was more poignant than he realized: 'Younger brother, how many children do you and your wife have now? If possible, can some one of you write back to me?'[56]

This time Paul's letter did not go unanswered. But the news that he received from China was not what he had expected to hear. It certainly filled some of the gaps in his knowledge, though largely in unwelcome ways. And, partly as a result, it took time before many of the personally and politically sensitive details were revealed. Indeed, not until our visits to the province of Jiangxi in 2007 and 2008 were we able to piece together the full story.

Not for the first time, the family's story is intimately—and tragically— intertwined with the modern history of China. Following Mao's ascendancy as leader of the People's Republic of China in 1949, the next three years saw over one hundred million acres of land confiscated from farms belonging to wealthy farmers and landlords like the He family. With the aim of putting the peasant on an equal footing with the landlord, land was re-distributed on a per capita basis. Sometimes this process, known as the Land Reform, was instigated by party-led cadres who, during their visit to a village, would not only investigate landownership but also take the opportunity to spread their own propaganda about the inequity of its distribution. At other times members of a village took it upon themselves to break up the large agricultural holdings.

There was much settling of old scores during the process. Landlords and previous high-ranking officials living in Jiangxi were singled out for revenge. This was, after all, where Mao and his nascent army had been forced to leave their refuge in the southern area of the province and commence their Long

---

[56]   Paul Ho to He Buxiu, 2 February 1972, in possession of He Tangxiang.

March to western China. It was also where, in 1941, the Communist Party's organizational apparatus had been completely destroyed by Chiang Kai-shek's Republican Army.

With Mao now in power, the land was re-distributed. The result was 'grim and startling,' as a British journalist of liberal inclinations, James Cameron, noted on his tour through China in 1950-1951. 'The drumhead courts in the village squares, the desperate ad-hoc tribunals with denunciation taking the place of evidence and the piled-up hate and bitterness of years overflowing' could only be assuaged, Cameron reported, 'by the sight of the kneeling landlords and the crisp smell of gunpowder.'[57]

It was at some point during 1950 that Paul's high-born family came in for this sort of treatment. Dispossession was not the worst of it. Paul's brother, Buxiu, was not only forcibly evicted from the ancestral home by officials from the prefecture of Xiacun but then thrown into jail. A few days after his incarceration news reached Hejiacun that He Buxiu was dead. He had been brutally executed.

Buxiu's death at the age of twenty-eight was a tragedy for the entire He family. Fu had now lost two of her sons—one exiled, one dead—and, with them, her own security. Zhilan had lost her brother. Furthermore, Honglian, Tangxiang, Xiangbao and their mother Gu, who were already under suspicion because their father, Buji, was living in Taiwan, now had an uncle and brother-in-law who had been executed as a criminal.

With Buxiu's death, the only 'adult' male left in the He family compound was Buji's eleven-year-old son, Tangxiang. In reconstructing the reasons for Buxiu's arrest and murder with various members of the family on my visits to China, I found Tangxiang's testimony impressive in its insight and lack of rancor. Though deeply moved in recollecting these painful experiences, he also displays detachment in making sense of the story, and resists any temptation to blame his father's absence for the tribulations of the family. Nevertheless he still weeps as he graphically recalls how his uncle was arrested, dragged before the whole village, taken away and shot.

It emerges that Buxiu, who had known for days that he was in danger, might have escaped. And even after his arrest, he might have been saved if county officials had been notified and their support enlisted. But there was no telephone in Hejiacun. Moreover, even if Buxiu could have left the village before

---

[57]   James Cameron, *Mandarin Red* (London: Michael Joseph, 1955) p. 168

his arrest, Tangxiang is certain that he would never have done so. Following the death of his first wife, Hu, he had recently remarried. His new wife, Xie, had a child—Mingwu—on the way. Buxiu not only felt responsible for her. There were two children from his first marriage to care for, as well as his own mother, Fu; and there was also the wife and three children of his fugitive brother, Buji.

Buxiu's chances of lying low and surviving by keeping his head down were suddenly scuppered by random events in the neighborhood. A vigilante group had kidnapped a Communist Party official and were hiding him in the hills above Songlin. Tensions were high. The district officials were under pressure to find the culprit. Unfortunately the man they chose to arrest was innocent.

Yet it was no coincidence that Buxiu became the village's scapegoat. There was only one adult male living on the He family compound so, as Tangxiang puts it, 'we were considered weak.' Moreover, he ruefully cites his family's reputation for being honest and kind: 'We never used our fists but kept to ourselves because we wanted to stay out of trouble. So even though we were the most wealthy family in the village, it was still possible for people to beat us up.'

Following Buxiu's murder the family were thrown out of their ancestral home. They were given a new label—'bad class background' or 'unclean class origins'. And with it they were given a new place to live—a pigsty. 'We cleaned out the manure,' Tangxiang recalls, 'we waited for the mud floor to dry, then we moved in.' This unsightly and unwholesome dwelling was to remain the family's home for the next twenty-five years. They lost all of their belongings—with the notable exception of the family genealogy, which they took care to hide.

Just a schoolboy in 1950, Tangxiang suddenly found himself not only the head of the family but the sole breadwinner of his extended family. 'I had never worked on a farm so I did not have any tools,' he explains in a matter-of-fact way, avoiding pathos. A former tenant on the He family farm who belonged to the mutual aid team took pity on the boy. He taught him how to plant rice and to hoe a field—all on land that had once belonged to Tangxiang's immediate family. Tangxiang learned quickly. His compact physique became powerful, giving him a strength well beyond his years. Eventually he acquired his own tools. A prize item was a plough, but since there was no draft animal available, it was Tangxiang himself who pulled it through the red earth.

Tangxiang's mother and his grandmother added to his modest earnings by taking in sewing. Even so, things went from bad to worse. In the early 1950s the He family, along with almost everyone else who lived on the land in China, found themselves starving. This was not because there was an absolute shortage of food. It was because the food that was not consumed by people living in the cities was exported. Mao did this in the hope of making China into a superpower and an industrial, rather than an agrarian base. Needless to say his plan failed.

The resulting famine was, Tangxiang recalls, 'a disaster for the whole family.' His mother and grandmother had to beg for their clothing—and sometimes for their food. The family was reduced to eating sweet potato leaves, tree bark and wild grass. 'I don't know how we got through the five or six years,' Tangxiang told me as he rapidly shook his head from side to side as if wiping out the memory of those years.

In this desperate situation, with too many mouths to feed, Paul's first family had been broken up. His former wife, Gu, moved out in 1955. She went to a nearby village where she married a former tenant farmer who had worked on the family's farm and in the following year gave birth to the first of three children. While the second marriage protected Gu from the ridicule and gossip to which many 'single' women were subjected in new as in old China, Tangxiang claims that his mother had not only been forced into the marriage, but that her new husband beat her. Also in 1955, Gu's sixteen-year-old daughter, Honglian, left home. She willingly married the high school teacher, Li Wutang, with whom she had seven children. Tangxiang and his wife Chang Jin Xiang, whom he married in 1962, along with his younger sister Xiangbao, remained in the pigsty with their grandmother, Fu, and Buxiu's widow and her three orphaned children.

It was in this deliberately degrading habitation that the small but stocky Tangxiang had received his father's 1963 letter. Though he told me that he had been 'relieved to know that father was alive and well,' any attempt to reply to his father's letter had been out of the question. 'The kids were scared to get it,' as Paul later came to appreciate and acknowledged, 'so they burn it.' While his letter had reassured the remnant of his family that he was alive, it brought them little help. Instead, the news that he was now living in the United States, which it revealed to the district officials, was to reactivate suspicion against the family in the following years.

Their troubles again came to a head after Mao launched the Cultural Revolution in 1966, in order to regain power in the wake of the disastrous Great Leap Forward that saw thirty million Chinese starve to death. Mao's call 'to sweep away the four olds'—old culture, old habits, old customs and old ideas—saw youthful Red Guards ransacking homes and destroying anything they considered to be remnants of the former landlord class.

Initially this did not impinge upon the lives of Tangxiang and his family. On the contrary, it seemed for the moment that Tangxiang was recognized as a model worker—rather in the way that his half-brothers, David, Phillip and Sidney, would become "model-minority" Americans.

After the founding of the commune system in 1959, all farms were amalgamated into this structure. Below the level of the commune came that of the production brigade, usually linked to a particular village, and an even smaller unit called the production team. Tangxiang overcame the handicap of having a 'bad class background' through sheer effort. 'I can tolerate and endure a lot of hardship,'—or "eating bitter" as the Chinese put it. Indeed, one experience that united the whole family throughout the years, whether in China, Taiwan or the United States, was a resilient capacity for "eating bitter."

'I am always the best and the fastest,'Tangxiang told me. While most workers planted one acre of rice a day, on a good day Tangxiang planted three. At the year-end assessment meetings, when every aspect of an individual's work was discussed and the production teams were regrouped, everyone fought to have Tangxiang on their production team. 'I was top out of 117 laborers,' he proudly told me. Within a few years, Tangxiang became the note-taker for the village's eight production teams. This entailed keeping a daily record of every worker's output. And, after teaching himself how to do calculations on the abacus, he was put in charge of the Hejiacun Production Brigade's accounts: 'all of the money in and out.'

Tangxiang had clearly inherited his father's sense of confidence along with his industriousness and intelligence. But these attributes did little to protect him when several Red Guard members in his own village—all of them distant relatives, as one would expect in Hejiacun—demonstrated that 'even among dragons there are nine varieties.' And, as the proverb quoted in *The Dream of the Red Chamber* continues: 'it is easy to realize that there are snakes and vipers creeping around among the dragons of the family school, and that high and low were mixed together.'[58]

When I interviewed Tangxiang on my first visit to China, he would not elaborate on what had happened to him during the Cultural Revolution, saying only that he had had a bad time. Only when I returned to China a year later did I realize what an understatement this had been, as he now told me more of the sad story. During the 'Cleansing of the Class Ranks Campaign' in the late 1960s, Tangxiang was denounced several times at 'struggle meetings.' On at least two

---

[58]   Hung Lou Meng, *The Dream of the Red Chamber* (Westport Connecticut: Greenwood Press, 1958, originally published 1791) p. 65

occasions he was 'crowned' with a dunce hat, then paraded around the village. 'The Red Guards who made these charges,' Tangxiang recalled, 'were people I knew in the village who belonged to the extended family.' These were the people who 'accused me of having a father living overseas.' They demanded that Tangxiang write self-criticism essays confessing to his "sins". On one occasion Tangxiang was 'very badly beaten.' Unable to get proper medical attention for his cuts and bruises, he resorted to an old cure: in keeping with the old proverb—'Bitter medicine cures illnesses'—Tangxiang drank his own urine.

When Tangxiang recalls these horrific events today he does not blame his father. Nor does he later take revenge on the 'snakes and vipers' in Hejiacun who humiliated and beat him. Even though Mao had done his best to break down the family and to eradicate ancestor worship and filial piety, Tangxiang never forgot who his father was and who his ancestors had been.

One irony is that Paul Ho's long-desired residence in the United States, so propitious in its effects on his second family, should have proved equally unpropitious for the less fortunate members of his first family. But though his second letter, in 1963, had quite inadvertently inflicted this perverse effect upon them, his instinct to write for a third time was vindicated. In the different political climate of 1972, Tangxiang was very pleased to receive a letter from his father. Even better, he was able at last to respond. It was to open the door, in due course, to direct contact—and also mutual assistance—between the two branches of the family.

David and Phillip at Houli

David and Phillip, Taiwan

Paul, David and Phillip,
Sanborn Avenue, Los Angeles

CHAPTER 6

'Man does but Heaven sees'

人在做 天在看

It is lucky that Paul and Sonia Ho both cherish such vivid memories of their lives and their families, lucky too that they have been willing to confide their recollections so freely to their biographer. For I realized from the start that I would have to depend largely upon them in the absence of written materials that had not survived the uprooting of their families across two continents. I had accordingly been delighted to discover that the family in Songlin, though reduced to living in a pigsty, had safeguarded a copy of their genealogy throughout their time of persecution. This document certainly proved its worth. But it was a formal record; it did not capture voices across the years.

Not that voices were lacking or silent, as I immediately discovered at the Xinyu guesthouse, during my initial chaotic meeting with Paul's first family in the spring of 2007. It was late in the evening of Paul's eighty-eighth birthday, after a convivial dinner to which everyone had been invited. Phones were ringing and everyone seemed to be speaking at the same time, making translation particularly difficult. The piercing voice of Paul's short, trim and well turned-out youngest daughter, Xiangbao, soared above every other voice. Proud to be the eldest male child, Tangxiang was clearly been pleased to be there and was continually bobbing up and down as he called out, 'I know more than my father! I know more than my father!' It was a sobering moment when Paul's nephew Ming Wu who was born in April

1951 responded: 'I never met *my* father, he was murdered while I was in my mother's womb.'

Once Tangxiang got going he could not be stopped. He talked to me that night; he talked to me the following day, even during our visit to his father's primary school where we were mobbed by dozens of children all wanting to shake our hands, eagerly proffered for reasons that they would perhaps have had difficulty in explaining. He talked as we walked along the high bank of Yuan River and admired the crudely sculpted heads of Confucius, Mencius and the founder of Taoism, Lancious; and he talked as our small party viewed the delicate water color paintings and dry-brush drawings of Fu Baoshi at the museum dedicated to the artist's life and work.

Tangxiang not only talked, revealing things that he had thought about over the last fifty years but had little opportunity to discuss. He also put pen to paper, in the manner of the self-examination or self-criticism essays that were an unpleasant feature of Mao's China. In doing so Tangxiang revealed, as he had promised, that he indeed knew things that his father did not know. Prompted by our discussions, eager to help us further, he then provided the answer to a biographer's prayer when he showed up one morning with a large plastic bag in his hand.

Wrapped among the brittle pages of a canary-yellow newspaper were thirty-odd letters that Paul Ho had written to his family between 2 February 1972 and 7 July 1983. At this time—certainly until the late 1970s—few families in China had been allowed to use the mail, let alone to receive correspondence from the outside world. But finding these documents was a great coup for a more personal reason. Until then I had nothing written by Paul himself in past decades, nothing that captured his command of his native language. Justifiably proud of his spoken English, Paul always resisted allowing me to speak to him through a Chinese-speaking interpreter; and I relished his grasp of demotic American-English, at once graphic, lively and to the point. But I wanted to 'hear' his Chinese voice, and this now became possible, once we had photocopied the letters on an antiquated machine and brought them home for expert translation.

I was hardly surprised later by the appraisal I was given of their style and composition. It was fully in keeping with Paul's earlier reputation as an accomplished calligrapher: that his characters were confirmed to be well formed—'executed with ease and fluency'—or that his use of language read like that of an educated Chinese scholar of his generation. Moreover, as I had suspected, the overall tone of his letters was judged 'typical of a Chinese father talking to his son, with authority as a teacher or instructor.'[59] I felt that I had now come as close as a non-Chinese speaking person (with only a smattering of the language) could get to appreciating how Paul Ho thought and wrote during these critical years. And I was hopeful that quotation of the English translations would be able to convey the distinctive voice in which Paul expressed himself in Chinese.

Paul's first letter home in February 1972, of course, like those sent in 1956 and 1963, is addressed to his deceased brother. 'These many years I have been roaming abroad and had not written to you,' he tells Buxiu, which is perhaps a polite way of ignoring the lack of response to the previous letters. 'I beg you to forgive me. In fact, I have never for a moment forgotten the motherland, the old home and you.'[60] By the time he writes again, in the following month—evidently in response to news from his son Tangxiang—Paul is a sadder and wiser man: he now realizes that his brother has been dead for more than twenty years; that the family home is now occupied by someone else; and that his children have been forced to abandon their schooling in order to work on the land.

It is Tangxiang who thus sustains a correspondence that stretches over the next eleven years. It captures Paul's initial responses as the curtain of ignorance about his family is at last lifted. 'I was so happy to see my mother's photograph that I wept,' he writes. He quickly learns that Tangxiang, Honglian and Xiangbao have children of their own—'I find it hard to believe that I already have ten grandchildren. I do not feel old at all. You see I still have a five year old son.'[61] Paul readily assumes the role of grandfather as well as that of father, brother and son. The letters also show Paul not content to wallow in the guilt that he undoubtedly feels, instead responding with his customary resilience to a predicament of which he tries to get the full measure through persistent inquiries and practical suggestions.

Once he grasps that his middle-aged sister, Zhilan, is going blind and that his mother is ailing, he looks for remedies. Paul asks Tangxiang to let him know 'the

[59] Bill Liu to Maria Tippett, 1 September 2008. All letters quoted below translated by Diana Lary; the original translations were refined and revised by the Chinese translator and scholar, William Liu.
[60] Paul Ho to He Buxiu, 2 February 1972.
[61] Paul Ho to He Tangxiang, March.

degree of myopia' of his sister, Zhilan so that he can send her a pair of glasses.[62] 'You are the older brother,' Paul reminds him on another occasion, 'you must look out for her.'[63] Paul is equally full of confident advice to his daughters. 'In your spare time,' he lectures Honglian, now the mother of seven children, 'you must spend more time reading and writing.' And he likewise tells Xiangbao, after learning that her first husband is dead: 'The sensible thing to do would be to marry again; it is very difficult to bring up children on one's own.'[64] Her own reply does not survive, but we can tell that a letter from her reached Los Angeles from the prompt comment of her father, the inveterate schoolteacher: 'Xiangbao's letter is written very well; the characters are good, and the phrases are good.'[65]

Paul's continual worry about the welfare of his ailing mother naturally takes priority. Learning that Fu has recurrent bouts of bronchitis, Paul urges Tangxiang to ensure that *Popo* [grandmother] receives proper attention.

> The cold does not go away, you cannot stop coughing. As a result it gets worse and worse. Ways of alleviation: (1) Wear one more padded coat; (2) every morning and every evening soak your feet in hot water, especially important in the evening; (3) we sent twenty *Xiaoyan* [anti-inflamatory] pills. Every day after breakfast swallow one pill, it can stop the throat infection. After it has stopped, immediately stop taking it. It will only work 24 hours after you first take it. Generally within three days (six pills) the coughing will stop. If it works, write and tell me, and we will buy some more.[66]

Similar advice, in his role as long-distance medical adviser, intersperses the letters throughout. His mother's health is a continual concern to him, his fear that he will never again see her alive an unspoken sub-text to many of the greetings he sends. 'Please tell Popo, the old person, to pass the days calmly, health is number one.'[67]

---

[62] Paul Ho to [addressee missing] 5 May 1973
[63] Paul Ho to He Tangxiang, 18 July 1973
[64] Paul Ho to He Tangxiang, Yusheng, Honglian, Xuangbao, Jinlian, 12 June 1973
[65] Paul Ho to He Tangxiang, 6 October 1973
[66] Paul Ho [addressee missing] 6 Novemeber 1973.
[67] Paul Ho to He Tangxiang 18 July 1973

Now all too aware that the family no longer occupies the ancestral home, Paul encourages Tangxiang to build a new one. Furthermore, himself taking on the role of the traditional geomancer who divined the significance of the *feng-shui*, Paul advises exactly where to put it. 'As for the site of the house, the level ground in front of the north gate is higher and drier,' he writes, as though he had never left the village that he once knew so well. 'But to the east are fields, and in the fields is water, and they may be damp. What about the place where we used to have two haystacks? It is also dry, beside the two big trees?' He not only retains an accurate visual memory of Hejiacun, and brings a keen sense of economy to bear, but shows that his sense of *feng-shui* is unimpaired. 'The new type of houses should have cellars as they are warm in the winter and cool in the summer and could save money. The kitchen should be separated by a wall, to ensure the coolness of the living room and the bedrooms,' he stipulates. 'In the courtyard there should be space for flowers, which are pretty to look at and may contribute to a person's health.'[68]

All well and good; but, as Paul now renewed these links and belatedly discovered the plight of his relatives, where was the money to come from to execute his long-range plans? If he were to dispense more tangible assistance than simple advice to his family in Hejiacun, there would be an obvious impact upon his family in Los Angeles. In particular, what did Sonia think? Indeed, what did Sonia know?

* * *

In 1971 Paul had secured a position with a leading supplier of media technologies, Bell and Howell, at 11255 West Olympic Boulevard, Los Angeles. This was the address he used in his surviving letters to Songlin of February and March 1972. The replies that he received from Tangxiang were thus sent to Paul at his workplace, and initially he said nothing about them at home.

Acknowledging the fact that he had another family was never going to be easy. And why should he have taken the risk of alienating his second wife of twenty years, the mother of three young sons at an impressionable age, all of whose reactions would be totally unpredictable? There is no doubt that Paul himself carried a burden of guilt. He did not pretend to himself that his responsibilities to his first family in Jiangxi had neatly terminated with his own

[68] Paul Ho to He Tangxiang, 5 June 1974

departure, as his cravings for news of them sufficiently show. Unburdening himself to Sonia sooner would have released some of the emotional strain, if only by freeing him to acknowledge his own past before he had arrived in Taiwan—a story which he had never been able to recount except by editing out any stray, telltale allusion to an earlier marriage, still less to the birth of three earlier children. For a man who enjoyed anecdotes and was proud of his family lineage, the need to be watchful of any indiscretion was an inhibition that he had lived with every day throughout the long years during which he had alone nursed his unmentionable secrets.

This was hardly a unique predicament. Maintaining silence on such matters was by no means unusual among Chinese immigrants in that era. In Amy Tan's novel *The Bonesetter's Daughter*, it is a female character, Gaoling, who explains to her niece (herself the product of an irregular union) that her husband had been kept in ignorance of her first marriage: 'How could I tell him that I was still married? Your uncle would then question if we are really married, if I am a bigamist, if our children are—well, like your mother.' Gaoling felt that 'it was too late to go back and explain what should be forgotten anyway.'[69]

Paul Ho had long found himself in a comparable position but suddenly faced a dilemma. For over twenty years he had concealed his first marriage from his second wife—his only wife in the eyes of American law, which recognized the legitimate status of her three children. If he had twice before been prompted to try and contact his family in Songlin, that was likewise a matter that he did not need to reveal to Sonia at the time, for nothing had resulted. As long as he could postpone a crucially awkward decision, he did so. Twice, inaction prevailed; but the third time, a crisis could no longer be averted. What changed the situation in 1972 was the two-way correspondence that now ensued, generating its own momentum, creating expectations in Jiangxi that provoked revelations in Los Angeles.

When I spoke to Sonia about this delicate matter—it was a warm March morning in 2008 at Sun Moon Lake in Taiwan—she told me her side of the story. At some point Paul inadvertently brought some correspondence from Tangxiang to Sanborn Avenue. During the course of looking for something else, Sonia discovered the letters. From that moment on, there was no doubt in Sonia's mind that her husband had another wife and another three children

---

[69] Amy Tan, *The Bonesetter's Daughter* (London: Harper Perennial, 2004, first published 2001) p. 217

in China—and that, rather like her mother Lou, she was wife number two. The impact was emotionally devastating. 'Nine out of ten women would have divorced him,' Sonia told me, 'but I had three boys, they needed a father, like I did myself.'

Steeling herself to self-discipline, Sonia did not immediately reveal her discovery to Paul. 'He think I didn't know', she told me, her thoughts focused on her own children. 'When I found the letters I didn't tell my kids.' For this was a further barrier to simply disclosing the full situation. She could not know what David at twenty, or Phillip at eighteen, would make of it, still less how the infant Sidney could handle puzzling information which she imagined might provoke tantrums. Like Paul himself, Sonia too opted for only so much disclosure as seemed necessary in the circumstances. Again, there are literary parallels. Wayson Choy writes in his novel *All That Matters*: 'Doors and windows were shut on the past and should never be opened.'[70]

Had Sonia learned about her husband's first family while still living in Taiwan, would it have been less of a blow? After all, most of Sonia's aunts shared a husband with another woman. Her cousin, Lu Ching Shuang, had married a Mainlander who had left a family in China. But all that had been in Taiwan. Sonia was now living in North America, where having more than one wife was not only unacceptable, it was illegal. Here she was without the support of her deceased mother, her aunts, her favorite cousin I-wen and her best friend Lin Li Tai; though perhaps it was some consolation that she had avoided losing face in front of her family and friends—let alone her formidable grandmother, Lin Pen, who had long ago suspected her granddaughter's husband of having a wife and family in the first place.

Paul and Sonia could not have gone on for very long without clearing the air between themselves about the letters and what they revealed. Sonia could not possibly have discovered any replies from Hejiacun earlier than March 1972, and within three or at most four months Paul's side of the correspondence (which is all that survives) is very differently framed. It is surely significant that, by the time Paul wrote (probably for the fifth time) on 23 June 1972, he referred to a new possibility. 'On the matter of returning to the motherland to see the family,

---

[70] Wayson Choy, *All that Matters* (Toronto: Anchor, 2005 first published in 2004) p. 116

I want to set a provisional date,' he told Tangxiang. 'I know that my mother misses me very much and wants to see me.'[71]

Crucially, Paul now gave his home address, 2042 Sanborn Avenue, and told Tangxiang to use it in reply. Once the possibility of returning to China had been raised, Paul must have realized that Sonia had to be told. After all, she might well want to accompany her husband to China and to meet his much-talked-about mother Fu. And what then? What would happen if they arrived in Hejiacun and Paul's first three children—and possibly even the former wife, Gu—were there to greet them? Paul's ordeal in making his confession to Sonia—so long evaded, so long dreaded—was obviously eased in the outcome by the fact that she was already prepared for the information that he belatedly imparted. The crisis in their marriage was surmounted with a stoicism on Sonia's part for which Paul had reason to be lastingly thankful.

There is a gap of almost a year in the surviving correspondence (nothing between June 1972 and May 1973). But from the summer of 1973, with plans for a visit to China maturing, Sonia's name was added to the letters' closing salutation: from Father Buji and Mother Shuang-ru. Moreover, not only was Sonia brought into the picture but, having accepted the situation, she became characteristically active in making positive proposals. 'When Mother saw the photographs of Xiangbao and Honglian she was moved,' Paul told them. 'She wants me to bring Xiangbao to America, but under the present circumstances that is still impossible.' But they did now promise to send up to twenty dollars a month—again a matter on which Paul could hardly have acted without Sonia's support. 'Everyone here is very concerned about Popo,' Paul wrote in conclusion. 'Little Chunyi (Sidney) talks about his grandmother every day, and asks the old person to pass the days calmly, and look after her health.'[72]

There is a certain amount of ventriloquism in such remarks. The suggestion is nonetheless clear that little Sidney had been told about his grandmother. Why not? It was no doubt an innocent surprise for a six-year-old boy to discover the existence of his only surviving grandparent, living in faraway China. And obviously David and Philip had also been told about Popo, though not, it seems, about the old lady's full roster of descendants. If the existence of one elder half-brother and two half-sisters was not at this stage revealed to the boys,

---

[71]   Paul Ho to Tangxiang, 23 June 1972.
[72]   Paul Ho to his first family, 12 June 1973.

their own academic progress was proudly reported back to Songlin. Thus in September 1973:

> Oldest Younger Brother (Dayi) will graduate next year from Cal. Tech. He is now 20. After four years at medical school he will then be a real doctor. Second Younger Brother (Hongyi) is now 18. He is studying at California State University [UCLA]. Next term he will be in the second year of university. Third Younger Brother (Chunyi) is now 6. Next term he will enter the first grade of primary school. Their grades are all astonishingly high, and they follow Chairman Mao's thought very closely.[73]

More ventriloquism, of course, is evident in the last comment, which should hardly be taken literally. What needs to be remembered in reading any of these letters is that Paul wrote with other readers in mind, apart from his family. He was aware from the start that his letters would inevitably be scrutinized by the party officials living in his native province. In his very first letter Paul wrote: 'When I see and hear the scale of China's progress, it made me so very happy that I was brought to tears.'[74] And Nixon's visit to China was duly hailed as 'the crystallization and proof of the strength of Chairman Mao and the Chinese Communist Party.'[75] As soon as he received replies from Tangxiang (which have not survived), Paul knew what tone was appropriate, and thus what to say himself:

> In the next letter you and your siblings wrote together you have confirmed to me the circumstances of the progress made by the Motherland. For example before Liberation our home was a backward village, poor, suffering, the people worked but without the slightest hope. Now under the leadership of the Communist Party, there is a dam, a railway, a highway, electric lighting, a clinic, an old people's home. People like me living away want to thank

---

[73] Paul Ho to He Tangxiang, 3 September 1973.
[74] Paul Ho to He Tangxiang, 17 February 1972
[75] Paul Ho (fragment), 9 March 1972.

the thought and the energy of Chairman Mao and the Chinese Communist Party.[76]

The fact that Paul incorporated such utterances in ostensibly private letters to his family demonstrates only that he, like them, knew the game that had to be played if he were ever to return for a visit to Xinyu. By May 1973 he was also writing directly to the Xinyu County Revolutionary Committee, copied to the Commerce Department, copied to the local Xinyuxian commune—and prudently copied also to his own children. It was the familiar sort of encomium— 'Our whole family often learn about the progress and the strengthening of the Motherland under the leadership of Chairman Mao and the Communist Party from newspapers and films, and our delight is difficult to describe'—designed at once to please the party officials and to reassure his vulnerable family that contact with him would not add to their troubles.[77]

It is natural, then, that Tangxiang played the same faux-patriotic game as Paul on the other side of the correspondence. For example, in spring of 1975, when he viewed a photograph of Phillip and David sporting the (slightly) longer hair of the 'American teenager style' and wearing casual clothes—a significant contrast to an earlier photograph of the short-haired boys dressed in dark suits—Tangxiang expressed his disapproval. Not missing a hit in this verbal game of ping-pong, Paul assured his eldest son that 'Mother and I are also uncomfortable with them.'[78]

No one was spared during the Cultural Revolution. Even the revered Madame Sun Yat-sen confided to a friend in 1972 that 'One must be always on the alert since there are persons who consider it their *duty* to report every little happening.'[79] The Xinyu County Revolutionary Committee screened every letter to and from Paul Ho. When they found something that they did not like, they literally cut it out of the letter. Sometimes Tangxiang received complete letters; at other times mere fragments. The Committee not only vetted both sides of the correspondence; they wrote directly to Paul. They evidently told him how

---

[76]   Paul Ho to He Tangxiang, 23 June 1972.
[77]   Paul Ho, copy in letter of 5 May 1973,
[78]   Paul Ho to He Tangxiang, 13 March 1975
[79]   Churchill College Archives, Cambridge University, SEYR 3/3, Madame Sun Yat-sen to Lady Seymour, 10 May 1972.

the county of Xinyu now had twenty or thirty large and small factories.[80] And they boasted about similar developments throughout the mother country as well as in Hejiacun itself. Mindful that it was important to toe the party line if the family line of communication was to be kept open, Paul became a master at mimicking what was being fed to him by the Committee, and likewise what he heard when he tuned in to the China-based radio stations. Thus in one letter of early 1974, he dwelt on the current recession in the USA and other western countries, in contrast to China's plenty; and, in a reference to the Russians, with whom the Chinese had fallen out in the late 1960s, commented that 'these are all proofs that the "big noses" are really awful.'[81] Adept at echoing the rhetoric of the Revolutionary Committee, Tangxiang continued to emphasize the economic prosperity of Hejiacun village.

Paul, however, realized that the family needed tangible assistance, and Sonia supported him in giving it. He sent his grand-daughter Xilan an English language textbook. He posted several watches to Tangxiang; for although they only cost ten dollars each, they were highly valued in a society where one observer found only thirty-six watches among 3,610 people in one of Jiangxi's work brigades.[82] When it became possible for Paul to send money to China, he dipped into his pocket. Initially the amounts were small: five dollars for his mother Fu and for each of his children; fifteen dollars for minor repairs to the pigsty; fifty dollars to help Tangxiang pay back the money he had borrowed from his aunt ten years previously to cover the costs of his marriage to Zhang Jinxiang.

In July 1973, a bigger responsibility loomed: to make the customary contingency plans about Popo. She was, of course, grandmother not only of Tangxiang, and of his three American-based half-brothers, but also of their two cousins (or 'brothers' in Chinese parlance), the sons of the Paul's murdered brother, Buxiu.

> In your last letter [Paul responded] you talked about planning to go
> to Jiulongshan next month to buy fir planks, and when you come
> back to use them to make a coffin for her. According to ritual, this

---

[80]   Paul Ho to He Tangxiang 23 December 1973

[81]   Paul Ho to He Tangxiang, Dixiang and Yousheng, 18 January 1974.

[82]   Mobo C.f. Gao Gao *Village, A Portrait of Rural Life in Modern China* (London: Hurst & Company, 1999) p. 68

is my business, and I should give the money and make the effort. Now that you and your brothers are planning to make the effort, I don't know how to thank you. I have already sent $100, and I think that within a few days of your receiving this letter, the bank in Xiacun will inform you that you can get the money. If that is not enough, please write and tell me because this is the least of my duties as a son.[83]

*   *   *

Paul's concern for his mother was by this time injecting new urgency into the plans for an early return visit. In September 1973 he wrote again:

In your letter I learnt that Mother suffered a serious attack of bronchitis in July, and had to be in bed for over a week. As a result Aunt, Honglian, Xiangbao, Xilian and others all came back to look after the old person. Only I, so far away in a foreign land, did not return to care for her. This makes me very sad. Please tell Popo to look after her health from now on, to pass the days calmly. Next year I will definitely come back to the motherland to visit her . . . The commune is preparing to help us to resolve the question of Popo's coffin—when we heard this it made me weep with gratitude. I do not know how to repay their kindness.[84]

Paul's initial promise to return to China for the Spring Festival in 1974 could not be honored. He cited problems in taking special leave since both he and Sonia had exhausted their normal entitlement. But this was not the whole story.

It was, of course, not unusual for Chinese sojourners to want to return to the village of their birth. The traditional belief was that people should remain loyal to their native place, even after generations of separation. Nor was it unusual for returnees to contribute to the wellbeing of their immediate relatives as well as to their village. When the Australian-based Mobo C.F. Gao returned to Jiangxi

---

[83]   Paul Ho to He Tangxiang, 18 July 1973
[84]   Paul Ho to He Tangxiang, 3 September 1973.

Province in the late 1970s, so he recalled, 'the village and local government officials either explicitly or implicitly asked me to donate money for setting up a school and for some irrigation projects.'[85]

Nonetheless, Paul was finding it difficult to obtain the necessary documents to enter China. The State Department was not the problem. Although Washington had in 1952 restricted travel to China, by 1972 virtually any American citizen was permitted to go. Paul had been optimistic about receiving the necessary documents from the Chinese side because at the Tenth CCP Congress in August 1973, Chou Enlai had demonstrated increased confidence over his country's rapprochement with America. True, in the years before Mao's death in 1976, during the ascendancy of his heir Den Xiaoping, a number of free market reforms known as Gaige Kaifang or 'Reform and Opening' would make travel to China easier. But diplomatic relations—and hence ease of travel—between the two countries would not be formalized until the winter of 1978. Thus Paul's initial request, in February 1974, for the 'Introduction for Return to Native Village' document from the Chinese liaison office in Washington proved only the beginning of a long process; and he reported in the summer of 1974 that his efforts had still yielded no results.[86]

This did not lessen the financial subventions to Songlin that Paul pledged— quite the reverse. In December 1973 he had adroitly combined a paean of praise to the leadership of Chairman Mao and the Chinese Communist Party with advice on how to go about building a new house—after discussion with the local party comrades. And he added: 'if you need money, I can take care of it.'[87]

The project progressed during 1974, with Paul's intimate participation and Sonia's general approval. But it is quite likely that this commitment served to defer their own travel. 'Mother and I will slowly think this over and make a plan,' Paul wrote in June. 'Because we are still not clear what the costs of going back to China will be.' Indeed they explained their financial position in some detail to Tangxiang (and no doubt for the benefit of party officials who might entertain inflated ideas about their capacity as donors). Their total net income, he explained, was $15,000, after paying annual taxes of around $10,000.

---

[85]   Mobo C.f. Gao, *Gao Village, A Portrait of Rural Life in Modern China* (London: Hurst & Company, 1999) p. 249

[86]   Paul Ho to He Tangxiang 18 July 1974; Paul's application letter of 12 February 1974 survives.

[87]   Paul Ho [addressee missing] 23 December 1973.

The Ho family was thus far from wealthy, given their commitments. They currently had two sons at university. Having earned a Bachelor of Science degree in physics from the California Institute of Technology in 1974, David was about to embark on a medical degree at the Harvard-MIT Division of Health Sciences and Technology in Boston. 'He will have to take some money with him, and we have to buy the plane ticket,' Paul told Tangxiang; and added: 'Mother says wait until Oldest Younger Brother graduates and becomes a doctor, then we will be much more comfortable.'[88] Phillip was now attending the Los Angeles campus of the University of California (UCLA) closer to home. Like David, Phillip completed his advanced training with the help of scholarships; but he still needed help. Moreover, Paul and Sonia had not yet paid off the mortgage on their Sanborn Avenue home, so the account they gave of their rather stretched finances rings true.

Nevertheless, in July 1974, Paul sent Tangxiang five hundred dollars to begin constructing the much-needed home for the extended family in Songlin. This was a substantial sum, considering that the average annual income in China was well under five hundred dollars a year. It was at once an immediate practical help, a token of their good faith and a hint to the commune of further support to come.

Paul played every card in his hand in paving the way for a visit, sooner or (as it now seemed) somewhat later. He knew, of course, that in his youth it was not uncommon for western sojourners—like Chen Yixi, who had brought not only his fortune but also technical expertise back to his native province of Guangdong—to be hailed as local heroes.[89] And Paul knew too that the PRC had no compunction in reclaiming internationally famous sojourner-scientists like the Nobel Prize laureate Zhenning (Frank) Yang.

As the momentum of the Cultural Revolution slowly diminished in the 1970s, it seemed that everyone, from leading government officials in Beijing to inhabitants of China's most remote villages, was as hungry for international recognition as for financial contributions and technical information. Just as Paul Ho was obviously no millionaire, so he was plainly not an internationally renowned scientist. But the Xinyu County Revolutionary Committee knew that he was an electrical engineer who had told his son: 'I will make all my

<hr>

88 Paul Ho to He Tangxiang 5 June 1974.
89 Madeline Y Hsu, *Dreaming of Gold, Dreaming of Home* (Stanford, California: Stanford University Press 2000) p. 1

electronic knowledge and skill available to the Motherland.'[90] By May 1974 he was writing to thank them for their support for his proposed visit; in August he sent them a copy of a letter to the Electronic Engineering Department at China's prestigious Qinghua University in Beijing, explaining his work; and in September his offer to provide the Revolutionary Committee with technological assistance was renewed.

Paul's efforts to persuade the Committee of his allegiance to the PRC knew no bounds when, in the spring of 1975, it looked as though Beijing was going to issue him and Sonia with an 'Introduction for Return to Native Village.' Lest Chinese officials suspect him of harboring any patriotism towards Taiwan, Paul promptly called the Taiwanese government a 'traitorous clique' that spread lies and rumors about the Communist Party. 'People abroad, including foreigners all praise Chairman Mao and the Communist Party for their magnanimity,' Paul declaimed, 'that they not only cherish the people, they even cherish the enemy and they truly follow the principle of "all patriots belong to one big family, whether they rally to the common cause early or late", and they follow their words with action.'

Such ideological posturing, costless when it merely dealt in generalities, was now brought much nearer home. In the same letter, Paul at last gave the Committee what they wanted to hear about his view of his brother Buxiu's execution. 'I think (1), the main reason was that he wasn't able to stand on the side of the masses and those who were exploited and he did not think favorably of the benefit of the laboring class.' He wrote dismissively of 'the typical Confucian society that was rotten to the core' and of the inevitability of revolution. 'And (2),' so Paul duly enumerated, 'the secondary reason was that our ancestors accumulated such a vast amount of property' which needed to be returned to the people. 'In the early days I did have some ideas to do so, but could not carry it out, so in the end I could not save him,' Paul claimed. 'I only thought of leaving, to substantiate myself and be self-reliant and work hard for others, to stand on the side of the exploited workers. Mother has always done the same.'[91]

It would be easy now to mock the sort of charade that had to be performed; but the fragmentary state of the surviving letters is the stark evidence that precautions were not needless, and that any word out of place simply could not

---

[90] Paul Ho to He Tangxiang, 3 September 1973
[91] Paul Ho to He Tangxiang, 13 May 1975

be risked. Paul was correct, therefore, in his intuitions about the situation—more so than he could fully have anticipated until he later discovered the real story of the family's treatment. For it had been only three years since the Red Guards had beaten Tangxiang, had paraded him through the village wearing a dunce hat, and had denounced him at 'speak bitterness' meetings. The Cultural Revolution could not yet be presumed to have run its course.

It was under these circumstances, in early 1975, that Paul played his last card. He knew that, in his own local area, the brigade, the commune and the revolutionary committee had all been persuaded to press Beijing for an answer on his application. He also knew that, as well as satisfying the ideological tests, he needed the technological argument. It was now that he repeatedly stressed the progress on his own project: 'The Chinese-English typewriter that I have invented is under continuous development day and night.'[92] In February he told Tangxiang—and hence the Committee who read all of his letters—that over the last two years he had been working 'day and night' on this electronic typewriter.[93] He mentioned it in each successive letter, adding more detail, and acknowledging that there were other designs in the field. 'Some will demand $20,000 to $30,000 USD to make the design,' he wrote in the same letter in which he discussed Buxiu's execution; 'I think theirs is a design that serves the capitalists. I want to do the design for the masses, a design that is cheap and easy to operate.'[94]

*　　*　　*

In an era when the keyboard simply activates the digital technology of the computer to which it is linked, it may be difficult to imagine the difficulties that had long inhibited the development of a typewriter that could cope with Chinese characters. Not that the Chinese were unaware of the challenge, long before western technology came along. In the 11th century AD, four centuries before Gutenberg made history in the West by printing the first bible, the Chinese were making moveable type out of clay tablets and mass-producing books. Economists have argued that, rather like other inventions that anticipated those in the West, few of the pioneering printing presses were built, and the

---

[92]　Paul Ho to He Tangxiang, 1 January 1975.
[93]　Paul Ho to He Tangxiang 11 February 1975
[94]　Paul Ho to He Tangxiang, 13 May 1975.

secrets were often subsequently lost, because of the absence of institutions—such as universities—to protect those individuals who were advancing knowledge in ways that challenged established authority, notably the Imperial court.[95]

The problem was intractable, in the West as much as the East, so long as the relevant technology was mechanical. Thus the only kind of 'Chinese typewriter' available as late as the early 1970s was not much of an improvement over the Underwood Company's 1926 Chinese typewriter, or even the clay tablets the Chinese had used for printing so many centuries earlier. In 1970 the Chinese typewriter was a large and cumbersome machine, fitted with a mechanical arm that moved in four directions over a rectangular font containing more than two thousand small metal blocks, each one bearing a single character. The operator positioned the arm over a character, grabbed it, raised it into the air, then struck it against a sheet of paper. According to one report in 1973, 'the chief skill required for using the Chinese typewriter is knowing exactly where to find each character.'[96] Another was simply patience. None of this seemed very promising.

As a result, the use of the Chinese written language was obviously handicapped. A possible answer lay in the application of pioneering work on digital information technology. In 1956 the Chinese government had introduced a Twelve-Year Science Plan that had among its four objectives the development of an electronic computer industry; and in 1958, the Institute of Computer Technology in Beijing assembled a prototype computer—fourteen years after scientists in the West had built the first one. But further development was curtailed by the onset of the Cultural Revolution. In 1966 universities became riven with ideological conflicts and were closed down. The State Science and Technology Commission was dismantled. The prestigious Chinese Academy of Sciences saw the number of its institutes fall from over a hundred to forty-one. Accused of having nothing to contribute to society, scientists were consigned to 'the stinking ninth category,' as a prime target of the Red Guards. Scientific research was lost; equipment was destroyed; scientists themselves were beaten up, imprisoned and sent to the countryside for 're-education' through manual work. The pattern was all too familiar. It reeked of the kind of Imperial control

[95] Richard G. Lipsey, Kenneth I. Carlaw & Clifford T. Bekar, *Economic Transformations* (New York: Oxford University Press, 2005) pp 281-282; also see Simon Winchester *The Man Who Loved China* (New York, HarperCollins, 2008) pp 260-1

[96] 'Coming to grips with a Chinese typewriter,' *The Times* (London) 8 May 1973, p. 8

that saw China's first emperor, Qin Shihuang, burn books—and the scholars who wrote them too.

The climate for scientists and other professionals did not improve until 1971. During Henry Kissinger's secret visit to China that summer, the Chinese had been fascinated by the American delegation's photocopy machine. Accustomed to copying everything by hand, the Chinese were pleased when Kissinger left the machine behind.[97] It was a demonstration of the gap that had opened up in information technology. That year, too, some universities began re-opening. A year later, following the Shanghai Communiqué, scientific exchange programs between the PRC and the United States were established. And three years after that, in 1975, China set up a Computer Industry Bureau. Though China was now prepared to open its doors to western technology and know-how, there was still a shortage of engineers competent to operate foreign equipment, still less to undertake the research necessary to improve upon foreign technology and adapt it to China's needs. Hence the readiness of a few highly-placed scientists in Beijing to take an interest in the pioneering work claimed by a little known engineer of Chinese origin living in southern California—especially since Paul Ho professed eagerness to bring his invention to his ancestral homeland.

Paul had come up with his big idea while working for Bell and Howell Laboratory, where he was designing magnetic tape-heads for tape recorders. Some time in early 1972 or early 1973, the company won a contract with the US Defense Department. They wanted a special set of codes written on an inch-wide magnetic tape and Paul was asked to help design them. Each code would correspond to a particular matrix, created digitally—either black or white in each component square—thus producing a pattern or shape unique to that particular code. These patterns, of course, had no literal relevance so far as Bell and Howell were concerned—they were being applied to problems of submarine navigation. Paul Ho's insight was that the same digital technology could be applied to create Chinese characters, each one linked to a particular code on the keyboard.

Bell and Howell's contract with the Defense Department was for two years. Paul completed his part of the project in six months. This left him with a year and a half to adapt what he had meanwhile learned to the building of his own computer. Paul used an IBM machine for this purpose. To help him, he took a short course, at the extension department at UCLA in April 1973, on the

---

[97]   Margaret MacMillan, *Nixon in China* (Toronto: Penguin, 2006) p. 151

design, implementation and application of mini-computer systems. Then, over the next year-and-a-half, he began developing his own system.

Like many brilliant ideas, the essence was simple—at least in retrospect. By November 1974 Paul was ready to patent his invention.[98] His own surviving explanation of it makes the fundamental principle very clear. He shows a matrix, looking rather like a crossword puzzle, with sixteen squares across and sixteen squares down, each one either black or white. A digital representation of each square—either 0 or 1—is how a computer would handle this information. With these 256 squares at his disposal, Paul was thus able to create a unique image of a stylized Chinese character, which a computer could easily represent, store or print. And each character was then assigned a four-number code—in principle from 0000 to 9999, thus providing initially for a vocabulary of up to ten thousand expressions. A dictionary linking the Chinese words with the code numbers was thus the key to making this system operational. Once the operator had mastered the codes, the rest was done digitally on the computer itself.

Paul usually called this 'a multilingual typewriter and printer.'[99] This description, which he used in his correspondence to China in 1975, makes clear the phonetic basis of his procedure. He was using the Pinyin transcription of Chinese to create a system of classification by the sound of the word; and on this basis, to assign each code on the keyboard a unique phonetic significance. From this it was a short step in theory—though immensely laborious in practice—to complete the links that transcribed each written character, each with its own phonetic significance. In principle this could cope with the transcription of any sounds in any language, not just Chinese, so Paul's description of his invention as multilingual is obviously accurate; but in calling it a typewriter, he was simply using the word familiar at that time. In fact no conventional mechanical typewriter could have done what he was using digital technology to achieve. Eventually Paul was to adopt the term Multilingual Phonetic Word Processor for his invention.

In its final form, the Ho Input Method allowed the user to type what were called 'whole words', based on the phonetic Pinyin system of writing Chinese, into the computer. This was a refinement of the original method, more sophisticated but also more complex. It is clear that, in order to cope with the transcription

[98]   OSCII (Oriental Standard Code for Information Interchange), document dated November 1974.
[99]   Paul Ho to Tangxiang, 1 January 1975.

of 13,053 classical characters, the work of creating appropriate codes would be immense; but as with Paul's five-sentence word structure in learning English, he sought to simplify the process, concentrating, in the assignment of codes, on what was common usage. As he later admitted, it might take a week for the user to learn the codes, but he insisted: 'Pain for the short term is better than pain for the long term.' Paul's system thus had a potential for speed: it would be easy to input forty to fifty characters a minute. Moreover, he claimed that 'if you don't have to look at the keyboard, it would not be difficult to input over 100 words.' He envisaged the system's extension to tens of thousands of medical, biochemical and legal terms—'I will provide wings for you, tiger!'[100]

Such visionary applications lay in the future in 1975. What he could offer at that time was a method; and what was needed to develop it was operational support, not only in applying suitable technology on the computing side but in producing a comprehensive code-book or dictionary. All this demanded heavy investment in time and money over the years; in the end Paul would use over $10,000 of his own money on the project. In March 1975 Paul told Tangxiang that, due to the economic downturn and rising prices, he had had to 'stop moving forward temporarily' on his invention.[101]

Initially, Paul had attempted to generate interest in his invention in America. He approached Bell and Howell but he sadly recalls, 'they were not interested.' When he told them that he would travel to China and present his idea there, 'they said OK.' So in the spring of 1975 Paul asked officials at the Liaison Office of the People's Republic of China in Washington, D.C. to present his invention to two named officials at the Chinese Electronic Institute in Beijing: Chen Guolu and—an important future contact—its chairman, Deng Guojun.[102] As noted earlier, he had already written to Qinghua University with an offer, as he put it to Tangxiang, to 'hand over . . . all the circuits and the plans' of his invention.[103]

In the mid-1970s China's Computer Industry Bureau was less interested in making prototypes incorporating up-to-date technology than they were on providing standard lines of products in large quantities. Paul Ho's invention—'for the masses', as he had put it—fitted this template, apparently congruent with

---

[100] Paul Ho *Multi-lingual Phonetic WordProcessor* (2008)
[101] Paul Ho to He Tangxiang, 13 March 1975.
[102] Paul Ho to The Liaison Office of the People's Republic of China, 10 June 1975
[103] Paul Ho to He Tangxiang 11 February 1975

the goals of the computer industry. The Chinese therefore dispatched two engineers (Ying Dungje and Li Deji) to Los Angeles in order to inspect Paul's work; and they were to report back to the same man he had already contacted at the Chinese Electronic Institute, its chairman, Deng Guojun. Satisfied with what they saw, they took the bold step of inviting Paul Ho to give a series of lectures on his invention to scientists in Beijing. Paul agreed to do so on one condition: that when his lectures were over he would be allowed to visit his home province of Jiangxi, the city of Xinyu, and his native Hejiacun village at Songlin. The Chinese officials now agreed to all of this.

It was thus on 6 June 1975 that the hitherto elusive 'Introduction for Return to Native Village' certificates were issued from the China Liaison Office in Washington. The invitation to visit China came at the right time for Paul and Sonia. They could spare the time since they had been saving up their vacation entitlement. David and Phillip had finished the school year at their respective universities and were free to look after seven-year-old Sidney. So in July 1975, with almost two solid months of paid leave, Paul and Sonia traveled to Hong Kong (still a British colony at that time) en route to Shanghai. That they were able to make this journey could hardly have been predicted even a few years previously. It was to be Sonia's first visit to China, of course, and Paul's first visit since he had sailed out of Shanghai fully twenty-eight years earlier.

Paul, David, Phillip and Sidney

Paul and Tangxiang, Xinyu, 2007

CHAPTER 7

'Falling leaves return to the roots'

落葉歸根

When Paul and Sonia Ho touched down at Shanghai airport in the early summer of 1975, it was with mixed emotions. 'Scared' was how Paul frankly put it, admitting the doubts that suddenly assailed him about his long-awaited, eagerly anticipated return to his native China—'the country invite me there to treat me bad? I don't know.' What protection would his American citizenship offer against possible victimization? 'I was frightened,' he admitted, and his fears soared when a female government official addressed him by name as he stepped on to the tarmac. 'How do you know my name,?' Paul asked as soon as the woman had introduced herself. The official replied that she had his photograph and had come to greet them, using the word jia. But, what with her unfamiliar Shanghai accent and his own dark imaginings, what Paul heard was jian, which conveys the sense of detention and imprisonment—'I thought they had come to arrest me.' At this, the usually serene Sonia became as frightened as her husband. 'I told you not to come,' she whispered to Paul in Taiwanese, as they were briskly ushered past the customs officials who were examining the belongings of all the other passengers. 'When we are in jail,' Paul thought, 'they can check the bags any time.'

The alarming incident turned out to be an innocent misunderstanding, quickly dispelled when the official made clear that she was simply there to welcome the honored He Buji back to China. His own nervous apprehensions, however, had not materialized out of thin air but out of the obvious possibilities of the situation. He continued to believe that if he had not left China in 1947 his reputation for justice and fairness—demonstrated so many years earlier as a boy in Hejiacun and later as a student in Zunyi—would have protected him from the abuse that was meted out to the sons of landlords. Yet an alternative scenario is all too easy to envisage.

Even if he had escaped persecution and possible execution by the PRC for having 'a bad class background', Buji would surely have been punished in some way for participating under GMD colors in the Resistance War. He might well have shared the fate of his schoolmate, Yang Chenyuan (whom we met at their wartime school site in 2007), with his experience of banishment to northeastern China in 1953 for having been a soldier in the Republican Army, undergoing detention for a grueling thirty-four years. Quite possibly the outspoken Buji would have run into trouble in the late 1950s during the Anti-Rightist Campaign, when, after asking his compatriots to speak up and criticize the regime in the spring of 1957, Mao brutally turned on those who had expressed their views. If Buji had succeeded in becoming an engineer in China, he might well, like the father of the writer and broadcaster Xinran, have been accused of being a 'reactionary technical authority.'[104] Or if, having finished his studies in America, Paul had then chosen to return immediately to China, he could easily have shared the fate of the American-educated Wu Ningkun, who offered his 'expertise and conscience' to the PRC; for when Wu returned to China he found himself 'denounced as an enemy of the people,' then detained for several years in a reform-through-labor camp.[105] The example of the famous physicist and human rights activist, Xu Liangying, who spent years in prison and saw his life's work destroyed, is particularly telling, lending an awful credibility to the speculation of Phillip Ho: 'given my father's upbringing, intellect, feistiness, and righteousness . . . he would have become a dissident like Xu.'

Instead, Paul's eventual homecoming proved to be a triumph, once its first few alarming minutes at Shanghai airport had been put behind him. He and Sonia were now introduced to Mr. Hu, their police 'minder', who would be with them for the next forty-one days. When they arrived in Beijing the following day they were housed in a Chinese hotel dating from the Qing dynasty. Reserved for foreign guests and high-ranking government officials, this impressive building seemed to Paul 'just like a palace.'

---

[104] Xinran *The Good Women of China* (London: Vintage, 2002) p. 167.
[105] Wu Ningkun *A Single Tear* (London: Little Brown & Company, 1993) p. 341

Over the course of several days, Paul spent most mornings at Beijing's Electronic Institute, where he gave a series of lectures to upwards of one hundred technicians and scientists, unveiling at least some of the secrets of the English-Chinese computer. Paul had taken out a patent on his invention just before leaving Los Angeles. He was, of course, fully aware that China did not at that time subscribe to the international conventions that would recognize a patent taken out in the United States, which did not yet officially recognize the PRC. He also knew that researchers in China seldom disclosed their methodology when they published their findings. He did not, therefore, reveal how he had built his system. He did however, as he recalls, tell his audience 'how to put the connector; how to use the hex number for each Chinese character; then after that how to store in the computer—about 6,763 characters—then use Pinyin to type it out.' During the course of imparting this information Paul received a positive response. As he assured me with justified satisfaction, 'all these scientists were very interested.'

When Paul was not lecturing, he and Sonia were taken to see what the Chinese call their 'cultural relics'. Like most tourists in Beijing, they drove thirty-five miles north of the city and walked along the Great Wall. Photographs show Paul battling to the top of one steep section, up to the fort on the top of a hill, while Sonia waits prudently below, conserving her energy. They visited the Forbidden City, itself a monument to imperial power, viewing the lavish buildings and the Nine Dragon Wall. The camera catches them strolling through the gardens and pavilions of the Summer Palace built by the tyrannical Dowager Empress at the end of the nineteenth century; it shows them visiting the tombs of the Ming Emperors and the recently restored Lama Temple; and it shows how empty of other tourists these now crowded sites were in the 1970s. They were VIPs, treated royally. Paul's dry response—'I think I like to be King'—was typically understated about the emotive impact upon a man of fifty-six who had lived in exile for exactly half his life.

Every evening Paul and Sonia savored their favorite dishes in the hotel's magnificent dining room. After one lavish dinner held in their honor, their minder Mr. Hu took the couple to a traditional Chinese opera; after another, he saw to it that Paul and Sonia viewed a patriotic film celebrating the defeat of Chiang Kai-shek's beleaguered army by the Communist forces.

Throughout their entire visit to China, Paul and Sonia were never alone. 'Everywhere we went,' Paul recalled, 'there were plain-clothes policemen to protect us.' Protection was a two-way concept. On the one hand, the couple could be viewed by many members of Chinese society as 'running dogs of the capitalists', 'reactionary technical authorities', or even more heinous threats to good Communists. 'They have to protect us,' Paul reasoned; 'if something happens the government are in real trouble.'

The visitors were also being protected, of course, from seeing too much for themselves, or from penetrating the great wall of Chinese propaganda. The Cultural Revolution, it should be remembered, was only gradually winding down and its ideological gears had not yet been thrown into reverse. It was not just that, as Paul recalls, 'everyone was talking about Mao.' Patriotic songs like 'The East is Red' were blasted through public spaces. Popular slogans—'The People's Government is for the People' and 'The People's Liberation Army are the sons and brothers of the People'—were painted in simplified characters on the sides of buildings. There were also endless parades during which, as one observer noted, the marchers shouted 'down with this, up with that, here a victory, there an alarm.'[106] Big character posters bore accusations and denunciations of men and women who now lost their jobs and their families. Branded as traitors to the revolution, people were forced to pose 'airplane fashion' (bending forward, with arms raised backwards above the shoulders) before jeering crowds, and to write confessional depositions. Little did Paul yet realize how closely this paralleled the treatment of his own eldest son, Tangxiang.

For the weeks of their official visit to Beijing, then, Paul and Sonia were regaled as official visitors, plied alike with official hospitality and official restrictions. For Paul, naturally, this was an important mark of his acceptance in the land of his birth; but the return of the native was a story with a more personal aspect too. The next leg of their pilgrimage began when Paul and Sonia boarded the train for a six-hour journey to Hangzhou; and though Mao's voice, extolling the merits of living in New China, was pumped into their compartment during their entire journey, there was now a change of tempo and a shift of focus. In Hangzhou, as beautiful as ever, they viewed Paul's favorite student haunts (much as I was to do on my visit with him there in 2007). After a further week of intensive sightseeing, he and Sonia finally continued south on the train to Paul's hometown, Xinyu, expecting nothing more than a quiet reunion with a few members of his family.

*　　*　　*

---

[106] *Op. Cit., Chinese Profiles*, p. 227

Instead, they were met by a furor. If Paul and Sonia were exhausted by the time they arrived in Xinyu, their tiredness vanished when the train pulled into the station and they were caught up in the excitement. There were literally hundreds of people crowded onto the station platform, as Paul vividly remembers. Asked how everyone knew that he was arriving, he said that it was 'just like people in the market, everybody come automatically, word of mouth.' It was a welcome that exceeded his wildest dreams.

When Paul and Sonia stepped off the train, the secretary of the Xinyu Municipal Government, Fei Hua, stepped forward at the head of a reception committee. This time there was no doubt that he was there to greet them, not to arrest them. Paul and Sonia were then led by Fei Hua and his entourage to a building adjacent to the station platform.

There, standing in the centre of a small reception room, were the children of Paul's first family. Tangxiang, now thirty-six, bore evident marks of the troubles he had suffered, most recently in the Cultural Revolution; his elder sister Honglian, now thirty-seven and resembling her mother Gu, was there too, as was their younger sister, Xiangbao, now thirty-three and with a closer resemblance to her father than any of her siblings. Paul's sister Zhilan was also with them. They had all been anxiously awaiting his arrival for what seemed like hours.

When Paul entered the room, he did not at first recognize any of them. It was twenty-eight years since he had last seen them in Songlin—three young children and their aunt, then in her early twenties. As it gradually dawned on him who they were, Paul reacted with a restraint that would only surprise someone who did not know him, with Chinese formality masking deep feelings that he only hinted at—'I didn't do anything, they didn't say anything.' Perhaps there was no need for mere words; according to Tangxiang, the meeting was 'very emotional.' It was, at any rate, as emotional as was prudent, given the presence of government officials—ostensibly protective, possibly threatening, certainly inhibiting—as Paul remembered, 'everybody still scared to talk.' It was to be much later before they felt free to do so.

Any embarrassment was short-lived. Fei Hua and the other officials quickly ushered Paul and Sonia out of the waiting room. It was at this point that Paul took measure of the sheer size of the crowd that had gathered. People not only lined the station platform and filled the entrance hall. There were literally thousands in front of the station and packed into the surrounding streets. Indeed, the crowd was so large and so boisterous that, in the course of leading his guests from the foyer of the station to a nearby government vehicle, Fei

Hua lost his shoe. 'Somebody just stepped on his foot,' Paul recalled with a grin, 'he lost it!'

Even after Sonia, Paul and the officials had squeezed into the waiting van, they made slow progress. This was because, in the crowd's efforts to get a glimpse of the renowned He Buji, some people were sitting on the roof of the vehicle, while others were pressing against the windows. The happy occasion showed signs of turning ugly when the dense pressure of the crowd against the vehicle broke one of its windows. It was at this point that the driver put his foot on the accelerator. Miraculously, the crowd parted and no one was injured as the vehicle picked up speed.

The scale of this welcome came as a surprise; and the size of the crowd that had spontaneously assembled still seems striking. Tangxiang provides a simple explanation: 'because it was so rare to have foreign visitors—they were a novelty.' This is quite true. The hundreds of people who flocked to Xinyu Railway Station knew little of the outside world and were curious to see someone from abroad. He Buji was the first Native-born sojourner to return to Xinyu since the founding of the PRC in 1949. Moreover, it was known that he had just come from faraway Beijing, where he had briefed government scientists on his new invention. For most Chinese, as Mobo Gao observed when he returned to Jiangxi Province a few years later, 'their overwhelming impression of a foreign country or a foreigner is of their wealth and material superiority.'[107] Paul and Sonia were not only a novelty; like most 'ocean ghosts' from North America, they were held in some awe as presumably opulent and technologically sophisticated.

They spent the first few days in Xinyu's government guesthouse. The pattern that had been established in Beijing was resumed. They were honored at lavish banquets, treated to heavy doses of movies and plays celebrating Mao's China, and taken to view two steel plants of which the city were very proud. They were even driven to the southern part of the province to see Mao's early Communist stronghold at Futian. It was not until Paul's third day in Xinyu—more than a month after arriving in China—that the ulterior purpose of his homecoming visit was to be fulfilled. After legendary Beijing, emotive Hangzhou and populous Xinyu, it was at last time to revisit tiny, neglected Songlin—truly to come home.

---

[107] Mobo C. F. Gao, *Gao Village, A Portrait of Rural Life in Modern China* (London: Hurst & Company, 1999) p. 249

The village is less than a fifteen minute drive from Xinyu. The government officials who transported Paul and Sonia to Hejiacun drove into the main square and stopped in front of the largest building, the ancestral hall. The entire village—all descendants of the He family, albeit from different branches of the same genealogical tree—welcomed Paul and Sonia with cymbals and firecrackers. Paul did not yet know that, only six years earlier, some of these same people had beaten his son Tangxiang and paraded him through the square where they were now standing; and Paul had not yet been told how, two decades before that, older members of the clan had expelled his mother Fu and her family from the ancestral home.

Once the smoke from the firecrackers had cleared and the din from the cymbals had stopped, Paul looked around him. In his correspondence with Tangxiang three years previously, written with an eye to the Communist censors, Paul had claimed that 'before Liberation our home was a backward village' and had fulsomely rejoiced to learn that 'under the leadership of the Communist Party, there is a dam, a railway, a highway, electric lighting, a clinic, an old people's home.'[108] Now he could compare the evidence of his own eyes as he saw the new Hejiacun for himself. 'It was so poor; everything there is poor,' he recalled with a pained wince. The once-beautiful ancestral hall where Paul had paid his respects to previous generations of his family was only a shell of its former glory. And when Paul walked down the lane leading off from the hall to the building that had housed his extended family he noted that part of it was being used as a cowshed.

Paul was able to pause in front of his old home before proceeding to the end of the lane where he saw the new house that had been built for his mother. Its construction had, of course, been made possible by his financial contribution from far away. Thankfully, he was 'very happy' when he viewed the modest three-room house, and it was particularly pleasing to find that, acting quite spontaneously, Tangxiang had located it on the very spot that his father had in mind for it.

When I first saw the building in 2007, it had been extended in order to accommodate several more rooms. Otherwise, as Paul assured me, it had not altered since he first set eyes on it in the summer of 1975. Like virtually every other building in the village, then as now, it was without electricity, and without any source of heat. The rooms had mud-baked floors. There was no running

---

108   Paul Ho to He Tangxiang, 23 June 1972.

water or sanitation. Yet by 2007 a door at the centre of the building led to the He Village Little Health Centre. A glass-fronted cabinet displaying traditional medicines indicated that Buxiu's grandson Hong was carrying on the profession that had made his great-grandfather (Wenge) an asset to the village more than fifty years earlier—and a calling that his first cousin once removed, Dr David Ho, was pursuing in the United States.

On the right-hand side of the Health Centre was a sealed door behind which, I was told, were two rooms that had been added to the building (though I did not discover why or when, or who had occupied them, until my next visit to China a year later.) On the left-hand side of the Health Centre, the door was open, leading into a room with exposed beams, blackened from the burning of incense. With the exception of a photograph of Paul's mother Fu—a modern-day ancestral tablet in her honor—the room was bare. A second room at the back of the building was larger, furnished with beds (in a rather unkempt state), a table and a few cooking utensils.

This was Fu's last home. She had just moved there from the pigsty at the time of her son's visit in the summer of 1975 and it was from her new abode that she emerged to greet him. For fear of over-exciting her, Tangxiang had only told his grandmother the previous day of the planned visit. Fu may have had a restless night after hearing this news but she had risen early and spent the early hours of the morning preparing one of her son's favorite dishes. When she heard voices in the lane, announcing the arrival of visitors, the old lady rushed to the front door still wearing her apron.

Paul had some idea of how his mother would look after almost thirty years of separation because Tangxiang had sent him a picture some three years earlier. But the woman who stood before him now bore little similarity to this photograph. Though Paul was glad that Fu appeared to be in relatively good health, he was shocked to discover how much older she looked than her seventy-five years.

The story of their reunion on that warm August morning remains memorable—so much so that rival versions were given to me at different times. Sonia told me that Paul fell to his knees and, between sobs, asked his mother to forgive him for being an un-filial son. Yet Paul's typically understated account simply has him stepping forward, embracing his mother and kissing her cheek. As with the meeting with his children, although 'very excited,' he insisted that 'she didn't say anything and I didn't say anything.'

For one of the primary goals of Mao's Cultural Revolution had been to destroy the family unit, with its Confucian trappings of filial piety. After the 1975 visit to Hejiacun it was clear that this had clearly not been achieved with the He family. Paul's mother Fu, his sister Zhilan, his own children, the children of his deceased brother, and the progeny of their respective families—all openly acknowledged the returning Buji as head of the He clan. Moreover, they embraced his wife Sonia, as she warmly acknowledges—'I feel like a family and they are very nice to me.' Indeed, during the couple's first night in the village, Sonia slept with Fu: 'I feel I am supposed to.' It was a mark of acceptance on both sides.

During the ensuing days in Hejiacun, Paul and Sonia shared two rooms with Fu in a brand-new government building, constructed especially for their use. This was certainly better than Fu's own humble dwelling, and better propaganda too from the government's point of view. It was here that Paul, Sonia and Fu slept and ate their meals. It was here, too, that Paul was introduced to the husband, Luo Keng, of his sister, Zhilan and their daughter Guixiang; here that he met the spouses of his own children, and the children of his murdered brother Buxiu; and here that he met his grandchildren, many of whom were older than his own eight-year-old son, Sidney.

More comfortable here than in the waiting room at Xinyu Railway Station, the relatives now felt free to ask questions. Paul's mother, as he recalled, quizzed him about the long years of separation and silence: 'What you do in Taiwan?' 'Why you go to America?' 'What you do there?' Paul did not ask her or any other member of the family how they had spent the intervening years. 'We don't talk about anything,' he admitted; 'I am scared; I don't want to ask.' But it was not just the presence of Mr Hu and his colleagues, always trying to keep within ear-shot, that stopped Paul and his family from revisiting the past. As the writer Wayson Choy reminds us in *All that Matters*, reticence was inbred among this hard-pressed generation of Chinese—'there was always an understanding that some things could never possibly be told, that what mattered was that one had done whatever had been needed to survive.'[109] Paul's reunion with his Chinese family observed the same discretion: 'The people who come back from overseas,' he told me, 'they just keep quiet; don't say anything.'

Tacitly agreeing to ignore the last twenty-eight years for the moment, Paul's family found it easier to talk about, and openly pay tribute to, the family's ancestors. They took him to visit the grave of his father, the venerable He Wenge. Those who could climb Laojinshan made their way up the hill that Paul

---

[109] Wayson Choy *All that Matters* (Toronto: Anchor, 2005 first published in 2004) p. 116

remembered as resembling the shape of a tiger. When they arrived at Wenge's grave, they burned joss sticks, piled sods of earth behind the headstone and offered food. Then the small party bowed in order of seniority. Paul was the first to step forward—'I bow three times on knees and three times on feet'—and his grandchildren were the last. Paul would also have liked to pay his respects to his uncle He Duanyou, but the grave of his old teacher had unfortunately been situated near the entrance of the village, where it had been disrupted by the construction of a recent road.

There remained, of course, one further member of Paul's family: his first wife, Gu. Now unwell and bent over from years of hard work, Gu had traveled some thirty miles from a village to the east of Songlin for the occasion. But, under the watchful eyes of Fei Hua and the other policemen, she never had an opportunity to greet her former husband. As Paul explained, 'those guys keep me away from her.' While Gu had to be satisfied with viewing her first husband from a distance, the police presence did not prevent her from meeting Paul's second wife, Sonia. It was Tangxiang who introduced the two women and, since Sonia did not understand the local dialect, he acted as interpreter.

If Tangxiang was worried about Sonia's reaction, his fears were soon allayed by her magnanimous response. Sonia knew that Gu was twelve years older than herself but was surprised to discover how much older she looked than Paul, virtually the same age. It was one sign of her spending the last two decades with an abusive husband and living apart from her first three children. Knowing that Gu, unlike herself, was an accomplished seamstress, Sonia gave her some material. She also gave her 400 Yuan. Only fifty dollars in American currency, to Gu it represented more than the annual income of a farmer. Tangxiang notes with satisfaction that Sonia found his mother, Gu, to be 'a really honest, kind woman.'

'In China, face can be lost, sold, bought, borrowed, given or denied,' as Adeline Yen Mah reflects in her memoir *A Thousand Pieces of Gold*. 'Most of all, face must be preserved, especially in front of an audience composed of one's own henchmen.'[110] It was a maxim that the various levels of government had tacitly observed throughout the trip. The compliments of Paul's visit to Beijing—'They treat me like king,' he had noted with pride—were sustained in Xinyu. Tangxiang could see that the government officials had taken his father's visit 'very seriously',

---

[110] Adeline Yen Mah *A Thousand Pieces of Gold* (London: Harper Prennial 2004, first published in 2002) p. 243

as evidenced by the overwhelming reception that took place at the train station, by the banquets, by the construction of a government house for Paul and Sonia's use. At one level, this was an exercise in face-saving by a government that had been responsible for the execution of Paul's brother Buxiu, for the expulsion of Paul's wife Gu and his mother Fu from the family's ancestral home. Everyone studiously—or prudently—avoided talking about these things. But implicitly an accommodation had been reached whereby nobody lost face and further contact could be facilitated.

By the end of their two-month-long journey, therefore, Paul and Sonia, despite their initial fears, had achieved much. They had buried the past and come to terms with the present.

*   *   *

There was more excitement for Paul and Sonia when they returned to Los Angeles. If it seemed a novelty for foreigners to come to Xinyu, it was also a novelty in 1975 for Americans to come home from a private visit to China, so long inaccessible to Westerners. Paul spoke about his trip to the local association of alumni of National Zhejiang University drawing together exiled Chinese in Los Angeles. 'You went there,' they told Paul, 'you have guts!' The neighbors who filled the small living room of the Sanborn Avenue house were likewise impressed when they saw the slideshow. Here was the diminutive employee whom they saw commuting to Bell and Howell daily, now shown addressing a large gathering of scientists in the capital city of Red China; here was their neighbor, with his mysteriously exotic education, showing his wife his student haunts in the fabled city of Hangzhou amid the serene splendor of its West Lake; and here were the quiet couple who lived so modestly on Sanborn Avenue pictured in the midst of a surging throng of people at Xinyu Railway Station, enjoying a hero's welcome.

Paul put an official gloss on the matter when he resumed his correspondence with Tangxiang: 'We told them in great detail about the real circumstances of the motherland's progress, the people's lives and the treatment given to Overseas Chinese by the government and people of the Motherland.'[111] It was a game that had to be played, with his various moves coordinated so as to achieve multiple objectives, personal and professional alike.

---

[111]   Paul Ho to He Tangxiang, 16 October 1975

Friends and neighbors were not the only people who took an interest in Paul and Sonia's trip to China. Knowing that Bell and Howell had sensitive government contracts relating to national defense and that one of its electrical engineers had just spent almost two months in China, Paul was approached by an officer of the Central Intelligence Agency (CIA). According to American export regulations any equipment that might possibly be adapted for military use had to be licensed by the Commerce Department. The seven ensuing interviews to which Paul was subjected by the CIA in the mid-1970s must have awakened disturbing memories of being interviewed while a student in Colorado.

This time, however, Paul was not being taken for a cook or a laundryman. He was being viewed as a spy. Why had he gone to Beijing? 'They ask me about my lectures and want to know about my software and hardware,' he recalled. 'You tell them how to do it?' they asked him. Paul assured the CIA officer that he had not shown the scientists in Beijing how to build the computer. In fact he had a perfect answer. He had made sure not to reveal the information, in his own interests, because China did not recognize patents; but on the other hand, he was able to point out that the relevant information was available for any American to see, precisely because it had been patented in the United States. The CIA official was not so easily baffled by mere logic and his investigation did not stop here. The Agency contacted Bell and Howell. Paul's employer confirmed that Paul Ho had offered his invention to them but that they had not been interested. Paul was gratified that they also indicated that they valued their employee—'he is very smart; he is very smart'—which was some consolation to glean from this worrying episode.

After their first visit to China, life for Paul and Sonia would never be the same. On their first visit to China village and government officials had discreetly asked Paul for financial assistance. He happily funded the planting of an orange grove located at the base of the hill beneath his father's grave and later established the He Buji Educational Foundation for the purpose of awarding four scholarships a year to students proceeding to university.

There were also inescapable ongoing obligations towards his Jiangxi family that he knew would raise their status and give them a better life. Modest amounts of cash were contributed to the He family celebration of the Spring Festival and of family weddings. When the practice of maintaining a family genealogy was revived in the late 1970s, Paul paid his youngest daughter's school-teacher husband, Chen Sicong, to update his branch of the He family's genealogy.

Sonia and her three children, David, Phillip and Sidney now found their place in the family record.

It all came at a price for people on limited salaries; and their own sons were obviously the prime commitment for Paul and Sonia. Only eight years old when his parents returned from China in 1975, Sidney was still in primary school, so money had to be set aside to complete his education and meanwhile his elder brothers were only slowly becoming independent. Phillip did not receive his first degree from UCLA until 1976 and was then in graduate school for a year before entering dental school.[112] Traveling to and from the University of Pennsylvania, where he qualified as a dentist in 1981, required help and there would be the problem to face of setting him up in a practice.

David's career, though replete with early signs of exceptional promise, was equally slow to unfold as he amassed the appropriate professional qualifications. He still had two years to complete as a medical student at Harvard when he got married in 1976 to a student from Glendal City College, Susan (Sue-yu) Kuo. Born in 1952, the same year as David, Susan would go to be an accomplished botanical artist, was the Taiwanese-born daughter of a distinguished surgeon and was no stranger to the Ho family. 'Susan's family knows my family in Taiwan,' Sonia proudly told me, hinting that someone had made a point of introducing the young students. Susan had helped look after Sidney during his parents' six-week absence in China. The young couple returned to Los Angeles in 1978, after David had gained his medical degree, when he entered the UCLA School of Medicine for a four-year period undergoing clinical training in internal medicine and infectious diseases. Susan's parents provided much-needed support, notably in helping them purchase a stylish California-Spanish house on Live Oak Drive, in the Los Feliz Hills, which was hardly the kind of property that an impecunious young doctor would have been able to afford.

The elder boys were now intent on following in their parents' footsteps, retracing their family roots. In the summer of 1976 Phillip went to Taiwan: 'It was eleven years after we had left and it was thrilling seeing old relations.' He visited Houli where he and David had been photographed on the steps

---

[112] It should be noted that during his year in graduate school Phillip was doing research in biochemistry on active sites of enzymes—an area of study that his brother, David, pursued to a greater length with his work on proteze inhibitors.

of the mausoleum and where he now met his great aunt the last remaining Buddhist nun. He reacquainted himself with his mother's three half sisters and with the other relatives on his mother's side of the family who were still living.

Two years later, in 1978, David and Susan accompanied Paul on his second visit to China. It was important for Paul that his eldest son should meet his grandmother, see the village of his father's birth and pay his respect to his grandfather's grave. David recalls how exciting it was to meet his grandmother, despite attendant difficulties. When Fu greeted the young couple at the door of her modest home she offered David a bowl of raw eggs; it was impossible to refuse, but he became ill. During the course of making several trips to the outhouse—'much to the amusement of the rest of the village'—the ice was broken between David and his grandmother. 'I could only speak the Taiwan dialect and Mandarin, so we had a lot of trouble communicating,' he admits. 'It was mostly through body language.' David was thus aware of a large, friendly, curious extended family—but not in a position to establish the exact relationships between them and himself.

As well as obvious family ties, Paul's continuing interest in electronics also drew him back to his home province. He offered the Ministry of Electronics and the Municipality in Xinyu advice on matters relating to computer technology. They in turn agreed to assist him. Paul needed someone to help him assign each Chinese character with a coded number in programming his computer. During the 1975 visit, Chen Sicong, the husband of his youngest daughter, Xiangbao, had offered to help his father-in-law. So had the local officials, who readily seconded two students to assist Chen Sicong. Indeed Paul had spent the final days of this visit in Xinyu, instructing Chen and the students on how to convert 6,763 characters into coded numbers.

Since then, the climate had been slowly changing, the Cold War eventually thawing. Both sides gradually warmed towards cooperation. For example, in 1976 the American firm, Control Data Corporation, had applied for permission to sell their Control Data Cyber 73 computer—a system that would calculate oil exploration and detect earthquakes—to China. They were refused permission to do so by the US authorities. It took them another four years and many assurances that their system was not adaptable for military purposes before the government agreed—but it happened. By this time Mao was dead. China's new leader, Deng Xiaoping, with his pragmatic approach, reconciling Leninism with openness to innovation, acknowledged in a much-publicized speech in 1978 that China had fallen behind the technological advances of industrial nations.

Deng thus urged 'a new respect for foreign science and a new determination to learn from other countries.'[113]

In Los Angeles, Paul continued to work on the computer. He took out further patents as well as setting up a series of companies to exploit his invention: Chinese Information System Company (1978) which became Sino Data System Company in 1981 and two years later he was to found Data Ho Incorporated. Money had to be found for the costs of further development. 'I am still working night and day on the Chinese computer,' Paul told Tangxiang in January 1981, with a view to taking part 'in the motherland's four modernizations'—industry, agriculture, defense and science.[114]

One manifestation of Deng's determination to open China to the outside world was seen in the establishment of a Chinese Consulate-General in 1979 in two American cities. Based in Houston, Texas, and San Francisco, these consulates were devoted to the exchange of science and technology, and to promoting trade. Accompanied by Phillip, who had helped his father build the keyboard in the garage at Sanborn Avenue, Paul made the four-hundred mile journey to San Francisco. 'In 1981 we drove into the back door of the consulate,' Phillip recalls, in cloak-and-dagger style, 'my father performed for them, showed them what he could do.' Aware that doing business in China required that you had to work closely with the government, Paul had meanwhile kept up his contacts with the Electronics Institute in Beijing. As a result, it sent its chief engineer, Chen Liwei, to Los Angeles in early 1981. Paul's recollection was that Chen, who stayed at their house in Sanborn Avenue, 'questioned me in detail' over the course of a week together.

It did the trick. Within a few months, Paul and Sonia were back in Beijing, again as guests of the government, and 'were treated so good.' Paul gave a demonstration of the most recent generation of the Ho Input Method to the Institute. Photographs from 1981 show him, along with his IBM computer and printer, which he had brought with him in specially-built wooden crates, standing before an evidently enthusiastic audience. All dressed in blue jackets and trousers, the men and women crane forward, listening intently as Paul, with his customary animation, explains the uses of his English-Chinese computer.

---

[113] Richard Bauer *Burying Mao, Chinese Politics in the Age of Deng Xiaoping* (Princeton: Princeton University Press, 1994) pp. xii, 6

[114] Paul Ho to He Tangxiang 20 January 1981

Impressed with what they saw, a government agency calling itself the China Computer Technology Service Company (hereafter CCTSC) drew up a contract. On 12 December 1981 Paul, as head of the Sino Data System Company, was presented with an agreement with CCTSC for the development of a Chinese word processor. It was an attractive proposal from Paul's point of view. As CEO he would be responsible for 'the research and production operations to be set up in Los Angeles.' CCTSC would send to California and subsidize 'three persons to further the research on a Chinese character terminal, to open up the market, and to train personnel.' Furthermore 'the profits from all of the products manufactured and sold in America will belong to Mr Ho.'[115] Paul duly handed over his patents to CCTSC, signed the contract, and was given a banquet by the Deputy Minister of Technology, Li Rui. It seemed that he had finally scaled the summit of his ambitions.

Alas, it was a false summit. After Paul and Sonia returned home, nothing happened. The three engineers from China did not appear in Los Angeles. The 'joint venture company' with Sino Data System Company was never set up. And Paul had no further contact with the CCTSC. 'No it doesn't happen,' he said ruefully, 'they just cheat and they want my patent.' According to Phillip, it soon became clear that they had no intention of paying him. Paul sought legal advice. His lawyer, he reported, said 'but you exchanged your work with the government—it is not yours now.' After his hopes had been built up during his third visit to China in 1981, this was a cruel disappointment—and a disillusionment too with the good faith of those with whom he had dealt. Maybe the fault lay as much in the sheer confusion introduced by the baffling series of administrative reorganizations in the Chinese government at that juncture, during which it was easy for business to fall between the cracks and get lost. But the impact on Paul himself was understandably severe. 'After a while, he became resigned to the fact that he wouldn't be paid,' Phillip attests. 'It was heart-breaking for us—Sid and I lived through it.'

*　　*　　*

There were other blows at this time. In 1975 Paul had promised his mother Fu that he would see her again, and did so when he visited Hejiacun in 1978

---

[115] Contract between Sino Data System Company and China Computer Technology Service Company, 12 December 1981.

and 1981, when earlier worries about her health had been allayed. Fu had not appeared to Paul appreciably older or weaker than she had been in 1975: 'Mother was in good health.' Nonetheless, Paul did not need to be told when, at the age of eighty-one, she died in her sleep on 29 December 1982. 'On the night of my mother's death,' he maintained 'I dreamed that she was dying.' In his dream he told her that it was 'OK' to be buried on the unpopular site that she had chosen for her grave so many years earlier. Although Paul's frequent visits had made some amends for all those years that he had been abroad, it did not diminish his feelings of guilt, as he confided in an unusually forthcoming letter to Tangxiang's daughter Xilian:

> During her time of suffering she did not know that I was alive or dead abroad. When she was starving I did not support her. When she was ill I did not care for her. When she left this world I was not with her to say farewell to her. I really am a child who is guilty of a crime that even death cannot atone for, completely un-filial. When I think of this, I feel so bad that I could die.[116]

Paul's retirement from Bell and Howell came a few months after his mother's death, marking the end of his professional employment. Though now sixty-four, his US passport had always lopped three years off his age and he could easily have passed for a much younger man. His energy was still directed into his work on the computer program, despite the setbacks that he had suffered. But his attention was naturally increasingly focused on family matters, looking forward as well as back: watching over his student son Sidney who would embark on a degree in economics at UCLA in 1985; helping Phillip to raise the $10,000 that he needed to set up a practice as a dentist in Santa Barbara, where he moved after qualifying in 1981; and a continuing responsibility, felt even more keenly as he grew older, towards the younger generation of his family in Jiangxi. And all of this required cash, at a time when his salary ceased.

In 1982 Paul and Sonia had moved house. This came about not because of any lack of affection for their family home in Sanborn Avenue but because, with David's move from UCLA to a research post at the Massachusetts General Hospital in Boston, the house on Live Oak Drive now became vacant. Whether they would return to California was uncertain at the time, so Paul and Sonia,

---

[116]   Paul Ho to He Xilain, 7 July 1983

together with Sidney, agreed to move in instead (which may well have eased their cash-flow through the rental income of their Sanborn Avenue house). But they never felt wholly comfortable in this palatial home. There were no nearby shops; the up-market area ensured that neighbors were kept at a distance; and Sonia felt that, despite the lovely view to the distant Hollywood Hills, the house was simply too large.

Meanwhile, in Jiangxi the housing crisis was rather more pressing than that in Beverly Hills. Maybe Tangxiang was no longer living in a pigsty but Paul and Sonia had become aware of his unsatisfactory conditions on their first visit, and of his wish to move from Hejiacun into Xinyu. 'You need to build the house,' Paul told him at once.[117] But it took much longer to make this plan practicable and the burden on Paul and Sonia was increased by the series of remittances that they sent, on a scale that was now enhanced. Tangxiang's house was eventually to cost them $18,000 (American dollars), a considerable sum, given other claims upon their resources. It is little wonder that Paul felt the pinch, and also the need to convey the fact. 'My financial situation is difficult,' he told his granddaughter Xilian in 1983.[118]

During their first trip to China, Paul and Sonia had promised to bring Tangxiang's eldest son Chungen and his daughter Xilian to America in order to learn English. This proved to be no easy matter. 'The American Immigration Law allows one to apply for children, but not for grandchildren,' Paul told Xilian. 'So the grandchildren can only come with my son.'[119] As Phillip confirms, Tangxiang 'wanted to make a better life for his children' so he agreed to come with the children. It was a plan with a rationale that Phillip now understands better than he did at the time.

For it was the prospective arrival of Tangxiang and his son Chungen in America that finally broke a thirty-year silence. It prompted Sonia to tell David and Phillip about their father's first family. Sonia's telling left the boys with the impression that their father's first wife, Gu, had died, but they now knew that they had one brother and two sisters in China. 'David and Phil did not say anything,' Sonia recalls. This is perhaps because, for Phillip, 'it didn't come as a great surprise.' For David, who had visited Hejiacun in 1978, there came the

---

[117] Paul Ho to He Tangxiang, 16 October 1975

[118] Paul Ho to He Xilain, 7 July 1983.

[119] Paul Ho to He Xilain 7 July 1983; Xilian did not accompany either of her brothers to America.

sudden realization that Tangxiang, whom he had met as a 'cousin,' was actually a half-brother (though the fact that Chinese usage is sometimes ambiguous on the distinction between 'brother' and 'cousin' had no doubt conspired with his own lack of the local dialect to keep him in the dark). No one told Sidney, now in his late teens; his brothers agree, 'because we did not know how he would take it.' And when Tangxiang later arrived, Sidney—like David before him—'wasn't quite sure who he was.'

Thus enlightened about the extent of his family connections, Phillip set out with his father on his own first visit to China in 1987. Now a successful dentist in Santa Barbara, he had been married for three years to Michi (Mei-chi Tseng), like Susan of Taiwanese birth and known through her parents to Sonia, and herself a recent immigrant to the United States. She did not accompany her husband on this visit to Jiangxi, though was to go on later occasions (including that on which I met her in 2007). For Phillip, the 1987 trip had special significance. Even though, having viewed his parents' photographs of Hejiacun, he found the fabric of the village much as he expected, he was moved by the experience. 'I drank the water from the village well,' he recalls. 'I thought of how many generations of my family had tilled the soil and worked the land; and as I was walking through the village I knew that I had deep roots in this village.'

Above all, there was the direct human contact—'I met my half sisters'— and a meeting with Tangxiang, now singled out as his half-brother rather than the 'cousin' whom David had previously encountered. Paul, Phillip and Tangxiang were to travel back together. Tangxiang remembers clearly that he arrived in Los Angeles on 17 May 1987, the first step towards securing his green card. It was a key part of the whole plan that he was now accompanied by his son, Chungen, who later told Phillip, 'It was the best day of my life when I arrived in America.' Tangxiang at first moved in with his father and step-mother in the spacious house on Live Oak Drive, where Sidney still lived as a student, and where Chungen began his own keenly anticipated new life on the Gold Mountain.

Known as Ken or Michael in North America, Chungen, entered high school.[120] Tangxiang remained with his son for a few weeks and helped his

---

[120] Sherwood arrived in America two years after his brother, Ken. He later studied, spent four years in the Army then trained as an accountant, a profession he pursues to this day. Ken continues to make his home in Los Angeles where he is involved in the automobile business.

father, who was working on his Chinese dictionary. But Tangxiang needed some sort of employment if he was to get his green card and thereby establish his son's residency in America, so he moved north to Santa Barbara, where he took a job in a motel owned by Phillip's father-in-law. After a few months there, Tangxiang moved across the country, again finding a new job as a result of family connections, at the Huawang Restaurant in Washington DC. This is where he lived and worked for the next two years.

None of this was easy. For Tangxiang to succeed in America was, as the Chinese saying goes, like "climbing up to heaven without a ladder." He possessed no marketable skills. He did not speak English. He had little formal education. He was handicapped by racism. Moreover, working for low wages at the back of a restaurant gave him no sense of achievement, earned him no work points in order to measure his productivity, and effectively constrained him from learning English. Too old to adapt as his own father had done so many years earlier, Tangxiang had no path to cultural integration into American society.

'In America,' Lindo Jong observes in Amy Tan's novel, *The Joy Luck Club*, 'nobody says you have to keep the circumstances somebody else gives you.'[121] By contrast, in provincial cities like Xinyu, and in rural communities like Hejiacun, there was, at least in the mid-1980s, no sense of upward mobility. Every major decision was made by someone else. This meant that the concept of self-sufficiency was as alien to Tangxiang as much as the ability to control one's destiny. Even this was not the worst of the problems for a man deprived of any social contacts beyond the Chinese back-kitchen. Without the companionship of his wife, Zhang Jinxiang, Tangxiang was acutely lonely.

Not surprisingly, he did not settle in the United States himself. After two years in Washington, having satisfied the qualifying period to establish his son in America and to help another son, Xiaowu or Sherwood, to immigrate a few years later, Tangxiang returned to the house in Xinyu that his father had bought for him. There he picked up his role as head of the family, prompting his father to further good works.

During the visit, Paul asked Tangxiang to see to it that his mother, Gu, was moved back to Hejiacun where she could be close to her children. Thus some time in the mid-1990s Fu's former house was extended to more than double its original size in order to accommodate Gu and her family. 'They all shared a

---

[121] Amy Tan *The Joy Luck Club* (London: Vintage 1998, first published 1989) p. 254

kitchen that was on the side of the building,' Tangxiang told me in 2008 (thus explaining why I had earlier found just a sealed door on the right-hand side of the health centre). This is where Paul caught a glimpse of his former wife in 1998. I asked him what happened when he saw Gu, who was to die two years later. What could he possibly say after so long to a woman who had borne his three children? Knowing Paul I was not surprised when he answered: 'There were a lot of people; we didn't talk, nothing; just look.'

What's in a look? Everything and nothing. A look backward can change little, beyond recognizing circumstances and acknowledging outcomes that cannot be wished away. A look forward can change everything, mastering difficulties and overcoming setbacks that can sometimes be willed away. In the life of Paul Ho reflection had been less evident than action, contemplation less than ambition and the dynamics of his own nature did not change in old age.

* * *

It is not known what happened to the computer that Paul Ho left with the China Computer Technology Service Company in Beijing in 1981. It is indisputable, however, that he did not give up, as his flow of books and articles about his invention formidably testifies. Introduction to MWP (1995) was published when Paul was seventy-six; Multi-lingual Phonetic Word Processor (2008) was published when he was eighty-nine. [122]) Well into his seventies, Paul was attending conferences in Beijing at which he gave papers. [123] And in the mid-1990s when he was invited by the Southern California Chinese School Teacher Association to give a talk about Chinese characters and their computerization in writing he impressed at least one student.

When he entered the classroom Tse Tung assumed that the man who had developed the software program that phonetically combined the spelling of multiple-character phrases would be a relatively young person. However Tung

---

[122] Paul Ho *Introduction to MWP, the Jewel of the Chinese Computer* (Jiangxi Post Secondary Publications, 1995) and Paul Ho *Multi-lingual Phonetic WordProcessor* (2008)

[123] Two papers which Paul Ho gave were, 'Ho's Code for Multilingual Word Processor and Communications,' presented to the 1983 *International Conference on Chinese Information Processing* in Beijing; and '4-Key Method,' to the same conference in October 1992.

encountered a man in his late seventies. This not only reinforced Tung's view that creativity and intellectual curiosity did not diminish with age. Since 'all other Chinese software players, including the all mighty Microsoft' were now following what Paul Ho was now calling his 'Grand-View Garden'—a tribute to the greatest Chinese author, Cao Xueqin—it reminded Tung of Warren Buffett's belief that 'someone is sitting in the shade today because someone planted a tree a long time ago.'[124]

Paul's pioneering work not only impressed students like Tse Tung. He succeeded in winning abiding recognition in his home province. In 1985 he was invited to become technical advisor to the Computer Research Institute at Jiangxi University and, three years later, senior advisor for the Jiangxi Information Technology Development Company. Still as active as ever, in 1994 Paul Ho took up a visiting professorship at Nanchang University. This was the very city that he had first entered as an ambitious young student, seeking to get a foothold on the ladder of learning, pushed on a rustic one-wheel cart, over sixty years previously.

---

[124] Tse Tung to Phillip Ho, 13 November 2009

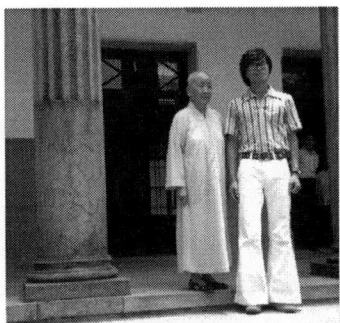

Phillip visiting Buddhist nun at
Lu Family Temple, Taiwan, 1976

Tangxiang and son Chungen (Ken) in Washington

Paul and Sonia, Great Wall, 1975

Paul demonstrating the Ho Imput
Method in Beijing, 1981

David and Susan in China 1978

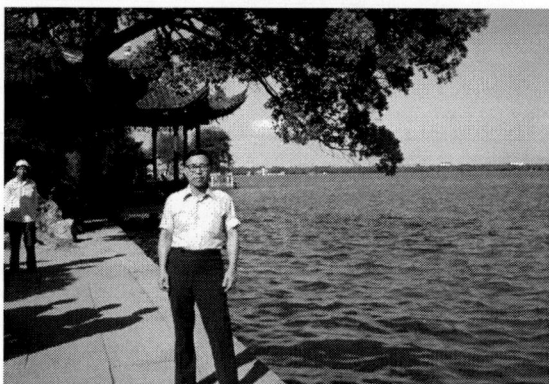

Paul West Lake, Hangzhou 81

Sonia and Fu, Hejiacun, 1975

Epilogue

There can be no doubt that Paul and Sonia Ho always liked to be at home—wherever that was. When the dancer Jin Xing insists that Chinese immigrants prefer to pass their final years 'back home', she means in China, because 'abroad we're in someone else's home.'[125] Yet Los Angeles remained home for Paul and Sonia, as any visitor to their two-storey condominium to the east of the city would immediately realize.

It was in 1987 that they decided to move to the district of Alhambra. Sonia enjoys pointing out that their North Palm Avenue home is only one block from fashionable Pasadena; yet their condominium is unpretentious and modest in size, certainly compared with the house that they vacated at Live Oak Drive. This was, of course, the property of David and Susan, and was to be reoccupied by their own growing family—Kathryn Kai-ling was aged nine, Jonathan nearly six, and Jaclyn just a few months old—when David gave up his position at Massachusetts General Hospital in Boston in 1987. He moved back to California as a professor at UCLA's School of Medicine where he had previously gained his clinical experience by serving as a resident at Cedars-Sinai Medical Center.

At this juncture, Paul and Sonia did not return to the Sanborn Avenue house, from which they continued to receive a useful rental income. Instead, they were free to move into a smaller house. Their youngest son, Sidney, aged twenty, was soon to graduate from UCLA in economics; indeed, within a few years, he would be living on the opposite side of the country. Nor was there further need

---

[125] Jin Xing *Shanghai Tango, A Memoir* (*London*: Atlantic Books, 2005) p. 137.

—

to accommodate Tangxiang's sons, now known as Ken and Sherwood, who were making lives for themselves with less help from their grandparents. Having seen to it that their own children were raised as Americans in a socially mixed area of the city, Paul and Sonia could now live in the area of the city where they felt most comfortable.

Not for nothing did Alhambra become known as the 'Chinese Beverly Hills.' Along with the cities of San Marino and Monterey Park, also located in the San Gabriel Valley, the district supports the largest suburban group of ethnic Chinese people in North America. Paul and Sonia could walk from their North Palm Avenue home to a Chinese bank; they could eat in Chinese restaurants and buy food in Chinese supermarkets nearby.

Their condominium, where members of their family could be found most weekends, unostentatiously reflected their own identity as the elders of a Chinese American family that had remarkable achievements to its credit. The white leather furniture was comfortable. The glass-topped tables, on which Sonia served endless cups of High Mountain Tea, were strewn with copies of Los Angeles' *Chinese Daily News*. Their move to Alhambra brought the elderly couple into the heart of the uptown Chinese community, with friends who gathered every Monday to play mahjong.

But few knew better that life is not just a game. Near their front door is a waist-high pile of cardboard boxes waiting for Sonia's attention. Despite her retirement after the onset of liver troubles, she still pursues her business interests, now assisting her middle son, to whom she was particularly close. Phillip admits that he 'always liked to fiddle with things'; helping his father fiddle with the Chinese-English computer had occupied him in his student days. Thus it is not surprising that, working as a dentist, Phillip took to developing his own innovations when the tools seemed unsuitable. When Phillip set up the Ho Dental Company at his home in Santa Barbara, a parallel company, handling the distribution of the dental equipment that he got manufactured from his designs, was also established by his enterprising mother. The work is done mainly by telephone and clearly provides satisfaction all round 'A little income,' Sonia says with a modest shrug.

Against one wall of their living room is an enormous flat-screen television, ensuring that they keep abreast of the news—from China and Taiwan as well as in America. Beside it are hung two amateur portraits of Paul and Sonia, very creditably rendered in oil by their great-granddaughter, Stephanie (who lives with her father Ken, her brother William and her mother Connie in a bungalow in nearby South Pasadena). On the opposite wall of this compact room is a finely woven tapestry, depicting the skyline of Shanghai, the port from which the young man known as Buji boarded a ship bound for Taiwan in 1947. Then aged twenty-eight, he was to see another twenty-eight years elapse before he was able to return to his native China.

* * *

The Strait of Taiwan is much easier to cross and re-cross these days. Direct air travel, recently established, marks a further step in easing restrictions that for much of Paul Ho's life separated the three territories—China, Taiwan and the USA—where he made his career. From 1998 Paul and Sonia's visits to China were more frequent and for longer periods of time. This was facilitated by official hospitality, recognizing their family's distinction. Following the naming of the Xinyu Middle School after their son David—or Dayi as he is known in China—the couple were given the use of an apartment in a fashionable area of Xinyu. 'It suits us like cream,' Sonia told me as we walked through the spacious three-bedroom third-floor apartment in the spring of 2008. It was here that she and Paul played two games of mahjong a day with Tangxiang, Xiangbao and other relatives, mirroring the pattern of their life in Alhambra.

One obvious difference was that from their Xinyu apartment Paul and Sonia could easily travel to Hejiacun and pay their respects to the ancestors at Fu's graveside. Correspondingly, for Sonia a visit back home really meant going to Taiwan. Paul too had felt more comfortable there, especially after the government lifted martial law in 1987, banishing some of the demons that had haunted his attempts to make a career under the Chiang Kai-shek regime. It is for Sonia that the sites of memory in Taiwan have a special significance.

On one of his own regular journeys from New York to Taiwan and China, David stopped over in Los Angeles. During his short visit with his parents, he asked them where they wanted their ashes deposited after their death. There was nothing surprising when Sonia said that she wanted her ashes to be placed in an urn in the Lu family mausoleum in Houli, next to her mother's. Nor, in keeping with Paul's reverence for his mother Fu, was it surprising that he wanted his ashes to be scattered below his mother's grave, next to the pond where, so many years earlier, he had taken refuge from the bandits and met the Christ-like figure whom he thanked for his salvation. Both, then, had chosen to go back to their childhood homes; but their choices—so they struck the family philosopher, Phillip—reflected the different ways in which they had lived their lives. 'My Mom neat, organized and purposeful,' Phillip commented, whereas his father's decision to scatter his ashes seemed 'liberating, free from the burdens of emotional ties, with the general location being the only reluctant ode to sentimentality.'

This was one way of going home: a posthumous return that would ultimately take each of them back to the beginning of a long journey, and in so doing keep faith with deep-rooted Chinese traditions. Yet much of their own lives had been devoted to ensuring that their descendants enjoyed the opportunity of a better life in the United States. It was plainly the sacrifices made by the parents that enabled David Ho and his brothers to climb the ladder of success and to integrate, to an extent that was not an option for the parents, into American life. Paul felt gratified, in his role as head of the family, that the public celebration of David's achievements had brought honor to all of them, not least to their ancestors. Such feelings, at once proud and modest, had inspired him, in the Chinese tradition, to choose a final name for himself. The boy who had been known as Rongda ('glorious prospects'), the young man known as Buji ('step by step') wanted to be remembered after his death as Jisheng—'second generation better than me.'

*   *   *

In the spring of 2008 I had an opportunity to observe at first hand the impact of David Ho's groundbreaking work on HIV/AIDS. On this expedition to China, accompanying David and his wife Susan, my husband Peter and I joined the AIDS benefactors Sally Tsui Wong Avery and her husband Dennis Avery. Together the six of us were to visit two of the most vulnerable areas of China: the province of Anhui, lying adjacent to the badly HIV-infected province of Henan, northwest of Shanghai; and then—taking us far into the inaccessible southwestern corner of the country—the province of Yunnan.

What we could not have foreseen was that, barely a week before our arrival, the Great Sichuan—or Wenchuan—Earthquake would hit western China on 12 May 2008. The newspapers and television news were suddenly full of reports of the well-publicized solicitations of 'Grandpa Wen', as the prime minister was now called; of pandas being moved to safe locations; of soldiers, medics and the public performing heroic rescue acts; and of countries from Japan and Taiwan to Canada and the United States sending supplies and rescue teams.

Once we flew west, our journey took us alarmingly close to the earthquake zone. We changed planes in Chongqing the day that an aftershock exceeding a magnitude of 6 on the Richter scale hit Sichuan's capital, Chengdu, to the north of the city, and the health officials whom we later met gave us chilling first-hand accounts of the disaster. But our mission had a very different focus: to look at the care of HIV orphans and the prevention of mother-to-child transmission of AIDS.

The first two days of our visit to Yunnan followed the protocol of a VIP visit, with accommodation in a modern luxury hotel in the provincial capital of Kunming. Our only qualm was having rooms on the twentieth floor of a high-rise building on the edge of an earthquake zone. Apart from this unease at the back of our minds, the fact that we were in the entourage of the famous Dr David Ho assuaged all difficulties and opened all doors. We met senior government health officials and witnessed the formal establishment of the Yunnan AIDS Initiative, the province's first non-governmental organization (NGO). We put on our best suits for the occasion, clapped in the right places (so we hoped), drank our glasses of champagne, posed for the official photographs.

But the real work soon became apparent. We quickly gathered that much of the drive came from Dr. Zhou Zengquan, an impressive figure who has worked in the field of HIV/AIDS for over ten years. With its team of over one hundred workers, this NGO is now implementing a rigorous program to tackle the prevention, testing and intervention of high-risk groups. Not only is it committed to the treatment of and care for adult HIV/AIDS patients but the organization has to cope with roughly five thousand orphaned children. Since March of 2007, with the assistance of the Aaron Diamond AIDS Research Center and the Elizabeth Glaser Pediatric AIDS Foundation, Zhou Zengquan and his colleagues have sought to implement the 'Prevention of Maternal and Pediatric AIDS Project' in six counties lying close to China's western border in Yunnan. It was one of these counties, Longchuan, which we would now visit. Dr. Zhou had prepared a full program that would keep us busy for the next few days.

Accompanied by Dr. Zhou, his capable physician wife and ADARC's China Programs Coordinator, Haoyu Qian, we flew out of Kunming's busy western-style airport, going as far southwest as it was possible to fly in China. On arrival, we saw at once that Mangshi airport does not rival the great air terminals of the world; but its bare metal shed is serviceable (except when it rains) and we wasted little time there on tedious security procedures. It may be the outpost of commercial flight to western China, but it was not our final destination. We now had a four-hour journey by van along the old Burma Road before we reached the heart of Yunnan's HIV epidemic, which began in Longchuan county in the late 1980s. The county is right on the Burmese border and our route brought us within sight of the border police: only boys, as they seemed, in their crisp uniforms, flourishing the arms and insignia of the military government of Myanmar (formerly Burma).

Now deep in Yunnan, we had certainly left behind the bright lights and high-end glitz of Shanghai, or even of Kunming. This was a far more simple, rural area of the province, though it was blessed with an eternal spring climate in which the natural vegetation flourishes with an almost surreal abundance. The subtropical forests enfolded us at times: giant banyans, rubber trees and forty kinds of bamboo. At one country restaurant, eating outdoors under a canopy to protect us from tropical showers, we were to find that every dish was made from a different kind of bamboo—and each one was delicious. Still, Longchuan is in one of the poorest parts of China. Seventy-seven per cent of the county is mountainous, erosion is a continual problem, and the sugar cane, coffee, and papaya industries struggle for profitability.

Moreover, the province of Yunnan is a victim of its political geography. An exposed western salient of China, it not only shares one border with Myanmar, but another with Vietnam and Laos—an area long known as the golden triangle. It is here that heroin is trafficked through China's porous border to Hong Kong. This is a longstanding problem. Opium, used in China for recreational purposes since the fifteenth century, became rampant during the seventeenth century and was subsequently outlawed in 1729. Even so the high drug purity of its refined version, heroin, has led people in this area to rapid addiction. What is new, however, is that many drug users now take the drug intravenously, that addiction is endemic among the sex trade workers, and that as many as eight out of ten of them are HIV positive.

As we bumped along the precipitous mountain track from Mangshi, David told us that he had two goals for our visit in Longchuan: to learn more about AIDS orphans and to observe the progress of the prevention of mother-to-child transmission of HIV. The virus is passed either *in utero*, during delivery, or while breastfeeding, to no fewer than one in three babies in untreated pregnancies. Proper pharmaceutical intervention can reduce the rate of infection in infants from 33 per cent to 2 per cent. On the face of it, then, a simple and effective remedy. We wanted to see whether this ambitious strategy was succeeding in practice.

As we made our way along the virtually deserted road, I was reminded of traveling, a year earlier, to Zunyi, the town where Paul Ho had spent his university days. Though we had followed the route of the Burma Road on that journey from Chongqing to Zunyi, we had had the luxury of traveling on a brand-new highway. There was little resemblance here in Longchuan to the

New Burma Road or to the infrastructure of the province of Guizhou. On our route to Longchuan we traveled along a single-lane, poorly-graded road that was hemmed in on both sides by a dense jungle growth. Another novelty for me was to enter a part of China where the population was not predominantly Han Chinese. Almost half of the population in this part of Yunnan is drawn from China's fifty or so ethnic minorities, most of whom remain disadvantaged and poor compared to the Han Chinese in their midst.

We were to have an opportunity to meet one of these groups when we visited Desa village in the township of Zhangfeng in Longchuan County. The Dai's cultural identity was quickly made apparent to us when, upon arriving in the village, we had to walk through a corridor of some twenty teenagers, giving us a traditional welcome by splashing us with water. Those of us towards the end of the line received particularly copious amounts, as the receptacles were emptied over us. Right at the back, my husband Peter felt particularly honored when he received a thorough drenching, in a spirit of cheerful hospitality, soaking his newly pressed cotton clothes (which soon dried in the hot sun).

After this dousing, we were led to the Youth and Cultural Activity Center. During the course of the next two hours the teenagers told us their stories. Only a few were living with a surviving parent; some were with grandparents; others were with caregivers; most were not in school. Only one boy, age eighteen, seemed to have any occupation; he proudly told us that as a butcher's assistant he was earning 400 RMB a month (say $70), which put him well above the poverty line. After we heard their stories we watched one lovely teenage Dai girl, gracefully dancing for us. Later, to the rhythm of deep-pitched drums, we joined the young adults in a traditional circle dance.

During the course of our visit to Longchuan, we found the warmth of our reception by the Dai repeated time and again. Nonetheless, the background to the music, to the spontaneous theatrical performances and to the ready smiles of the children was unmistakable deprivation. In the villages we met 'barefoot' or 'village' doctors with relatively little formal training in public health, pitted against the odds in trying to cope with the AIDS epidemic. We met caregivers who found it difficult to implement the regime of treatment properly under desperately poor conditions in which they lived. I particularly remember one grandmother, manifestly troubled by the failing health of her beloved granddaughter, yet tragically unable to link this with the necessity of regularly administering, every day without fail, the sequence of three pills necessary to comprise the 'AIDS cocktail'. Here, in the flesh, were the human, social, educational obstacles that stood in the way of effective treatment.

None of this came as news to David Ho, of course. It is a mark of his achievement to have seen the fallacy of the supposition that AIDS can simply be conquered by waving a pharmaceutical magic wand created in laboratories thousands of miles away. If he has become the public face of AIDS, especially in China, this is not some celebrity spin-off from his work but an integral part of getting across his message about the necessity of a strategy with political, social and economic dimensions—as well as good science, of course.

Our visit to Longchuan showed us this spectrum of activity. Thus we also encountered provincial health officials, as high as the deputy-governor level, and were given power-point lectures showing us that they had insufficient funds to meet the need of the AIDS orphans and see to the needs of their caregivers. One frustration that emerged among local officials was their difficulty in communicating with the central government. If only Beijing would listen to them! If only resources could be made available to cope with the epidemic! If only the new wealth of China could be mobilized to alleviate poverty in the old China where AIDS was one problem among many!

Towards the end of our visit to western Yunnan, there was a memorable meeting at Longchuan's Maternal Child Health Hospital. Many of the mothers who attended were HIV-positive. As we talked across the bare table, we heard stories of how they had walked many miles—and in some cases for days—through a jungle terrain that was infested with pythons, boa constrictors and tigers. The morning showers that we had dodged on our own short journey from the only hotel in town seemed embarrassingly trivial by comparison. But now a tremendous downpour began and the sound of the torrential rain competed with the chairs that scraped on the tiled floor whenever a child or mother rose to tell us their story.

Their first-hand accounts of abandonment, of abuse and of discrimination were harrowing. One child after another shed tears, all too many recalling that both of their parents had died as a result of AIDS—and they shed further tears when they heard stories from the other children that were touchingly similar to their own. Yet the gleam of light in the room was the fact that so many of these children were not themselves HIV-positive. One young woman stumbled in, late and wet, naturally upset, unnecessarily apologetic, determined to attend this gathering with her own HIV-free baby strapped on her back (like that of other mothers). When her turn came to speak, she wept when she recounted how no one in her village would touch her, sit on a bench that she had occupied, or employ her in any task, however menial. Yes, yes, others chimed in, corroborating her account of the shame, the humiliation and the despair that accompanied a medical diagnosis hard enough to bear in itself.

This particular woman spoke poignantly on these matters, articulating the feelings of many others in the room. And she did so again when—moved to tears by her own emotion—she explained why she had been determined to come that day. She plainly spoke for every mother in the room when she said that she simply wanted to seize this chance of meeting the great Dayi. They all clamored to thank the doctor who had brought a drug that gave hope in their fraught lives, a treatment that prevented them from transmitting the virus to their newborn children or was helping to keep their HIV-infected children alive.

My mind naturally went back to what David Ho had told a student during his talk at the eponymous Dayi Middle School in Xinyu a year previously. He had said then that his greatest satisfaction was having an HIV-positive patient tell him: 'you've saved my life.' And yet, on that wet morning in Longchuan, though David was not ungracious when he heard similar tributes, he simply got on with the job, turning to the immediate problems of the patients and what he could do to help them. 'How can we adjust this patient's drug?' he asked of one twelve-year-old girl who was clearly dying. 'How can we arrange to build an activity centre that will bring these thirty AIDS orphans in the Guangsong Village together more than once every other week?' And a more general worry: 'How can we help local doctors educate the caregivers about ensuring that they administer medicine correctly to HIV-positive children?' As I watched David, almost as outwardly undemonstrative as his father Paul, I thought of how much they each embodied traditions deeply rooted in China, and how much the internationally celebrated New York scientist remains his father's son.

* * *

Paul and Sonia may have seen David, living on the other side of the USA, less often than their other sons. Nonetheless he was never far from his parents' minds, and his image remained proudly displayed on the walls of their Alhambra home. The cover of *Time Magazine*, showing him as 'Person of the Year' in December 1996, is naturally prominent, as is a photograph of President Bill Clinton presenting David with the Presidential Citizens Medal a few years later at the White House. These were landmark events for his whole family, not least for his two brothers.

The only American-born son in the Ho family, Sidney is taller than David and Phillip. He was not initially interested in learning to speak Mandarin or

Taiwanese. For most of his life, he preferred eating hamburgers to his mother's famous chicken stir-fried rice, and he still prefers drinking coca-cola to High Mountain Tea. None of this is really surprising. One thinks of the fictional character in Betty Lee Sung's novel, *Mountain of Gold*, who cries 'Stop calling me Chinese,' because 'I have no interest in China, and it always rubs me the wrong way when strangers ask me if I'm Chinese or Japanese.'[126]

Yet Sidney's outlook had clearly been transformed by 2005 when he first visited China himself. Married for six years to the Japanese American, Lesley Mia Kurose, he and his wife, now living in San Francisco, were intrigued to join a family visit to Jiangxi. For Sidney it was an experience to which he now felt responsive and which became memorable: viewing what was left of the family's ancestral home in Hejiacun; meeting his half-sisters; discovering that Tangxiang was his half-brother—'until then I wasn't quite sure who he was.' He watched his father, at eighty-six, 'in the ninety degree weather just beat us up to the top of the hill' when they visited the grave of Paul's mother, Sidney's grandmother. Within three months of returning to San Francisco, Sidney and Lesley had quit their jobs and moved to Los Angeles, where their own young children, Emily and Charles, could in turn sustain a relationship with their grandparents.

It had been when Sidney moved to New York in 1993 that his attitude shifted. Aged twenty-six at the time, he went there in order to work under his brother David, fifteen years his elder and now getting into his stride in the work that was to establish his pre-eminent position in the treatment and public understanding of AIDS. In 1990, after three years back in California, David had been appointed Research Director and chief executive officer of the newly-founded Aaron Diamond AIDS Research Center (hereafter ADARC) in New York City. He needed someone whom he could trust implicitly as operations manager for the Center, and among those with suitable professional qualifications was his young brother, who got the job. There were already a number of Chinese employees at ADARC. It was in Manhattan, then, that Sidney came into contact with a group of young Mainland Chinese research scientists. 'We got to hang out, and when they spoke to one another they spoke Mandarin,' he recalls, almost with resignation to an inevitable fate. 'I learned Chinese from them—and gained an appreciation for Chinese food too.' And

---

[126] Betty Lee Sung *Mountain of Gold* (New York: Macmillan, 1967) p. 263

Sidney was thus at his brother's elbow throughout one of the most exciting phases of David's career.

*   *   *

When David had seen his first case of AIDS in 1980, it was as a medical resident at Cedars-Sinai Medical Center in Los Angeles. 'I didn't know what I was looking at,' he admits. But then, neither did anyone else. He has a keen recollection that, when curiosity drove him to investigate why so many of his homosexual patients were dying 'many people and colleagues said that I should focus on something else that would make my career.' It was prudent advice, boldly ignored. David continued to specialize in AIDS during his research career at Massachusetts General Hospital in the mid-1980s. He relied on his strong hunch that he was 'looking at something new and rare, something that came into a person's body and destroyed the immune system.'

We all know now that he was right—not uniquely right but among the pioneers worldwide who hunted down the truth about a worldwide plague. He saw the significance of the new breakthroughs around the world that were now opening up the field and brightening the prospects of effective treatment.

First there was the discovery, reported from France in 1983, that patients suffering from this mysterious ailment were being attacked in a peculiar way. Normally a virus (either DNA or RNA) would be expected to reproduce its own genome in a process known as transcription. But here the process is reversed and the pathogen reproduces its RNA genome by copying it into DNA—hence the term reverse transcription—and inserts this DNA copy into the chromosomes of the host cell. It is, in short, a retrovirus. As part of this process the virus kills a particular host cell, which is an essential part of the immune system. If this theory was correct, the retrovirus could wear down the immune system in a cumulatively devastating way. This was corroborated in the USA in the following year, firmly demonstrating that the onset of AIDS itself was triggered by a virus, subsequently known as HIV, and that this was indeed a retrovirus.[127] HIV was

---

[127] The controversy surrounding the discovery of the AIDS virus was revived with the awarding of the Nobel Prize in 2008 to Professor Françoise Barré and Professor Luc Montagnier of France. See, for example, 'Nobel awards revive HIV discovery row,' *The Guardian* (London, 7 October 2008)

thus able to replicate at a rate that—in some patients but not all—would subvert their natural immune systems.

David Ho has described the HIV life cycle as 'simple in concept but enormously complex in detail.'[128] The essential ideas, then, have a simplicity that only hindsight can disclose, but finding a path through the baffling complexity was the work of years. Not everyone who had HIV would develop AIDS, only those unlucky patients whose immune systems were eventually overwhelmed by the unchecked proliferation of the virus. But suppose that the odds could be shifted, knocking out the HIV faster than it could be produced, by developing the right drugs?

An early discovery on the pharmaceutical side had come in 1985. In the USA a drug called AZT had been developed to kill HIV; optimism that it was a sufficient preventive treatment increased when it sailed through the clinical testing procedures in only a couple of years or so. Alas, it proved insufficient in itself, disappointing clinicians desperate for cures that really worked. At Mass General, and then back again in Los Angeles, David Ho was among those in hot pursuit of more adequate forms of remedial therapy.

'We were fortunate enough to jump right in in 1984, when it was clear that a retrovirus was causing this,' he has said in one interview. 'So I was really at the right place at the right time on several occasions along this AIDS timeline.'[129] Nobody would believe that it was simply a question of luck. His own qualities gave him the capacity to seize his opportunities. He was fuelled by curiosity, supported by logical thinking, and driven by a strict work ethic. Personal as well as scientific qualities were important too.

Much of this was already apparent to those who knew the young scientist in his mid-thirties. But it took real insight and courage in 1990 to appoint David Ho, aged thirty-seven, to head the new research laboratories at ADARC. The key figure here was Irene Diamond, of whom David speaks with understandable respect and even awe. No scientist herself, she had enjoyed a long and close marriage to the philanthropist Aaron Diamond, after whom the center was named. Intended as their joint project, it was carried forward after his sudden death by his widow, in conjunction with New York's City Health Department.

---

[128]   David Ho, H'IV-1 at 25' *Cell* 133, May 16, 2008, p. 561.

[129]   Interview with David Ho, 'The age of aids' *Frontline*, Public Broadcasting Television, May 2006, p. 6.

It was Irene Diamond who picked David—who made David, as some would say. Certainly he could not have achieved so much, so quickly without her support, which was far more than financial. As he says with affection, she was a human dynamo, a force of nature in herself. They worked well together. David looks back with a well-justified confidence that if he 'understood what was going on scientifically,' he would make 'a good contribution.' Others readily acknowledge that he quickly grew into the job, not daunted by his task but stimulated by his challenge.

Backed by the formidable Irene Diamond, the young director was soon in the driving seat at ADARC. Situated in Manhattan, on the lower east side, it was formally part of Rockefeller University, but was given a free rein in pursuing its particular line of research. This remained true when the distinguished biologist Arnold Levine later took over as University President (1998-2002) because, as he told me, he recognized that David's ability to move in different spheres made him special. 'David understood the biology better than most clinicians and was essentially a researcher himself,' says Levine, with generous admiration of how the younger man built on this foundation.[130]

True, David's formal training had been unusually broad, with a solid grounding in physics, medicine and molecular biology, which allowed him to tackle the problem from various sides. Although working initially on the clinical side, his forte was in research, to which he brought leadership skills that could be projected in public—crucial in subsequently establishing him as the public face of AIDS research. Though open and unassuming in his behavior, and thus widely liked, what was really impressive was his intellectual self-confidence. And it was this, perhaps paradoxically, that allowed him to admit mistakes on occasions when he went down a blind alley or too hastily seized on an apparently promising line of research.

When he talks about it, David's vocabulary yields some insight about his motivation and his methods in a contest that was to absorb so much of his energies. This has been more than a tense game of chess or mahjong. He writes of mobilizing a 'therapeutic arsenal'.[131] Sometimes he speaks of the long war against HIV almost like the British General Montgomery, fascinated by a redoubtable opponent, used to speak of the German General Rommel. 'I have

---

[130]   Author's interview with Arnold J. Levine, Institute for Advanced Study, Princeton, 6 February 2009.

[131]   *Op. Cit.* 'HIV at 25', p. 563.

a lot of respect for this foe,' as David put it in one interview. 'It has beaten us again and again for a long, long time. And having studied it, I know it quite well, and I find it remarkable that it's so strategic in striking a key cell in our immune system.'[132]

There was never going to be a single set-piece battle that won this campaign. It was a war of movement, of constant skirmishing along an ever-changing front line, where the tactics too had to keep changing. A few fortunate patients carried the virus without ever developing the disease (AIDS); everything depended on how successfully their immune systems were repelling invasion over time. HIV was a protean challenge, taking on different forms at different times and places. David speaks of 'opportunistic infections', and of the way that HIV gets through the lines of defense by 'mimicking' the processes of the host cell that it is attacking. Even its error-prone mode of reproduction gives it an advantage, since it increases the range of variance through new mutations that are capable of infiltrating the barriers already in place. 'Darwinian evolution tells us if you have more variance, the fittest will survive,' David reflects ruefully. 'It's an adaptive mechanism.'[133]

These malign effects of natural selection thus needed to be thwarted by purposeful intervention. The degree of success of different treatments, with the different new drugs that were becoming available, was carefully monitored at ADARC. This mathematical modeling of the problem, though controversial in method, pointed towards a more effective response: not to wait for the single wonder drug that would alone do the trick but to deploy several at once. As David explains, 'if you start to combine the drugs and try to force the virus into a corner using multiple drugs, it is exceedingly difficult or statistically improbable for HIV to become resistant to all the drugs simultaneously.'[134] By 1995 this strategy was in place and ready for multiple testing, typically with a combination of three anti-retroviral drugs. Any one of them might be defeated by a random mutation in the HIV; the chance of two simultaneous mutations was far less likely; the chance of three simultaneous mutations entered the realm of statistical improbability.

And it worked! The results showed that this was indeed the way to suppress the virus in a patient, and to keep these levels down so low that HIV would not

---

[132]   *Op. Cit., Frontline*, p. 19.

[133]   *Op. Cit. Frontline*, p. 11.

[134]   *Op. Cit., Frontline*, p. 8.

lead on to AIDS. In 1996 the International AIDS conference in Vancouver gave ADARC its platform for publicizing these astonishing results, which provided the best news to date in tackling a menacing problem. It was a triumph for ADARC, which had created what is variously known as the triple anti-retroviral drug therapy, HAART, or popularly the 'AIDS cocktail'. It was a triumph, too, for Irene Diamond, with her staunch faith in the young director whom she had appointed.

David Ho well knows that his own contribution was neither unique nor immaculate. Others were working in the field, some with him as colleagues— others against him as competitors, or so it sometimes seemed.[135] Indeed some manifestation of competitive instinct is both natural and predictable, not least in someone from David's background who had a lot to prove, in every sense. He later publicly acknowledged possessing 'a bit of an underdog mentality.'[136] As his eldest child Kathryn feelingly puts it: 'Dad fought so hard for every point.' By 1996, it was clear that he had fought and won. David Ho's triumph, moreover, was not confined to scientific recognition from his peers, however well earned. It was now that he became a public figure.

* * *

At ADARC, Sidney Ho, was paid to be the Director's eyes and ears. He did his job well. When Sidney learned towards the end of 1996 that his elder brother was about to appear on the cover of *Time Magazine*, he sensed at once that 'from now on, all of our lives are going to be different.'

Overnight David became a celebrity. He received honorary degrees from universities around the world. In 1991 he had already received the prestigious scientific Ernst Jung Prize in Medicine. He now became the commencement speaker at the institutions that had helped shape his career: Caltech, MIT and

---

[135] See, for example, L.K Altman, 'Researcher Postpones Plan for Test' *New York Times* 23 January 1997; and more recently, Andrew Pollock, 'Scientists Say They've Found Elusive Protein That Might Help Fight AIDS', *New York Times*, 27 September 2002. Andrew Pollack, 'AIDS Researcher Partly Retracts Study that Caused Stir,' *New York Times* 23 January 2004.

[136] Howard Hua-Eaon with Dan Cray, Alice Park and Donald Shapiro. '1996 Dr David Ho', *Time Magazine*, December 30, 1996-January 6, 1997 Also see *Ibid.*, Christine Gorman 'Man of the Year The Disease Detective'

Harvard School of Public Health. He was elected to Taiwan's Academia Sinica; he became an honorary professor at China's Academy of Medical Science; and he was invited to become honorary dean or board member of medical schools in North America, China and Taiwan.

The cover of *Time Magazine* has a particular iconic status in American culture. Only one scientist has ever appeared alone on the cover, and only one Chinese American citizen: David Ho in each case.[137] Of course there were great rejoicings. It went largely unsaid that, only fifteen years earlier, almost every ivy-league educational institution in the country still imposed entrance restrictions on the number of high-achieving Chinese American applicants whom they were willing to admit to their universities. But the country was changing, as was shown by Clinton's statement as the new President in 1993 that he wanted a cabinet that 'looked like America'. David was celebrated for his work on AIDS not only because of his actual research but because his story symbolized a broader recognition of Chinese American achievement, status, and as an immigrant making good in the United States.

Back in Los Angeles, old Mr. Li placed the December issue of *Time* in the window of his corner grocery store in order to tell his customers that it was here that 'The Disease Detective,' as the magazine called David, had bought soft drinks on his way home from high school. 'The neatest thing was that my parents got to enjoy it,' Phillip comments, and David smilingly concurs: 'for them, it's probably the greatest thing since sliced bread.'

An undisputed expert on her son's success, Sonia was ready to help reporters account for it. 'He's kind of a genius,' she told *Time* writer Dan Cray in 1996, 'I'm not supposed to say that, but it's true.'[138] Her later revelation that the young genius 'would get unhappy if he received a grade of 99,' was reserved for a Chinese-speaking television audience. 'When he got home, he would throw down his satchel, go to his room and close the door,' she said. 'Then we would hear the sound of him hitting himself.'[139] David preferred to mention the 'values of drive and dedication, imprinted during early childhood' that were then allied

---

[137] In 1960 fifteen American Scientists were elected 'men of the year' as were the three Apollo 8 astronauts in 1968. Chiang Kai-shek and his wife Soong May-ling appeared on the cover of *Time Magazine* in 1937 and the modern architect of China, Deng Xiaoping, appeared twice on the cover: in 1978 and 1985.

[138] *Op. Cit., Time Magazine*, December 30, 1996-January 6, 1997.

[139] Sonia Ho 'Top Talk' *CCTV*, 'Dr. David Ho', 18 March 2007.

with 'the entrepreneurial spirit, creativity and imagination' that he had acquired during his university study in the United States.[140]

In 2001 Paul and Sonia accompanied David and his wife Susan to the White House for the presentation of the Presidential Citizens Medal. David's two brothers were also there: Phillip with his wife Michi and Sidney with Lesley. Formally, the citation dwelt on David Ho's 'tireless effort and commitment to helping others' during the course of unraveling 'much of the mystery of the virus, helping us understand how it behaves and how it has been treated.'[141] For President Clinton, these were not just sonorous words; he was to remain a key supporter of David's work.

For the Ho family, gathered in this august setting on privileged terms, the occasion evoked mixed reactions. It was a thrilling moment for Sonia when she set eyes on another of the twenty-eight recipients, her favorite movie star, Elizabeth Taylor—who greeted her former physician with the loud cry: 'David!' Sidney and Phillip were more impressed by meeting Mohamed Ali and by the moment when the former boxer ushered the entire family into an adjacent room, muttering: 'Beautiful, beautiful' as he admired the family. The one person who seemed to have betrayed least emotion was the 'strict father,' Paul, who observed the conventions of a long lifetime by keeping his feelings to himself.

*   *   *

The impact of David Ho's work on AIDS is worldwide. He has played a prominent part in dispelling theories about the transmission of the disease—showing that HIV could not, as popular belief often had it, be acquired through normal contact with an infected person. Above all, the 'AIDS cocktail' has given patients infected with the virus hope for a longer and healthier life. 'Thus, 1996 marked a turning point in the AIDS pandemic,' David has claimed, with obvious justice. 'AIDS-associated mortality has since dropped by 80%-90% in the US and Europe and, conservatively, more than 3 million person-years of life have been saved.'[142] By 2008 the cocktail cabinet was to contain some twenty-five approved retroviral drugs; or, to use David's own metaphor, the therapeutic

---

[140]   David D. Ho, 'Honorary Doctorate Address' Yang Ming University, 27 February 2008.

[141]   Citation of the Presidential Citizens Medal.

[142]   *Op. Cit.*, 'HIV-1 at 25', p.563.

arsenal at the disposal of clinicians was continually upgrading. But the principle of combining three therapies was still the same.

Wonderful progress, then, in the largely western countries that can afford such treatment. But it is under less prosperous conditions that the battle is currently being fought, as we saw for ourselves when accompanying David to Yunnan in 2008. We saw enough here, and in the province of Anhui, to understand why the 'China AIDS Initiative' that David helped launch in 2003 now has such priority.[143]

Our trip would not have been possible before 2003. In the early part of that year the deadly 'bird-flu' or SARS—Severe Acute Respiratory Syndrome—swept through the countryside of China and Taiwan. Now famous for his work on HIV/AIDS, David's advice was sought by health officials in these SARS-infected countries. Eager to help, David travelled no fewer than five times that spring to Taiwan, China and Hong Kong. During each of these visits he calmly assured health officials that they could control the virus if they induced their citizens to practice good public health measures such as frequent hand-washing.

David claims for himself no more than what he calls 'a calming influence' on health authorities. But the fact that such advice was followed, and that by September 2003 the pathogen had been contained, meant that David's role was celebrated. China's Vice Premier, Mrs. Wu Yi—who bears an uncanny resemblance to Sonia Ho—invited him to the Chinese leadership compound, known as Zhongnanhai, in Beijing. In the course of meeting her, David took the opportunity to raise the problem of AIDS in China. In particular, he now asked for permission to visit one of the worst infected areas of the country, the province of Henan.

It is an understatement to say that this request was a bold move on David's part. As early as 1985, AIDS cases in China had been reported in the western press—albeit with the cliché that it was only western tourists who were dying of the disease.[144] A decade later, the elderly Chinese physician, Gao Yaojie, broke the news to western reporters that an untreated HIV/AIDS epidemic had caused mass infections in the province of Henan, as a result of unclean practices

---

[143] The China AIDS Initiative comprises ADARC along with Hong Kong AIDS Foundation, Fuyang AIDS Orphan Salvation Association among other groups.

[144] *The Times* (London) 30 July 1985

affecting people paid as blood donors.[145] Gao's whistle-blowing forced admissions from the Ministry of Health that their officials had not bothered to screen the blood for the AIDS virus or other pathogens, and had thus allowed the virus to spread to the general population.[146] Later that year thousands of state-run medical institutions were ordered to discontinue these practices.

There was an obvious aftermath, which was officially ignored. Virtually nothing was done to treat the thousands of people who had been infected or to help the children who had been orphaned as a result of their parents' AIDS-related death. Only six years later, in the summer of 2001, did China edge towards the admission that they had an epidemic on their hands. And not until the autumn of that year, during an AIDS conference sponsored by the United Nations, did Chinese health officials acknowledge that they had an AIDS problem. Even then, they would not accept the estimate that over one and a half million people throughout the country were infected with the virus.[147]

Hence the significance of David's request, backed by his newly-won SARS credentials, to go to Henan himself. He was given privileged permission to visit the rural areas of the province in September 2003. There he saw the appalling extent to which at least one generation of rural poor, selling their blood to improve their standard of living, had been ravaged by the disease. He also observed how orphans—many infected with the virus—were now in the care of their grandparents or other care-giving relatives. Clearly AIDS was not just a medical problem; it was a social issue that, as David told a university audience several years later, 'got us out of our ivory towers and into the real world.'[148]

David exploited the leverage given by his unique access to China along with his special status in the USA. In New York he worked through the newly organized 'China AIDS Initiative.' In China, he enlisted the help of Peter Little, a publicist who knew the country well, in a key move to make

---

[145] Jim Yardley, 'Fighting Parallel Crises in China: AIDS and Apathy,' *New York Times* 30 December 2003

[146] Patrick E. Tyler, 'China Concedes Blood Serum Contained AIDS Virus,' *New York Times*, 25 October 1996

[147] 'China Admits its AIDS Epidemic,' *New York Times*, 26 August 2001; Elizabeth Rosenthal, 'China Seems Uncertain About Dealing Openly with AIDS,' *New York Times*, 14 November 2001.

[148] David Ho speaking at Harbour Front Center, Simon Fraser University on 21 January 2008.

senior members of the Chinese government publicly recognize the extent of the AIDS problem. Together they organized a one-day conference aimed at raising the public's awareness of AIDS, held at Beijing's Tsinghua University in November 2003.

This proved to be a key event. First, the Chinese executive deputy health minister, Gao Qiang, made a public commitment to provide HIV-positive patients with free medical treatment. Secondly, the American ex-President Bill Clinton, whom David had persuaded to be the guest speaker at the conference, offered to help broker a deal with foreign pharmaceutical companies, with the aim of enabling China to purchase anti-viral drugs. Even more striking, he publicly challenged residual belief that the disease could be acquired through normal physical contact. After he spoke, a twenty-one-year-old man came forward to ask a question, identifying himself as HIV positive. In a brilliant piece of theatre, the imposingly tall and charismatic ex-President showed no hesitation in giving his interlocutor a warm bear-hug.

David had been standing behind the podium when Clinton embraced the young man. As he witnessed this spontaneous gesture, he punched the air with his fist. Like everyone else in the room, David realized that it meant an official breakthrough over which the Chinese authorities would lose face unless they reciprocated. Indeed, it was not long before Prime Minister Wen Jiabao, and later President Hu Jintao, were prompted to make similar gestures.[149]

Here was an admission by the heads of the Chinese government that their country had an AIDS epidemic and that HIV carriers were not social lepers. The fact that the situation needed urgent attention was reinforced a few months later when Prime Minister Wen Jiabao gave the equivalent of the 'State of the Union Address' in March 2004. In it Wen promised to 'cool China's surging economy and focus more resources on the hundreds of millions of people left behind in the boom of the last decade.'[150] In words at least, there was recognition of the enormous gap in living standards that existed between China's urban dwellers and its rural poor, who make up almost 80 per cent of the population. In this more favorable official climate, the China AIDS Initiative was one

---

[149] A year later President Hu Jintao was shown on state television shaking hands with AIDS patients.

[150] Joseph Kahn, 'China's Leader Urges Shift in Development to Rural Areas,' *New York Times*, 5 March 2004

of the charitable organizations that soon became active in Henan and in the neighboring province of Anhui.

*   *   *

When we went to Anhui Province four years later, we saw the work that had been done—and the work that needed to be done. Again, the gap between conditions in Shanghai, where we had assembled, and those in rural China came as a shock, if not a surprise. After the short flight to Hefei airport, we traveled overland to the northwest area of the province. Our destination was Fuyang, which, with a population of 9.3 million people, is considered to be a 'small' city. With an average per capita income of less than $285 a year, Anhui is one of the poorest provinces.

Fuyang itself boasts a sort of misplaced affectation to emulate modes of outdated western culture which the Buckingham Palace Hotel perfectly embodies. Amid its shabby-genteel gilt, we were greeted by the well-dressed and affable Mrs. Zhang Ying. In 2003, we were told, Zhang gave up a successful business career to become founding chairman of the Fuyang Aids Orphan Salvation Association. Her role in it is prominent, as seen in the glossy brochure that she gave us, where she appears in every photograph: rescuing some four hundred AIDS orphans, nursing those who are infected with HIV, teaching children at the activity center that she established. Her "orphanage" is an umbrella term for all these activities, caring for children who would plainly be worse off without the assistance that she channels from the different charities that support her efforts.

Though the China AIDS Initiative had provided the initial funding for Zhang's work, other charitable organizations have taken over most of its funding. It was because its own pioneering role had been largely fulfilled in Anhui, that the China Aids Initiative was able to switch its own resources to the work that we saw commence in Yunnan. This is a rolling program, more optimistically seen as pump-priming, less optimistically seen as trying to staunch breaches in the dyke. That it is work that needs doing was not doubted by anyone in our visiting group in May 2008.

Our final destination one day was a small village, well outside Fuyang, reached long after the paved roads had petered into mud tracks. It made Paul Ho's dirt-poor Hejiacun look prosperous. We had come to see a ten-year-old boy and his twin sister, orphaned by AIDS, and now being brought up on their grandparents' farm. In the background we could see the family's one-room earthen-floor dwelling, with its leaking roof, and its only piece of furniture, quite incongruously, a flat-screen color television powered by a car battery.

Feeling that they should entertain us, the children showed us a few Kung-Fu kicks. Maybe they had seen the routine on television. Their graceful bends and twists were performed on a patch of mud-packed earth, in front of a barking dog that was pulling, in a menacing way, on a heavy chain. Feeling that we should entertain them, Dennis Avery performed a few magic tricks that he had learned as a boy. The children's pleasure—and their grandmother's pleasure too—at seeing Dennis make a coin disappear into thin air did little to raise our spirits.

What we saw made for a dismal picture. We saw the twins' aging grandparents who were clearly struggling to keep food on the table; we noticed with concern the bruise that darkened the young girl's left eye; we observed the children's lack of schooling—their small hands were needed on the farm and, in any case, there was no money to pay for their school fees. We did what we could to trade some tangible assistance against the promises that the children would at least be sent to school, that they have some opportunity to escape this life through the possibilities of education.

The need for David's ongoing commitment, not just to pioneer medical research, but to ameliorate social conditions in his ancestral China could not have been more tellingly illustrated that day. As we huddled under the shelter of the roof to avoid the rain, we noticed that the family shared their limited accommodation with a cow, which was now stirring. If they did not take the animal into the house, it was explained, they were afraid that it would be stolen. On my own first visit to China I had found the room where Paul Ho had been born in 1919 now occupied by a cow. As I stood with his son David, who had brought us back to China in 2008, I thought that the wheel had come full circle.

*   *   *

A year following that memorable trip to China in the spring of 2008, I met up with the Ho family once again. The occasion was the ninetieth birthday of Paul Ho. The day was Sunday the 29th of March and the place was the Garden of Flowing Fragrance at the Huntington in Pasadena.

The fact that Paul Ho was ninety was belied by his continuing vigor, his alertness and his unquenchable sense of fun. Here was a long life manifestly worth living to the full and worthy of commemoration by a large family spread over two continents. Since the Chinese custom is to count a new-born baby as already one year old, Paul's ninetieth birthday celebrations had already duly taken place during the visit that he and Sonia made in the spring of 2008 to Xinyu, with the members of his first family crowded around him for the occasion. But a western-style observance of the ninetieth anniversary itself was plainly demanded in the following year. Its form was the subject of long discussions among Paul's second family, especially David, Phillip and Sidney—and their children—who were conscious as ever of their special obligations.

I was not only flattered, but touched to find that Paul's biographer was to be included in this remarkable family gathering. Indeed, with my husband Peter, I accompanied Dennis Avery and Sally Tsui Wong Avery, alike the sponsors of the biographical project and major donors to the Garden of Flowing Fragrance. It was thanks to them that this beautiful Chinese garden, set in the midst of the Huntington's grounds on the San Marino hillside, was made available for Paul Ho's ninetieth birthday party.

The Huntington is world famous for its renowned collections of art, rare books, manuscripts and plants. But it is also only a few minutes' drive by car, along the boulevard and up the hill, from the home of Paul and Sonia Ho in Alhambra. It was the perfect venue for an event that brought together some honored travelers from longer distances with a larger number of other guests drawn from the immediate Los Angeles area.

True to the authentic Chinese tradition, the Garden of Flowing Fragrance respects the site in which it was created. It preserves the sheltering woods but enhances the original pond so that it becomes a majestic lake, surrounded by rocks from China's Lake Tai and crossed at strategic points by formal bridges, with fine stonework. The elegant Teahouse naturally commands the best view over the lake and through the trees with glimpses of mountains in the background that you could swear for a moment must be those of Paul's native Jiangxi rather than his adopted California.

Looking eagerly around at the fifty guests who congregated in the Teahouse on that spring evening, Paul had seized on connections that took him back through the decades. We were introduced to a group of distinguished senior figures whom we saw conversing happily together—they were Paul's old housemates, Wong Yao and Chen Guan from early immigrant days in California, now accompanied by their wives, all with little visible hint of the advanced years for which they kept apologizing. We were also pleased to meet some younger members of the Ho family whom we had not previously encountered, and we noticed how the grandchildren of both the first and second families formed a happily boisterous group at a large table on the terrace once dinner was served.

As Paul and Sonia contentedly circulated amid the throng, we saw the relief on the faces of their own three sons, each of whom was to make a characteristic speech during the course of the evening: David more practiced and attentive to detail; Phillip more spontaneous and intuitive in his comments; Sidney more businesslike and concerned that nothing should be forgotten. At the centre of all this attention, Paul and Sonia sat in evident appreciation of the whole occasion. The many courses of the fine dinner that was served by one of the city's best Chinese restaurants came and went, seemingly with no end in sight, first satisfying our hunger, then ministering to our greed. And the traditional Chinese music, performed by a group of young musicians, filled the Teahouse before drifting across the lake.

When dusk fell the musicians gathered up their instruments. The setting on the lakeside terrace now acquired a special kind of tranquility, punctuated throughout by the lively interventions of the younger guests. Sonia displayed her own serenity in taking in the whole scene, with its evocations of so many episodes in a marriage of over fifty years—and in the presence of offspring of an earlier family of whom she had long been unaware. Paul, more animated on the surface but as inscrutable as ever about his deeper emotions, saw around him the tangible evidence of the trajectory of his extraordinary life. So much was brought together in this poignant moment of commemoration, expressing the filial piety of sons who had not forgotten their Chinese roots in embracing the opportunities of their own life in the United States.

*   *   *

While it is true that David, Phillip and Sidney joined their parents on a memorable trip to China in May 2009, the birthday celebration at the Garden of Flowing Fragrance at the Huntington was to be the Ho family's last gathering. Less than six months later Paul was dead. He had developed complications following gastric resection for stomach cancer.

Paul had spent the previous four months in Xinyu in Jiangxi Province. He and Sonia had recently bought a high-storey apartment overlooking the Dayi School named in honor of their son, David. They were in the process of moving in when Paul fell ill. Following a short spell in hospital he was transferred to Los Angeles where he died on September 3.

Officials in Xinyu wasted no time in providing a fitting home for the ashes of He Buji. Within a month workers had constructed an imposing pavilion on the side of Laojinshan mountain—the burial site of Paul's father, He Wenge. Reached by climbing over three hundred steps, the pavilion offers a good view of Hejiacun and the surrounding farmlands that have been cultivated by the He clan since the twelfth century. Known as, *Ji1 Bu4 Ting2*, the name is not only a play on Buji; it acknowledges the Chinese notion that the slow accumulation of effort leads to significant accomplishments.

Several weeks following the inauguration of *Ji1 Bu4 Ting2* in Hejiacun, family and friends gathered at the California Institute of Technology in Pasadena. Paul Ho's memorial service in the splendid Athenaeum was a somber occasion. There were tributes from, among others, David, Phillip and Sidney who acknowledged that they were the direct beneficiaries of their father's many hardships, that his rich long life had provided them with a living roadmap; and that their father was not just a good man who had lived a simple life but a simple man who had lived an extraordinary one. Phillip and Michi's young daughter, Remi, sang and played the guitar. And, as Paul Ho's chronicler, I provided a biographical sketch of his life. Following the tributes the family made their way into the garden surrounding the Athenaeum. Each member clutched a long ribbon that was tied to a silver balloon. After a few minutes of silence, the guests joined the family in the garden. Then the balloons were released. All eyes were fixed on the balloons as they rose above the Athenaeum, the university, the city of Pasadena and the distant mountains. As I followed their fast ascent I was reminded of what Paul had witnessed following the death of his own father: 'The grave gave off a flame, which went up to the sky; many people in the village saw it.' Over seventy-five years later the same thing was happening again as Paul's own sons watched their father's spirit leave earth.

David Ho and far right Mrs. Zhang Ying in
Fuyan Aids Orphans Recreational Centre

back row, David, Phillip, Sidney;
front row, Honglian, Tangxiang, Xiangbao

Paul and Sonia, 2008

Paul Ho Pavilion: Ji1 Bu4 Ting2, Jiangxi Province, Hejiacun, China

BIBLIOGRAPHY

Baker, Hugh R. *Chinese Family and Kinship* (London: Macmillan, 1979)

Bates, Judy Fong *Midnight at the Dragon Café* (Toronto: McClelland and Stewart, 2004)

Bauer, Richard *Burying Mao, Chinese Politics in the Age of Deng Xiaoping* (Princeton: Princeton University Press, 1994)

Baum, Richard *Burying Mao* (Princeton: Princeton University Press, 1994)

Belden, Jack *China Shakes the World* (MNU: Monthly Review Press, 1970)

Benson, Lee Grayson *The American Image of China* (New York: Ungar, 1979)

Bosworth, Patricia 'Rebel With a Purse,' *Vanity Fair* (December 2000) 250-268

Bowles, Samuel *Colorado, Its Parks and Mountains* (Springfield, Massachusetts: Samuel Bowles and Co, 1869)

Cameron, James *Mandarin Red* (London: Michael Joseph, 1955)

Chang, Iris *The* Chinese *in America* (New York, Viking, 2003)

Chang, Jung and Jon Halliday *Mao* (London: Jonathan Cape 2005)

Chang, Leslie *Beyond the Narrow Gate* (New York) A Dutton Book, 1999)

Chen, Guidi and Wu Chuntao *Will the Boat Sink the Water* (London: Public Affairs, 2006)

Chen, Hsiang-shui *Chinatown No Moore* (Ithaca: Cornell University Press, 2000)

Chiang, Kai-shek *China's Destiny* (New York: Roy Publishers, 1947, first published 1942)

Chiang, Monlin, *Tides from the West* (New Haven: Yale University Press, 1947)

Jin, Ba *Cold Nights* (Seattle, University of Washington Press, 1978)

Ching, Frank *Ancestors* (New York: William Morrow and Company, 1988)

Ching, Leo T.S. *Becoming 'Japanese'* (Berkeley: University of California Press, 2001)

Chow, Ching-li *Journey in Tears* (New York: McGraw-Hill Book Company, 1975)

Choy, Wayson *All that Matters* (Toronto: Anchor, 2005 first published in 2004)

Churchill College Archives, Cambridge University, SEYR 3/3, Madame Sun Yat-sen

Churchill College Archives, Sir Horace James Seymour Papers (SEYR 3/2)

Corcuff, Stéphan edt. *Memories of the Future* (London: M.E. Sharpe, 2002)

Cripps, Sir Stafford 'Diaries,' Bodleian Library, Oxford University.

Daniels, Roger *Guarding the Golden Door* (New York: Hill and Wang, 2004)

Patricia Buckley *Women and the Family in Chinese History* (New York: Routledge, 2003)

Ebrey, Patricia Buckley *Women and the Family in Chinese History* (New York: Routledge, 2002)

Endicott, Stephen *James G. Endicott: Rebel Out of China* (Toronto: University of Toronto Press, 1982)

Fenn, Charles *At the Dragon's Gate* (Annapolis: Naval Institute Press, 2004)

Gao, Mobo C. F. *Gao Village, A Portrait of Rural Life in Modern China* (London: Hurst & Company, 1999)

Gorman, Christine 'Man of the Year The Disease Detective' *Time Magazine*, December 30, 1996-January 6, 1997

Han, Suyin *A Many-Splendoured Thing* (London: Jonathan Cape, 1952)

Han, Suyin *Destination Chungking* (London: Jonathan Cape, 1942; London: Granada Publishing, 1973)

Hessler, Peter *River Town, Two Years on the Yangtze* (New York: Harper Collins, 2001)

Ho, David 'David Ho Interview' *Frontline* (May 2006)

Ho, David 'The age of aids' *Frontline* (May 2006)

Ho, David 'The Chinese Experience,' *Bill Moyers special, Becoming American* (2003) Public Affairs Television

Ho, David, 'HIV-1 at 25' *Cell* 133, May 16, 2008

Ho, David, 'Honorary Doctorate Address' Yang Ming University, 27 February 2008

Ho, David, Paul Ho, Sonia Ho *et. al.* 'Top Talk' CCTV 18 March 2007

Ho, Paul *A Concise English Grammar* (Beijing: Beijing Higher Education Publishing Firm 2003)

Ho, Paul *Introduction to MWP, the Jewel of the Chinese Computer* (Jiangxi Post Secondary Publications, 1995)

Ho, Paul *Multi-lingual Phonetic WordProcessor* (2008)

Hsu, Madeline Y. *Dreaming of Gold, Dreaming of Home* (Stanford, California: Stanford University Press 2000)

Hua-Eaon, Howard with Dan Cray, Alice Park and Donald Shapiro. '1996 Dr David Ho', *Time Magazine*, December 30, 1996-January 6, 1997

Hung Lou Meng *The Dream of the Red Chamber* (Westport Connecticut: Greenwood Press, 1958, originally published 1791)

Israel, John *Student Nationalism in China 1927-1937* (Stanford: Stanford University Press 1966)

Jin, Ba *Selected Works of Ba Jin* (Beijing: Foreign Languages Press, 1988 first published in 1931)

Jin, Xing *Shanghai Tango, A Memoir (London*: Atlantic Books, 2005)

Kates, George N. *The Years That Were Fat* (New York: Harper, 1952)

Knapp, Ronald G. and Kai-yin Lo *House Home Family* (Honolulu: University of Hawai'i Press, 2005)

Ko, Dorothy *Cinderella's Sisters: A Revisionist History of Footbinding* (Berkeley: University of California Press, 2005)

Kwan, Michael David *Things That Must Not Be Forgotten* (Toronto: Macfarlane Walter and Ross, 2000)

Kwong, Peter and Dusanka Miscevic *Chinese American* (New York: The New Press, 2005)

Kwong, Peter and Dusanka Miscevic, *Chinese America* (New York: The New Press, 2005)

Kwong, Peter *The New Chinatown* (New York: Hill and Wang, 1987)

Lary, Diana *China's Republic* (Cambridge: University of Cambridge Press, 2007)

Lee, Rose Hum *The Chinese in the United States of America* (Oxford: Oxford University Press, 1960)

Levine, Arnold J. *Interview* 6 February 2009

Liao, Ping Hui and David der-wei Wang *Taiwan Under Japanese Colonial Rule* (New York: Columbia University Press, 2006)

Lin, Yutang *Chinatown Family* (New York: Mei Ya, 1948)

Lin, Yutang *From Pagan to Christian* (London: Heinemann, 1959)

Lin, Yutang, *Chinatown Chinese* (New York: Mei Ya, 1948)

Lipsey, Richard G. Kenneth I. Carlaw & Clifford T. Bekar, *Economic Transformations* (New York: Oxford University Press, 2005)

Liu, William *Grace in China* (Montgomery: Black Belt Press, 1999)

Louie, Andrea *Chineseness Across Borders* (Durham: Duke University Press 2004)

Lovell, Julia *The Great Wall* (London: Atlantic Books, 2006)

Lui, Zongren *Two Years in the Melting Pot* (San Francisco: China Books, 1988)

Ma, Laurence J.C. and Carolyn Cartier *The Chinese Diaspora* (New York: Rowman & Littlefield, 2003)

MacMillan, Margaret *Nixon in China* (Toronto: Penguin, 2006)

Mann, Susan *The Talented Women of the Zhang Family* (Berkeley: University of California Press, 2007)

Meskill, Johanna Menzel *A Chinese Pioneer Family* (Princeton: Princeton University Press, 1979)

Michael, Franz *China Press* (Shanghai, 23 January 1939)

Needham, Joseph and Dorothy Needham *Science Outpost* (London: Pilot Press, 1948)

Needham, Joseph *Chinese Science* (London: Pilot Press 1945)

Pan, Lynn *Sons of the Yellow Emperor* (London: Secker & Warburg 1990)

Pannell, Clifton W. *T'ai'chung, T'ai'wan* (Chicago: University of Chicago, 1973)

Pan, Lynn *Sons of the Yellow Emperor* (London: Secker & Warburg, 1990)

Pomfret, John *Chinese Lessons* (New York: Henry Holt, 2007)

Pruitt, Ida *A Daughter of Han* (Stanford: Stanford University Press, 1945)

Roberts, J.A.G. *China to Chinatown* (London: Reaktion Books, 2002)

Ronning, Chester *A Memoir of China in Revolution* (New York: Pantheon Books, 1974)

See, Lisa *Snow Flower and the Secret Fan* (London: Bloomsbury 2006)

Sheridan, Mary and Janet W. Salaff *Lives, Chinese Working Women* (Bloomington: Indiana University Press, 1985)

Sung, Betty Lee *Mountain of Gold* (New York: Macmillan, 1967)

Tan, Amy *The Bonesetter's Daughter* (London: Harper Perennial, 2001)

Tan, Amy *The Joy Luck Club (London: Vintage 1998, first published, 1989)*

Thogersen, Stig *A Country of Culture* (Ann Arbor: University of Michigan Press, 2002)

Wang, Kang, 'The Lianda Ethos' in *Chinese Education* Vol XXI (Summer 1988)

Wang, Gungwu, 'Among non-Chinese' *Daedalus* (September 1994)

Wang, Kang, 'The Lianda Ethos' in *Chinese Education* Vol XXI (Summer 1988)

Wang, L. Ling-chi, 'Roots and Changing Identity of the Chinese in the United States,' *Daedalus* (Spring 1991)

Wang, Ling-chi and Gungwu Wang *The Chinese Diaspora* Vol. 1 (Singapore: Times Academic Press, 1998)

Wang, Mei-ling T., *The Dust that Never Settles* (New York: University Press of America, 2001)

Wei, William 'History and Memory, The Story of Denver's Chinatown,' *Colorado Heritage* (Autumn 2002)

Wen, Yiduo, 'Reminiscences and Thoughts on Those Eight Years,' *Chinese Education* Vol XXI (Summer 1988)

Westad, Odd Arne *Decisive Encounters, The Chinese Civil War 1946-1950* (Stanford: Stanford University Press, 2003)

White, Theodore H. and Annalee Jacoby *Thunder Out of China* (New York: William Sloane, 1946)

White, Theodore *In Search of History* (New York: Harper and Row, 1978)

Wilson, Richard *Learning to be Chinese* (Cambridge, Mass, MIT Press, 1970)

Winchester, Simon *The Man Who Loved China* (New York: Harper Collins, 2008)

Wolf, Margery *The House of Lin* (Englewood Cliffs, New Jersey: Prentice-Hall, 1968)

Wolf, Margery *Women and the Family in Rural Taiwan* (Stanford: Stanford University Press 1972)

Wong, Jade Snow *Fifth Chinese Daughter* (New York: Hurst & Blackett, 1952)

Wu, David Yen-ho "The Construction of Chinese and non-Chinese Identities" *Daedalus* (Spring 1991)

Wu, Ningkun *A Single Tear* (London: Little Brown & Company, 1993)

Xinran *The Good Women of China* (London: Vintage, 2002)

Yee, Chiang *A Chinese Childhood* (London: Methuen, 1939)

Yen, Adeline Mah *A Thousand Pieces of Gold* (London: Harper Prennial, 2002)

Yung, Judy *Unbound Feet* (Berkeley: University of California Press, 1995)

Yung, Judy, Gordon H. Chang, and Him Mark Lai *Chinese American Voices* (Berkeley: University of California, 2006)

Zhang, Xinxin and Shang Ye *Chinese Profiles* (Beijing: Panda Books, 1986)

Edwards Brothers,Inc!
Thorofare, NJ 08086
26 August, 2010
BA2010238